From the Library of:

Author: *Kyle Franck*

Title: *From Pocket Change to Profit*

Date	Issued To:

THIS BOOK IS MEANT
TO BE PURCHASED,
ENJOYED, AND
THEN GIVEN TO
THE NEXT PERSON
FOR FREE.
LEARNING IS ABOUT
SHARING AFTER ALL!

Variety & Errors

FOR FREE ONLINE
NEWS, PRICES, INFORMATION
AND MORE ON
UNITED STATES CURRENCY
VISIT MY SITE:
VARIETYERRORS.COM

THANK YOU FOR BUYING MY GUIDE BOOK! PLEASE CUT THIS $100 BILL BOOKMARK OUT TO USE!

FROM POCKET CHANGE TO PROFIT

A GUIDE TO COINS, BANKNOTES, GOLD AND SILVER

ISBN: 979-8-218-15131-7
Copyright © 2023 by Kyle M. Franck
1st edition. 2023. All rights reserved.
Book Cover by Kyle Franck

Please contact KyleFranck@VarietyErrors.com with inquiries, business requests or other questions. Thanks for viewing our guide and good luck on your hunt for the next rare coin or banknote!

Table of Contents

Forward

This is simply the best hobby in the world! Anyone can get into it without major investments of either time or money. Ironic huh? Collecting money can be low cost.

Hear me out... I know books on how to collect currency and precious metals can be super boring. I personally love a good fiction novel compared to the normal, stuffy "how to" guide, but this book is meant to be different. Within these pages we will cover each U.S. coin type, error coins, banknote types, error banknotes and precious metals.

Learning about investments and currency collection doesn't have to be drab and boring. It can be light, easy and a fun way to connect with friends over something that everyone loves... money!

This book is not a price guide. It is a reference guide for general coin, banknote and precious metals information, with details on error coins and bills. This will help in identifying what coin or banknote you have, if it is an error, and how to care for it. If you are a veteran collector, grab this book for a friend and get them into our wonderful hobby!

I think many of us want to collect something that could potentially gain in value, but simply don't know where to start. Hopefully my guide will help in that respect!

Remember, this used to be referred to as the "hobby of kings and queens", after all. As far as I see it, we are all kings and queens of our own worlds, filled with endless opportunities to thrive within a universe of uncertainties. With this guide, I hope to teach you the knowledge you need to utilize coins, banknotes and precious metals as tools to turn your pocket change into huge profits! Thank you for picking up my guide!

Happy Treasure Hunting!

Introduction

This guide will cover many things to get you started in the journey of collecting currency and turning your pocket change into profit!

Numismatics has many avenues within it. Both coin and banknote collecting are equally as fun and profitable! With both coins and banknotes, grading is perhaps the single most important ingredient of value when it comes to collecting currency, so we will cover that too! Gold and silver collecting is also covered in this book, so hopefully there is something for everyone!

Back to the task at hand. I think many people know they want to collect, but do not know how to get started or what to look for when searching spare change and bills. This book covers just that! It's for us, the ones who want to turn their pocket change into more money!

This past time, hobby, way of life...

Whatever coin, banknote and precious metals collecting becomes to you, it is a fun- filled experience where the everyday person can find extraordinary things right in their pocket! Even in your common pocket change, there can be a variety of rare coins and banknotes found. Never assume old coins or banknotes found anywhere are not valuable due to appearance or condition. Many times, banknotes and coins can have quite a bit of damage can still command a heavy premium over face value!

Decide what you want to collect:

- Modern coin or banknote errors
- Defunct or Obsolete Currency
- Large or Small Face Banknotes

- Foreign coins or your home country's currency.
- Smaller denominations or larger denominations
- Circulated coins
- Uncirculated coins (UNC) which have been available in the United States since the 1950s.
- Proof sets which are uncirculated coins prepared especially for collectors and enthusiasts. Also, Silver proof sets which are very beautiful (more affordable than gold) and their value will increase (or decrease) as the value of silver increases (or decreases).
- And with a little research... many other varieties of currency and genres of collecting are open as well!

Now that I have given you some ideas on what to collect, let's get into the real good stuff!

The Basics

Introduction

Coin Anatomy

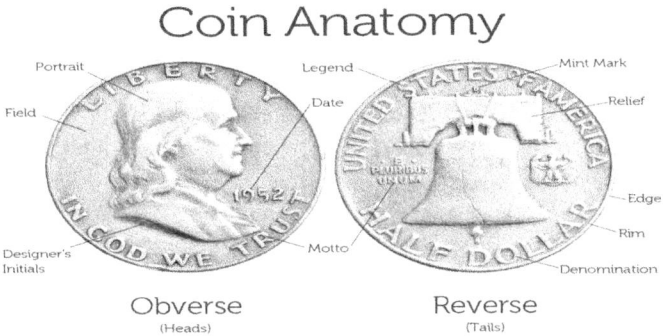

Obverse
(Heads)

Reverse
(Tails)

The United States Mint is nearly as old as the United States itself. After the founding of our country, the government realized immediately the need for unique coinage to build our national identity. By 1793, the first United States Mint building in Philadelphia, Pennsylvania, was erected. This first facility was tasked with producing all of the country's coinage, but before long was operating at full capacity, necessitating the creation of more facilities.

The United States Mint was established April 2, 1792, and is recognized all over the world. Primarily producing coins for the United States, the mint also strikes currency for other countries, as it has since shortly after being founded.

While the U.S. Mint got its start in Philadelphia, Pennsylvania, it quickly began to expand and needed additional facilities to continue operations. Many coins produced by the mint carry what is known as a mintmark, a piece of identification on the individual coin that shows the minting location.

How Are Coins Made?

All coins struck in the United States are struck by a pair of dies. A die is a steel rod with a face that is the same size as the coins that it will be striking. This steel rod will contain the design for one side of the coin. Two of these steel rods (dies) are needed to strike coins. One will have the obverse (front of the coin) design, and the other will have the reverse (back of the coin) design.

The dies are set up in a machine called a coining press so that a planchet (blank) will come between them. In the older coining presses one die would be positioned above the other. The upper die (hammer die) would come down with great force and strike the planchet while it was resting on the lower die (anvil die). The force of the hammer die striking the planchet on the anvil die would place the images from the dies onto the planchet and the result would be a coin as we know it.

In the newer coining presses the action of the hammer die is now side-to-side rather than up and down, but the process is still essentially the same, as is the result.

The reality is that the die varieties we enjoy collecting, which includes doubled dies, re- punched mint marks (RPMs), over mint marks (OMMs), re- punched dates (RPDs), over dates, (OVDs), and misplaced dates (MPDs), are the result of mishaps that occur in the process of making the dies that strike the coins. A working knowledge of the die making process will help us to see how the various die varieties resulted over the years.

What are Error Coins?

An error coin is a coin that was manufactured incorrectly by a mint. Many times called mint errors, error coins come in scores of "shapes, sizes and types." The sheer variety of minted errors adds excitement and uniqueness in collecting them.

Before buying a mint error, knowing the type of coin and the latest selling prices for similar coins is a sound idea. There is a bunch of error coin price guides out there that will help you associate value with your collection.

Die Variety

A Die Variety any variation in the normal design of a given coin, usually caused by errors in the preparation or maintenance of the coin dies. Typical die varieties include doubled dies; re-punched mint marks and dates; variations in the placement or alignment of mint-marks, letters and numbers, devices, etc.; changes to the die surfaces from over-polishing or die clashes; and a number of other minor variations in the final strike of the coin.

One must be careful not to confuse die varieties with error coins, which have variations in their appearance as a result of the manufacturing process itself, such as off-center strikes, wrong planchet types, planchet preparation mistakes, etc.

Doubled Die

Commonly searched for online and called, "Double Die". Doubled dies are a result of the way in which in the United States Mint's dies are created. Before 1997, die pairs (hammer die and anvil die) were made

by hubs that contained the raised elements that were intended to appear on the coin. The blank dies were heated (to soften the surfaces of them) and then were pressed against the hubs to transfer the design from the hub to the working dies.

One impression was not enough in every case to transfer the design elements from the hub to the die, so multiple impressions were required to transfer enough of the design. For this reason, after the first impression was made, the die was reheated and prepared for a second impression.

The mint workers would use guides to align the hub and the working die perfectly to prevent overlapping, or a doubled die. It is when mint workers failed to align dies properly during this process that doubled dies were produced. In many instances three to four impressions were required, which could but rarely led to tripled and quadrupled dies.

Modern coining methods have vastly reduced the frequency of these varieties due to the use of a single squeeze hubbing method during die creation, but doubled dies in modern United States coinage are still occurring.

With the new die making process, implemented after 1996, dies only required one impression of the hub to transfer all of the design from the hub to the die. But it has been discovered that the pressure created is so great, that some dies tend to slightly rotate during this process.

Additional Information:

Doubled dies are created a first image is imprinted and then an additional image is stamped on top of that. These are classified into eight accepted classes. These classes are outlined below.

Doubled Die Classes

Class 1, Rotated

> A class I doubled die results when the die receives an additional hubbing that is misaligned in a clockwise or counterclockwise   direction.

Class 2, Distorted

> A class 2 doubled die results when the hub's design moves toward the rim between "hubbings".

Class 3, Design

> A class 3 doubled die results when a hub bearing a different design stamps a die bearing another design.

Class 4, Offset

> A class 4 doubled die results when the die receives an additional hubbing that is misaligned in an offset direction.

Class 5, Pivoted

> A class 5 doubled die results when the die receives an additional hubbing that was misaligned via rotation with a pivot point near the rim.

Class 6, Distended

> A class 6 doubled die results when the die receives an additional hubbing from a hub that was distended.

Class 7, Modified

> A class 7 doubled die results when the hub is modified between the die's hubbings (e.g., a design element was chiseled off for various reasons).

Class 8, Tilted

> A class 8 doubled die results when a die and/or hub is tilted during a hubbing.

<u>Where Can I Get Coins and Banknotes?</u>

Ask Friends, Family and Other Enthusiasts

Ask people you know if they have old change (Early 60s silver coins and pre 50s pennies especially.), old collections, old banknotes (like $2 bills, silver certificates, etc.) or know of any locations for sales/ estate auctions besides eBay or common online markets. You would be surprised how many people have that old change jar somewhere in their home, waiting to be searched through!

Check with Your Local Bank or Credit Union

Many banks will sell you rolls or bags of coins at face value and you can also find a slew of old banknotes. Variety & Errors have found a TON of great variety and error coins and banknotes this way! It is shocking to think the bank would have great coin finds throughout this rolls and bags!

Expand Your Collection

You can also visit your local coin or gold dealer, hobby store, and individual collectors for buying coins. They typically sell banknotes and coins, but not always at the greatest prices however. These stores almost all the time there's a cheap coin bin that is suitable for kids and adults alike to search through.

Collecting Coins Out of Pocket Change

Once a modern coin has been in circulation, it is typically only worth its face value, although there are notable exceptions. Many varieties of

banknote and coins can be found in pocket change. To be honest, the entire Variety and Errors YouTube channel would have never been anything at all without the wonderful pocket money finds we come across in our searches.

Grading of Banknotes and Coins

Simply put... most people over grade their own currency. It is a simple fallacy we all have, the wishful perception of our finds being worth more than they really are. A qualified second opinion is something important to seek when determining the value for any currency you collect.

Buy the Information Before the Coin

This is an oft-used saying in numismatics that outlines the necessity of researching and understanding a coin before dropping money on it. One of the best ways to "buy and sell carefully" is to read up on the item before you buy the coin. Knowledge is power... and that applies greatly in the coin world. *Would you rather KNOW you have a rare and valuable coin, or THINK you have a rare and valuable coin?*

Go Out and Meet Other Coin Enthusiasts

That's right! This hobby is actually meant to get out and be social. There are conventions, meet up groups, social media outlets like Facebook and Twitter, along with many other great avenues for meeting new and interested people who are also into collecting coins. Check out your local coin store or search online for a Numismatics Association near you. Plus, currency hunting is always better with friends!

U.S. Coin Guide

Lincoln Cent
(1909 – Current)

The **Lincoln Cent**, also known as the penny, first started out in 1909 with the Wheat cent design by Victor David Brenner. Brenner's coveted "wheat cent" design is a favorite among collectors. The initial release of his design featured his initials "V.D.B.", which caused much controversy at the time and were later removed. VDB Lincoln Cents remain a valuable and highly sought after specimen for anyone's collection. If you're interested in the wheat cent, there is more information to follow! Let's start with the modern design you know today.

Lincoln Cent Memorial Reverse Design

The Lincoln Cent with the Lincoln Memorial reverse design was first released in 1959, on February 12th to commemorate the sesquicentennial of Abraham Lincoln's birth. (150th anniversary)

The reverse was designed by Frank Gasparro, who won the internal competition the Mint held between the Mint's engravers.

The design features the Lincoln Memorial from straight on, with a small Lincoln Memorial statue in the center. This is one of the few coins that feature the figure depicted on the coin on both the obverse and reverse sides!

Jefferson Nickels
(1938 – Current)

First minted in 1938, the early years of the **Jefferson Nickel** series have drawn a premium value for a while. Many dates and mintmarks of this coin series are worth 25 cents or more depending on condition and that alone is a stellar premium over face value.

Jefferson nickels began production in 1938 along-side the last of the Buffalo nickels, which are covered later. Introducing a new design featuring Thomas Jefferson on the obverse with Monticello, his Virginia estate, as the reverse design. These nickels have the deep relief of design elements as the previous Buffalo nickel and Jefferson's portrait is raised above the field of the coin.

Jefferson Nickel | Nickel-Copper Alloy

Jefferson nickels are made of a nickel-copper alloy (25% nickel with 75% copper) the same metal used since the first five cent nickel denomination was introduced with the Shield nickel in 1866. A very durable metal proven by longevity of surviving in circulation.

Three mints struck Jefferson nickels throughout the years. San Francisco mint, Denver mint in Colorado, and the Philadelphia mint. All varieties are valued separately, as each has key dates and specimens worth a wide range of values.

JEFFERSON NICKELS IN WAR TIME

"Wartime" Jefferson Nickels were released by the United States Mint during the years of 1942-1945. Each has a composition of 56% copper, 9% manganese and 35% silver for a total silver weight of 0.05626 ounces.

The creation of wartime Jefferson Nickels was owed to shortages of the metal nickel during World War II. The metal was used in the production of armor plating being manufactured for use in military equipment. Similarly, copper in pennies was shifted to war time use during this period as well.

Previous to the release of silver nickels during the war, five cent pieces of the United States were struck from a composition of 75% copper and 25% nickel. In fact, "Nickels", as we refer to them, owe this term to another war, the American Civil War, when five-cent coins were first composed from the metal nickel.

Jefferson Nickel Silver Coin Melt Values

Five-cent coins were not the first United States Mint strikes to contain nickel. Previous to their release, both cent and three-cent coins had compositions containing a percentage of this metal as well. In 1866, the United States Mint opted to use a cupro-nickel blend on the five cent coin as the United States struggled with a silver shortage.

Recognizing this inclusion of the transition metal, the American public began referring to five-cent coins as "nickels", a name which has stuck with the coins since.

The composition of nickels remained the same from its 1866 introduction until 1942. At that point, a substitute had to be found for the metal as it was in high demand for the war effort. By Congressional order, the United States Mint started exploring alternatives and found that a return to the use of silver would result in coins with basically the

same weight and electrical resistance as the pre-war releases. Thus, the United States Mint started producing nickels in 1942 from a 35% silver composition. These are always great to look for.

These new coins would be different from their predecessors by the inclusion of a large mintmark on the reverse side of the coin. The location and size of the mintmark would make them easier to identify for later removal from circulation after the war by the government, an action which never really materialized.

Other than the placement and size of the mintmark, remaining design elements were unchanged from the existing nickel. This includes an obverse portrait of Thomas Jefferson, the third President of the United States. The reverse showed an image of Monticello, Jefferson's estate home. These were added to the coin in 1938 and were designed by artist Felix Schlag.

Following World War II, five-cent coins returned to their previous cupro-nickel content. It should be noted that there are errors that came out of this era of nickels, where some 1942 and 1943 five-cent coins were also struck from a cupro-nickel composition rather than the standard 35% silver of those years.

Wartime silver Jefferson Nickels are desirable for simply what they are, but notably the silver metal content in the coins. As older and somewhat rare strikes, collectors are typically willing to pay a premium for the coins, especially if they are in good condition. Those that are in poor condition are also sought after as junk silver coins for the 0.05626 ounces of the precious metal in each.

Jefferson Nickel 1965 To 2003

A high relief design continues with Jefferson nickels in 1965. Obverse and reverse designs remain the same as in previous years starting in 1938. The designer's initials "FS" were added to the obverse just under the portrait of Jefferson in 1966.

2004 "Westward Journey" Jefferson Nickels Varieties

The "Westward Journey" series of nickels honoring the bicentennial of the Louisiana Purchase and the Lewis and Clark expedition, began in 2004. Nickels from 2004 and 2005 included four designs struck and released into circulation by both the Philadelphia and Denver mints.

First is the 2004 Peace Medal reverse showing the design of the Indian Peace Medal. Lewis and Clark carried special struck coins and gave these to Native Americans along their journey. The second reverse of the year features a 'keelboat' with Captains Lewis and Clark. These vessels were crucial for the time, used to navigate the treacherous and narrow waterways.

2005 "Westward Journey" Jefferson Nickel

In 2005, the third reverse design in the "Westward Journey" series was released. The American Bison reverse recognizes its importance to Native America culture. The obverse design is a new view of Jefferson facing left rather than right. "Liberty" inscribed on the field of the coin is based on Jefferson's own handwriting.

The Second design of 2005 is "Ocean in View"; commemorating the arrival of the expedition at the Pacific Ocean in 1805.

These coins have either Philadelphia Mint ("P" mintmark) or Denver Mint ("D" mintmark) s

"Return To Monticello" - 2006 To Present

During 2006, a new design "Return to Monticello" began, and continues, as the ongoing design of the Jefferson nickel series through current. Jefferson is portrayed in a three-quarter view as the obverse

design. His home, Monticello, is depicted as it is used on nickels in prior years.

Condition Of Modern Era Nickels

A big shift in collecting nickels is evident with the modern era Jefferson nickels. Mint state examples rule the market and most sought after by collectors. Circulated nickels, generally do not have a premium value assigned to them unless they are error coins or key dates in some form.

These circulated coins are GREAT for beginning and young collectors. Many dates and mints are found in circulation. This provides a good opportunity to get into a long running series of coin.

If you believe you have a desirable nickel, I would suggest getting it graded through a professional service. This gives evidence and certification to your find, ultimately raising its value in a variety of ways.

Roosevelt Dime
(1946 – Current)

Introduced in 1946, the **Roosevelt Dime** was hit with a post- war society not utilizing the coin as much as seen currently. Today, sought after Roosevelt Dimes are mostly valued for their 90% Silver content, but those in pristine condition are certainly collectible as well.

These coins have large production amounts and are easy to collect. Beginners can easily find a variety of key dates and notable coins in the modern dime series worth holding onto. Although millions of this little coin have been produced, many are in heavily circulated condition and have no major value to them.

Very high condition or graded specimens of Roosevelt Dimes will attract not only the most attention from collectors, but higher sell values.

ROOSEVELT DIME VALUES

The premium attached to a specific Roosevelt Dime depends completely upon who is buying the coin and the condition. Generally, these coins are affordable for any collector, simply because there are still so many to choose from and so many made.

On the open collectibles market, you can expect to find beautiful Roosevelt Dimes in absolutely pristine condition for around $5, though you can find very nice specimens for about $0.50 to $1.

Certain editions of the coin command higher values when found in excellent condition, but the $1-$5 price range is a good rule of thumb for a lot of regular dimes.

SOUGHT AFTER ROOSEVELT DIMES

With Roosevelt Dimes, most buyers are looking to buy coins in excellent condition, as availability of these is out there. In terms of professionally graded coins, Uncirculated pieces are most desired.

You can analyze the coin to put a rough grade on it. If the coin shines vividly and has sharp detail, it could possibly be an Uncirculated piece or high condition piece.

Washington Quarter
(1932, 1934 - Current)

The **Washington Quarter** was introduced in the 1930s and has remained in continuous circulation ever since. Of course, unlike clad quarters, Washington Quarters minted between 1932 and 1964 contain a good bit of Silver.

For collectors, the Silver content is less of importance than the coins' historical value. Early dates of these coins, in exceptional condition, are the most sought after.

Washington quarters of the early years are 90% silver forming a solid base and premium over face value. As a collectible; 1932 to 1964 dated quarters (the silver era) are popular with collectors assembling date and mintmark coin sets.

First era Washington quarters; 1932 to 1964 are 90% silver and a popular variety of the series with collectors. Availability of all dates and mintmark combinations attracts new and seasoned collectors. Mint state coins attract the most attention and are worth in line with initial mintage numbers. Know your mintmarks to help value these silver coins.

The condition has a large impact on Washington quarters value. A heavily worn "Good" condition coin - if a key date - has appeal to collectors over a better condition non key date. Mint state coins would be the most sought after.
To help you determine the rough condition of your coin, I have included an image below showing details of each grade.

Grading Set: Washington Quarters

Mint State   Extremely Fine   Fine   Good

Value is Condition

As you grade your quarters, you want to focus your attention on the rim of the coin. A full looking rim versus a more worn one can separate a coin in "Fine" condition from one in the slightly lower "Good" condition. Coins with minimal wear and circulation damage tend to command higher premiums.

Kennedy Half Dollars
(1964 - 1970)

Since the introduction, **Kennedy Half Dollars** have been a favorite of the public and collector alike. These coins were produced to commemorate John F. Kennedy in 1964.

The obverse of the coin has shown a portrait of President John F. Kennedy as designed by Chief Engraver of the U.S. Mint Gilroy Roberts. Obverse inscriptions include "LIBERTY," "IN GOD WE TRUST" and the year.

The reverse contains an image of the Presidential Seal as designed by Frank Gasparro. The seal is surrounded by the inscriptions of "UNITED STATES OF AMERICA" and "HALF DOLLAR."

Collectors will typically find that obtaining the 1964-1970 Kennedy Half Dollars is relatively easy and affordable even in higher grades. Those of lower quality are still valuable for their intrinsic silver coin melt values.

Silver Kennedy Half Dollars were produced by the United States Mint from 1964-1970, however, those coins dated 1965 and later were only composed of 40% silver. The 1964-dated Kennedy's were struck from a composition of 90% silver.

The obverse design on the Kennedy Half Dollar is a portrait of former President of the United States, John F. Kennedy. The reverse design of the coin has an image of the Presidential Seal. Each 40% silver coin contains 0.1479 ounces of the precious metal within it.

There was a change in metal content from 1964 to 1965 and was caused by an increase in the price of silver. This helped lead to the Coinage Act of 1965. That Act allowed the Treasury Department , and by extension the U.S. Mint, to eliminate silver from the dime and the quarter and allowed the half dollar to only contain 40% silver moving forward.

Kennedy Half Dollar Values

Prior to the aforementioned change, Kennedy Half Dollars were in great demand. That demand was caused by two major factors. First, President Kennedy had only been assassinated a few years prior to their introduction. They became a quasi- commemorative coin in memory of him.

Second, silver was already on the rise price wise prior to the coin coming out. Almost immediately after the firs Kennedy half dollars came out, the melt value exceeded the face value of the coin!

Due to huge demand for the coin, Congress allowed the mint to produce strikes of the 1964 Kennedy half well into the ladder end of 1965. After 1970, the United States removed all silver from produced coinage.

Half Cent Coins
(1793 - 1857)

Although this coin had a face value of 1/200th of a dollar and was the size of modern day quarter, the **Half Cent** served graciously in the world of circulated coinage for over half a century. One of the most interesting coins struck by the United States Mint is the Half Cent, first sanctioned through an act of Congress in 1792.

Though the Half Cent went through several iterations, it never strayed far from its original, simple design. A Half Cent was first produced in 1793. The coin's design by Henry Voigt, depicted Lady Liberty with blown hair loosely held by what some people think is a small cap and others think is bow – there are conflicting opinions as to which one it really is. Depending on what time of year a 1793 Half Cent was produced, the reverse side features either a ring of chain or a wreath, along with the face value. That chain element drew criticism at the time, for people associated it with the chains of slavery. These designs were later changed across multiple denominations of cent coins in favor of the wreath design.

Many people do not like the design of the Half Cent Coin. It seems comical and ill conceived. Aside from the issue with an original design referencing slavery, many people think the depiction of Lady Liberty is comical and disproportionate. This coin went through multiple design changes over the years and the latest issue was much more accepted by everyone I think.

Half Cent Importance

After the 1793 release of the first design for the Half Cent's subsequent disapproval, officials decided the next release should be altered. Following this initial change, would be a string a redesigns. These include:

- In 1793, Mint Director David Rittenhouse hired Joseph Wright to adapt the design the obverse of the 1794 Half Cent. Wright also depicted Lady Liberty, but unlike the 1793 version, her hair was well maintained and adorned with a Phrygian cap – a historic symbol of freedom.
- In 1796, Chief Engraver Robert Scot completely redesigned a great deal of the nation's coinage, including the Half Cent. Lady Liberty was still on the obverse, but she faced right and was more mature looking. It also featured her in more detail. The reverse still bore a wreath, but it was changed to an olive wreath symbolic of peace.
- In 1808, the coin would be redesigned again. That artwork is commonly referred to as the Classic Head design. The obverse features a left facing Lady Liberty with headgear not very dissimilar to a crown or mantle worn by ancient Greek athletes.
- In 1840 another redesign of this coin would happen after changes in metal composition and a dissatisfaction with the depiction of a mature Lady Liberty. She would be changed to have fashioned hair into a stylish tight braid. This design remained on the coin, unchanged, until the Half Cent was discontinued in the late 1850s.

Factors that effect the value of these coins is probably pretty obvious at this point. Ultimately, the value will be based on the year and design of the coin. Condition has a play as well, just like any other coin, but the age is the biggest determinate in valuing the Half Cent in your possession. For collectors, completing a collection of Half Cents is amazing! These coins were produced for more than 60 years and some or more then 200 years old, making them a wonderful addition to any collection!

Large Cent Coin
(1793 – 1857)

Large Cents are the same thing as modern day pennies as far as value, but the U.S. public did not adopt the name "Large Cent" very easily. Among the first coins produced by the United States Mint, the Large Cent had a face value of 1/100th of a dollar.

These coins were roughly the size of a half dollar and were made for over 60 years. The obverse of the coin depicted a right-facing Lady Liberty with her hair blown back as if by a strong wind. The coin's reverse caused great controversy upon its release, as it depicted a ring of chains. This initial design was not welcomed by most U.S. citizens, it is of particular importance to numismatists now. The U.S. Mint responded to public dissatisfaction and altered the design of both sides of the coin. The Large Cent's new reverse depicted an ornate wreath, which met with much greater favor than the ring of chains.

They saw a lot of circulation, but were eventually phased out in favor of the smaller cent. Every year from 1793 to 1857, with the exception of 1815, the U.S. Mint struck large quantities of Large Cent coins. The 1815 coin was unable to be produced due to an embargo set during the war of 1812. This stopped the use of copper planchets to produce coins and the back stock of these planchets had run out by the time they were required to produce the coin, so they simply did not happen. After the war ended in 1816, the Philadelphia mint began producing

the Large Cent again. Oddly, this would be the only mint to make the coins throughout their entire production!

VALUE OF THE LARGE CENT

Large Cents are extremely popular and easy to get a hold of. You can easily buy and sell these! Among coin enthusiasts, it is one of the most collected coins. These precious coins were among the first coins designated as the official coinage of the United States! Even in poor condition, these coins are valuable in any condition. These coins represent United States history itself and so they are great to have in your collection. Since the Large Cent in some years can be over 200 years old, you can understand why these are sought after. If you are looking to purchase a coin like this, you need to expect to spend between $1,000 to $2,000. In really good condition, these coins can be worth thousands of dollars!

If you have one of these coins or you end up coming across one of them, get it graded! Having a professional grading service certify the coin will undoubtedly qualify the condition and help in the event of selling the coin. It is much easier to establish a value for a graded coin since you can compare it to other coin sales featuring similarly graded Large Cents.

Flying Eagle Penny
(1857 - 1858)

Flying Eagle Cents are beautiful coins and I think anyone who is lucky enough to have one of these, should feel fortunate! Originally, pennies were made of purely of the metal copper, but by the mid-1800s, pure Copper coins were expensive to make and were subsequently phased out for different compositions of metals.

The mint began striking smaller pennies composed of Copper combined with other metals, commonly silver. During this time, gold and silver coins of foreign countries were still accepted as legal tender, but that was coming to a change as the U.S. began producing its own currency. Flying Eagle Pennies were at last produced in April 1857 and launched into circulation.

The obverse of the coin depicts an embolden eagle flying, the Flying Eagle Penny is a relatively plain coin with only the singular depictions on either side. On the reverse of the coin is an inscription saying, "United States of America", and the mintage year. The coin's reverse artwork is also pretty plain, featuring the one-cent face value within a wreath. A reed- like texture encircles both faces of the coin. Overall, the Flying Eagle Penny is extremely plain, but still very beautiful in its simplicity.

FLYING EAGLE PENNY VALUES

The Flying Eagle is a super weird coin in the history of U.S. currency. Despite many people loving the design and the intended use of the coin, it had many problems on the production line. Issues with minting these coins resulted in a change in design within a couple of years of its release. The coin was quickly discontinued and replaced by the Indian Head Penny. Due to this very short time in production and circulation, these coins are prized among collectors.

The finite supply of these coins, coupled with most of the ones found in the "wild" today are in poor shape. Another factor in its value to collectors is the depiction of the flying eagle itself. Many coin experts believe the Flying Eagle Penny was the first coin to ever feature a bird mid- flight. Across the globe previous to this point, birds had been used by many countries on their currency, but usually depicted in the form of a crest or bust. Many coin enthusiasts believe the Flying Eagle Penny is the first coin worldwide to feature an animal in "natural state".

The Flying Eagle Penny is not easy to find or obtain, especially in good condition. As you may know, pennies were used for a TON of transactions then, as they are now. For anyone trying to complete a set of pennies for their historical significance, having a Flying Eagle penny is a must. Now, keep in mind, these coins are generally close to $2,000 in most cases, so this addition will not be cheap. However, these coins will become the main feature in your collection if you are lucky enough to acquire one!

Indian Head Penny
(1859 – 1909)

There are quite a few penny designs out there and the **Indian Head** is definitely one the favorites among collectors. These coins have a wide variety of values and can be found pretty steadily when searching both local and online markets. These coins debuted in the years prior to the Civil War and were continued until shortly after the turn of the 20th century.

Indian Head pennies can be traced back to the Large Cent. (Also covered in this book.) Large Cents began in 1793, but were an odd coin due to the restriction of what metals were to be used as legal tender during the time. Being of mainly copper, it was a weird coin to the public, as gold and silver were still understood as the only precious metals to be used as tender. Things such as government tax payments and municipal fees had to be paid with a tender backed by gold and silver, something these cents didn't have.

The need for a different metal in later years drove the United States to reduce the size of the Large Cent, effectively phasing out that version of the coin. This need drove the mint to develop the Flying Eagle Penny, which was struck only from 1856-1858. This coin differed from previous pennies in that its metal content was less than 90% copper. Unfortunately, these coins quickly encountered design flaws and had to be replaced. Their replacement was the Indian Head Penny, which was launched on the market in 1859.

The design of the Indian Head Penny was conceived by James Longacre, the acting engraver of the United States Mint.

INDIAN HEAD PENNY VALUES

The Indian Head is hugely popular with collectors. For the longest time, my local coin shop here in North Carolina had a basket with old "junk" Indian Head Pennies for only a dollar. For collectors, the Indian Head Penny represents great historical significance of its era. The first years of this coin were produced just before the outbreak of the Civil War. Due to this, you will find some coins produced in the first few years of the Indian Head Cent's existence now command a much higher premium than other editions made during later years.

When it comes to values, these coins are all over the map. You can pick up later year coins from this series for only a few bucks, whereas high condition coins from the pre- Civil War period can command values in the thousands.

Lincoln Wheat Cent
(1909 – 1958)

The always popular **Lincoln Wheat Cent**, launched by the U.S. Mint in 1909, is beloved by casual collectors and serious enthusiasts alike. While some original pennies from 1909 have significant value (like the previously mentioned 1909 VDB pennies), there are other editions of the Lincoln that are highly sought after by coin collectors also. For instance, a 1933-D may have a value at or above $2.30, where as a slightly older 1931-S Lincoln cent could command $40 to $50 or more in the coin sales market. A huge difference for only a couple of years difference in age!

Of course, some mint years may be valued much higher than others, and other factors such as minting location, condition and the amount of pennies produced, play a large role in valuing your coins. In an obvious note, high quality condition coins will certainly command a higher premium in value over poorer condition coins.

VALUE OF LINCOLN PENNIES

Coin dealers and collectors are willing to pay a significant premium for superior condition or high graded Lincoln Wheat Pennies. The values of collectible wheat pennies in good condition range from a couple of dollars to thousands of dollars. If you own a Lincoln Wheat Penny, in great condition, from a desirable year, you may benefit from having your penny graded by an NGC or PCGS grading service. In having your wheat cent graded, you can compare it to historical auction sales of similar coins for a better valuation of what you have. The grading process is exacting, and takes into account very subtle grading points and will be discussed further later in this portion of the book.

LINCOLN WHEAT PENNY CONDITION

To gauge the grade of your Lincoln Wheat Penny, you need to really examine the coin. One simple detail to inspect is the wheat stalks on the coin's reverse side. If the lines at the tops of the wheat stalks remain crisp, clear and robust, the coin may be in extremely fine condition. If the parallel lines at the top of the wheat stalk are easily observable, the coin is likely in fine or perhaps even better condition.

If the penny bears significant circulation wear, the lines at the tops of the stalks are worn down or even worn away. In this case, the coin might be in good or a lesser condition.

Of course, the coin's other details must also be in excellent condition to be assigned a grade of extremely fine, with little to no signs of wear. Simply put, the better the overall condition of your Lincoln Wheat Penny, the more desirable it may be to dealers and collectors.

COIN GRADING IS VERY IMPORTANT

If you have a Lincoln Wheat Penny that you believe to be in excellent condition, submitting your coin to for professional grading may be a good idea. This goes for error and key date coins as well. (Errors will be discussed in a later section.)

I feel the fee charged fort these grading services are worth it, in most cases, because it usually adds a higher premium to your collectible coin when selling it. In short, coins that have been graded typically sell for higher premiums than non-graded coins, so the graded fee is a wash and generally pays for itself.

VALUES ARE RISING ON PENNIES

While on the subject of wheat pennies, let me mention my thoughts on the future of their values. The value of Lincoln Wheat Pennies constantly shifts due to demand and supply, like any other collectible. Over a period of years, wheat penny values may increase based on the trajectory of their historical values. This happens for numerous reasons, including new collectors entering the market or established collectors gaining an interest in the coin as whole or a certain variety of the coin.

Additionally, new varieties such as double-dies or over-dates may come to light, enhancing the attraction of Lincoln Wheat Pennies. New errors always drive us collectors crazy!

Two-Cent Piece
(1864 – 1873)

Two Cent coins were minted due to a need for the denomination at the time. They were quickly phased out in exchange for more usable one cent coins, but there limited run gives them some good value to collectors.

Despite being a limited mintage coin, these Two Cent Pieces have never really taken off on the market over the years and can easily be obtained. In higher conditions they go for around $150 to $200, but you can also get a coin in Very Good (VG) condition for around $40 in most cases, depending on year.

Two Cent Coin Value

Condition of this can mean the difference between a coin being worth $15 and a coin that is worth $500! You can put a general grade on your coin by looking at the inscriptions. The motto "IN GOD WE TRUST" can provide detail about the coin's condition. If these letters exhibit medium wear, the coin may be in good condition or similar.

If the coin has all letters present and readable but has some slight wear or fading, the coin may be in fine condition. A coin that has all letters present and easily discernible that has maintained a crisp and clean detail across both sides, might be considered extremely fine condition. You can also look at other details on the coin's surface such as the ribbon for any signs of wear and tear, as well as the edge, since this will help determine the overall condition of your Two Cent coin.

If you are lucky enough to come across one of these coins, it would best to get it graded by a certified professional grading service. This process will encapsulate the coin and certify the grade and condition of the coin. This will maximize the value you may receive if you go to sell the coin.

Three Cent Silver Coin
(1851 – 1872)

Bullion from the California Gold Rush came to the Eastern U.S. in considerable quantities beginning in the 1840s. Silver coins subsequently disappeared from circulation. This gave way to coins produced with smaller amounts of silver content and creating the first coin not intrinsically tied to its precious metal content, the Three Cent Silver. The **Three-Cent Silver**, also known as the three-cent piece or "trime", was struck by the Mint from 1851 to 1872, and as a proof coin in 1873.

The value of a Three Cent Silver Coin varies based on a variety of factors. The condition of the coin plays a part, but mainly the year of mintage. Coins from mid- 1850s in good condition sell for around $100, where a first year, 1851 can be seen selling for close to $500 in good condition! If you have a 3-Cent piece from any year in good condition, get it graded by a professional grading service. This will maximize sales value for the coin and encapsulate it from further wear.

These grading services will put your coin through a rigorous inspection process, allowing the expert to accurately gauge the coin's condition to the minutest standards. They will also verify the coin's Silver content and authenticity. When you have your coin graded, you can rest easy knowing you have the best information as to the coin's fair market value.

Three Cent Nickel
(1865 - 1889)

The copper-nickel Three-Cent Piece, often called a **Three Cent Nickel**, was designed by U.S. Mint Chief Engraver James B. Longacre. The Three Cent Nickel was a circulation coin produced by the United States from 1865 to 1889. From 1865 to 1873, the mint struck a three-cent Silver piece as well. These coins had a short mintage period and there are a few of them that are incredibly expensive.

The Three Cent Nickel was never popular with the public and was not used as much as intended in general circulation. Because of this, many of these coins can still be found in nearly perfect or Uncirculated condition, making them worth a lot of money!

The minting date of these coins can have a significant impact on the overall value of your coin. These coins are all valuable in their own right, but first year coins from this series are the most valuable.

The Three Cent Nickel was only minted for basically 25 years. While half of these mint years are relatively easy to obtain, there are a few years of production that are not as easy to come by. Three Cent Nickels from 1876 to 1889 are extremely valuable in comparison to the rest of the minted years. These saw less production, among other factors, and generally see higher sales prices.

Values for the common dates range from roughly $15 in good condition to $120+ in higher conditions. If you have a nickel from a collectible date, your coin may potentially be worth a minimum of $50. If your coin is of higher condition, you could be sitting on a coin worth hundreds, even ungraded!

Shield Nickel
(1866 - 1883)

The **Shield Nickel** is a really great coin for any collector. They hold good value and can be found for well under $100. The Shield Nickel is just one of the many five-cent coins produced by our mint, but I think its real value comes from its historic significance as one the earlier coins of its type.

SHIELD NICKEL HISTORY

The Shield Nickel was a later 5-cent coin released in 1866. During this time, they were often referred to as "half dimes". Production of this coin came after an almost immediate halt to minting coinage upon the onset of the Civil War in the United States during the 1860s.

During the Civil War, commerce and trade transactions changed to the use of negotiable assets and trade goods in the forms of tickets, stamps and tokens. Congress would later pass laws to abolish smaller three cent coins and replace them with other coinage. A new five- cent piece was authorized during this time as well, being the Shield Nickel in 1866.

SHIELD NICKEL DESIGN

The Shield Nickel is the first United States five- cent coin minted using a copper- nickel composition. This is the same composition of metals used in the production of modern nickels today.

The shield design was chosen as a strong patriotic representation. The reverse features a simpler design to showcase the face value with some minor details of sun rays. The shield was loosely based on the Great Seal of the United States. Maybe you will like these coins for their design!

POPULARITY AMONG COLLECTORS

Shield Nickels are collected for quite a few reasons, most notably, for their historical importance. These are one the first coins minted after the Civil War. Also, Shield Nickels were some of the first coins struck in nickel, not only a metal never used before, but also the basis of the term "nickel" used for the coins today.

Funny enough, the design of the coin was originally not favored by many, but is a huge driving force in the value today. Many collectors like them for the patriotic depiction of the shield itself. Beginning collectors can easily start with Shield Nickels due to the availability of the coin. There were plenty of Shield Nickels preserved over the years and these coins make an excellent introduction to numismatics for new collectors with a circulated condition price of around $20.

Liberty Head 'V' Nickel

(1883 - 1913)

V Nickels are a wonderful coin to collect in any condition! Although, you are not going to find these floating around in pocket change, you can come across them pretty steadily in local coin shops. These five-cent coin were minted by the United States Mint from 1883 to 1913. The values of these coins are heavily factored upon by date and scarcity, the same as many other coins. For example, early V nickels from pre- 1897 are going to be worth A LOT more than later ones. Many start at the $5 - $10 mark. 1885 V Nickels are noticeably more valuable, usually garnering sales prices around $500.

When you have a coin graded by a professional service, you will get a clearer idea of the value and an approximate grade assigned to the coin. This is done through a regimented and exacting process to determine the coins overall condition and authenticity.

V NICKEL VALUE AND CONDITION

If you want to put a rough value on your V Nickel, you must closely examine the coin and its condition. Begin this process is by carefully looking at the stars around the coin's edge. If the stars are worn, which is generally how you will find these, then you V Nickel is in Good condition. If the stars have good detail and have only minor wear, the coin is close to Fine.

If details are crisp and there is little to no wear at all on the coin, the condition is probably close to Extremely Fine. The entire coin needs to be examined in order to really "condition" it, but getting the coin graded by a professional service is ultimately the best idea.

YOUR V NICKEL COULD BE RARE

If you have an 1885 V Nickel... things are a bit different. This is VERY valuable coin. The 1885 V Nickel is super sought after by collectors and enthusiasts alike. These coins have a huge value sitting usually around $500 in even worn condition, to over $2,200 in cleaner condition. These are very hard to come by however, so get yours graded if you have one!

The 1886 V Nickel, the 1912 V Nickel and the 1912-S V Nickel are all popular. Each of these coins sells for over $100 in Good condition, so they are also ones to look for while out on the hunt!

Buffalo Nickel
(1913 - 1938)

The **Buffalo Nickel** is another one of those coins that has a great design on both the obverse and reverse. I really like them! Today, the Buffalo Nickel is extremely popular among collectors. For some, the challenge of assembling a complete set of Buffalo Nickels provides an unparalleled exhilaration.

Struck from 1913 to 1938, with its strong and rustic design by James E. Fraser, the Indian Head, or "Buffalo" nickel has long been a popular series. It is difficult to complete a set of these coins, but many people have. The earlier years, especially in good condition, will bear the highest cost.

BUFFALO NICKEL VALUE

The problem when finding Buffalo Nickels is that they are usually really beat up. This doesn't mean they are not valuable, though! Even in bad shape, they are all worth above face value. So if you can, grab any and all Buffalo Nickels when you see them.

There are a few different ways to collect Buffalo Nickels. You can obtain one of each, Type 1 and Type 2, for example. A date set, when complete, will have one of each year of production represented. This is probably the most popular way to collect them. More advanced collectors will search for each of the dates and mintmarks of the 64 Buffalo Nickels. The most advanced collectors will not only want one of each of the 64 date and mintmark issues, but also the 8 recognized varieties, which are the following:

- 1914/(3) "overdate"
- 1916 doubled die
- 1918/7-D
- 1935 doubled die reverse
- 1936-D 3-1/2 Legs
- 1937-D 3 Legs
- 1938-D/S

There are quite a few re-punched mintmarks found in this series as well, so be on the lookout for those. Proof coins from 1913-1916 and 1936 and 1937 are really good to have in your collection. The first five of these proofs that were minted were in a matte finish are the most valuable.

For starting collectors, this is great set to complete even if it has a few coins that will take some time to obtain. I know a few local coin stores that have baskets of Indian Head/ Buffalo Nickels on the counter full of good finds.

Bust Half Dime
(1794 – 1837)

The **Bust Half Dime** is the series of half dime pieces of United States currency used in circulation between 1794 and 1837. There were several varieties of the Bust Half Dime, including the Draped Bust with a small eagle on the reverse, the Draped Bust Half Dime with a heraldic eagle reverse and the Capped Bust Half Dime.

Including all major types, there are three separate early half dimes series, including the Flowing Hair (1794-1795), Draped Bust (1796-1805), and Capped Bust (1829-1837). There are also two sub- types within the Draped Bust series of Half Dimes. These include the Small Eagle Reverse (1796-1797) and Heraldic Eagle Reverse (1800-1805). These major types and the Draped Bust sub- types are all valuable and sought after. Many people try to complete various sets of these.

BUST HALF DIME VALUES

As with other Bust coins, the value of a Bust Half Dime widely varies based on the mintage year, type and condition. For example, a Capped Bust Half Dime from 1829 might go for around $50, whereas one from the earlier part of the series in 1796 would exceed $8,000 in a sale easily.

If you have a Bust Half Dime from a choice year, or a coin that seems to be in really good condition, consider having your coin professionally graded by a coin grading service such as PCGS or NGC. Coin grading qualifies the coin and certifies its condition. With coins that are old like this, grading will maximize the amount you may get when going to sell the coin. Good luck in completing your set!

Seated Liberty Dime
(1837 - 1873)

For nearly fifty years the **Liberty Seated Dime** was minted in the U.S. and saw wide circulation. These coins are undoubtedly an easy coin to start collecting. I love the text based design on these coins and have a few myself, although I am not lucky enough to have a completed collection. Someday... someday.

This coin was minted from 1837 to 1891 and struck at the mint facilities located in Philadelphia, New Orleans, San Francisco, and Carson City. The obverse features on this coin are a great depiction of Lady Liberty seated on a rock with a shield in one hand and a pole with a 'freedom' cap on the end of it. Oddly, Seated Liberty Dimes included no stars on the obverse side of the coin.

LIBERTY SEATED DIME VARIETY

The different years of mintage and the different designs for this coin can command different values. Of course, many collectors only want the highest quality of coins, but I find that decent circulated version of this coin are steadily out there and a great option for a beginning collector. Liberty Seated Dimes minted from 1860 to 1873 changed from having stars in the legend to "United States of America". This is known as Variety 1. If you have Seated Dimes that seem to be in great condition or is struck in the earliest years of the coin's mintage, have your coins graded by a professional coin grading service!

The Liberty Seated Dime series has a ton of great varieties to collect!

There are doubled dies (commonly called "double die"), misplaced digits, multi struck coins and, aside from errors, multiple mint locations to collect from!

The series was produced for 46 years in large quantities and many collectors believe there are plenty of new, exciting discoveries to be found when looking through Liberty Seated Dimes. Since really high grade/ condition coins draw large values, many lower condition coins can be easily picked up for around $20 to $30. The value of these coins has risen a few dollars per year, so collecting them also shows a lot of promise!

Barber Dime
(1892 – 1916)

You may have noticed a pattern in **Barber Silver Coins**, many share the same design features! This design, created by Chief Engraver Charles Barber, is depicted on dimes, quarters and half dollars. Barber Dimes were minted from 1892 to 1916 and contain 90% Silver, alloyed with 10% Copper.

Although there are several factors in making a Barber Dime valuable, the mintmark plays a huge role in this. The mintmark on this coin is under the wreath on the reverse (back side) of the coin.

Many Barber Dimes are worth good money. San Francisco mintmark coins tend to have higher values in good condition. 1909 S Barber Dimes can be worth in upwards of $150! Denver and New Orleans mintmarks are very valuable also, usually selling for around $90 and $110, respectively. The most common Barber Dime was minted in Philadelphia and bears no mint mark. These coins have values from less than $10 typically.

Barber Dimes can be found in a wide range of conditions and a wide range of prices. Obviously, you will want every high condition example of this coin, but I would suggest buying any of them you can. These high silver content coins are always a great investment!

Mercury Dime Values
(1916 – 1945)

I think **Mercury Dimes** are one the coolest busts featured on the obverse of a 10 cent coin! The value of a Mercury Dime varies greatly depending on its year of mintage, condition of the coin and mintmark.

If you have your Mercury Dime graded, that will definitely help associate a value to your coin. In most cases, you can reference coin sales of other Mercury dimes of the same grade, to see what they sold for. Getting a coin graded is always a good idea if it will be sold or added to a long standing collection as it qualifies and preserves the exact condition of the coin.

MERCURY DIME VALUE

There is huge opportunity to collect Mercury Dimes. They were minted in large quantities for most years of their production. The rarest Mercury Dimes are the following:

- 1916-D
- 1921
- 1921-D
- 1925-D

- 1926-S
- 1931-D
- 1942 over 41
- 1942 over 41-D

The best way to complete the set is to start with Philadelphia mintmark coins. These are abundant and pretty cheap per coin. You can then go to the others and fill them in.

All these coins are getting scarcer to find. Although there were many of them made, you will generally only find well circulated copies with major wear. If you are lucky enough to come across a Mercury Dime in great condition, you could have a real premium over face value. The aforementioned varieties of this coin are the most sought after, so if you have one of those, get it graded if you haven't already!

Twenty Cent Seated Liberty

(1875 – 1878)

Many people have never heard of the **20 Cent Piece**. So I thought it was a good start for this portion of the guide. Thomas Jefferson introduced this coin as part of a "decimal model" to U.S. currency.

Mass amounts of silver was coming from Nevada and this coin became available as that metal needed to be refined into a tangible coin for commerce. Struck from only 1875 to 1878, the Twenty Cent Piece has a super low mintage of only 1.4 million. This makes it one rare and valuable coin!

These coins are struck in 90% silver. They are extremely rare and generally do not see the auction block very often. This is not to say you cannot get one of these coins, they are just pricey in good condition. This coin would have saw a lot more mintage, but the quarter dollar was already accepted and circulating as a much stronger part of United States coinage. This made the Twenty Cent Piece redundant in many ways, not to mention it was almost the same exact physical size as the quarter!

The Philadelphia Mint produced only 38,500 examples in 1875 and survivors are scarce across all grades. Decent condition coins from this period are oddly found in pretty decent shape despite this low amount. High condition coins are of course, the most sought after.

Twenty Cent Coin Value

Twenty Cent coins have a wide range of prices. This is driven mainly by condition of the coin, as it was minted for such a short period of time. A first year, 1875 20 – Cent Piece, is worth about $250 in Very Good condition. We can then look at something like a Seated Liberty from 1876 in Uncirculated condition and it sells for over $10,000! Crazy!

Bust Quarters
(1796 – 1838)

Bust Quarters are an awesome coin to collect for multiple reasons. Since they were minted so long ago, their age alone gives them good value. They are generally seen selling for higher values than other quarter dollars. They are not easy to find in good condition, mainly due to the age and abundant use during their time in circulation.

This circulation lasted for almost 50 years! Bust quarters were used in a lot of daily commerce throughout the United States, so most found today are in poor condition. Even so, these coins were made during a hugely important portion of U.S. history and have intrinsic value for that as well!

When you usually find Bust Quarters, they will be in fair condition due to extensive use and age. This wear and tear can be seen with the naked eye. The price these coins can command ranges dramatically, as seen in some coins minted in later years of the series selling for only $100, whereas early iterations sell for close to $1,000 in high condition.

THE VALUE OF AN EARLY BUST QUARTER

It will be hard for a buyer to find an early Bust Quarter for less than $80 or so, unless it is absolutely worn out. For example, a coin from 1807 may be nearly impossible to find, but there may be thousands of the Bust quarter produced just one year later on the market. In general, a collector can expect to pay anywhere between $800 and $2,800 for an

Early Bust Quarter. Most collectors still desire the oldest and rarest of any given coin in the best possible condition, of course.

Early Bust pieces produced in 1819 and graded decently, like Extremely Fine condition, will sell for close to $900 more than one minted in the 1830s. This age gap, coupled with the scarcity of the 1819 Bust Quarter, adds up to an extreme difference in the premiums seen when selling these coins.

Every collector pays attention to condition and that goes for any collectible. Whether you collect coins or comic books, the condition drives a lot of the value in most cases. This may not be case with these, as all of the coins are well over 100 years old. So, I think collectors are a bit more lenient when it comes to condition when buying a Bust Quarter. Condition is still important of course, but like an original run Superman comic, it is understandable that nearly all of them will show wear or some sort. I mean, in the older days of mail order comics, they came rolled for goodness sake!

Seated Liberty Quarter

(1838 - 1891)

Quarter dollar coins of all types have been favorites among collectors since their introduction. I know I like my ever expanding Washington Quarter collection! These coins have played a huge part in commerce and the quite old The United States Mint has produced numerous types of quarters throughout history, but the **Seated Liberty** is one of the most popular. Introduced in 1838 and ending at the turn of the century, these coins are valuable and old.

Nearly every type of Seated Liberty is valuable to collectors, but there are key date and special versions that are most sought after. If you are lucky enough to obtain one of these in excellent condition, you could have multi- thousand dollar coin!

VALUE OF A SEATED LIBERTY

Seated Liberty quarters have age to them and as such, value no matter what year or condition. This does not mean they are crazy expensive in every regard. There's no fun to coin collecting if every older coin is outrageously expensive, right?

A lot of Seated Liberty Quarters can be purchased in good condition for around $30. Of course, excellent condition coins and graded coins will have different values entirely. I see these for sale regularly in coin stores as well, so you should be able to buy one at your local shop for the most part. Plus, you should always support local coin stores if possible!

HIGH VALUE SEATED LIBERTY QUARTERS

It can be a little difficult to put a precise value on your Seated Liberty unless it is graded, but there are a few that are quite a bit more valuable then others. For example, 1877 Seated Liberty Quarters are usually around $20- $30 in poorer condition, but the same year coin from the Carson City Mint (CC Mintmark) will be valued around $40.

SEATED LIBERTY QUARTER VALUES

These coins are becoming increasingly hard to find and even though some are cheaper in cost, desirable condition coins are getting super hard to find. These obviously won't be in your pocket change most likely, but I see these coins in shops and online all the time. If you don't have a local coin store, then online auction sites generally have vetted sellers to buy from and are also good places to sell your Seated Liberty Quarter. The future value of these is looking good as the poorer coins gain a few dollars in value each year and the better condition coins seem to always sell for good money.

Barber Quarter
(1892-1916)

Quarters have always been steadily used since their introduction into U.S. coinage. They are one of the most common forms of metal currency in circulation today and are highly collectible in a ton of ways!

Barber Quarters were minted from 1892 to 1916 and were designed by U.S. Mint Chief Engraver Charles E. Barber, hence the name, "Barber Quarter." Collectors really like these coins due to their historic prominence as a turn of the century coin and their short mintage period. Mint locations that struck this series of coins included Philadelphia, Denver, New Orleans and San Francisco. As with any other collectible coin, the value is the highest with top level condition. The good thing is, if you do not want to spend a fortune on one of these coins, you probably don't have to!

Generally, the starting price for a Barber is below $10, but some have been known to go for more than $1,500 if the coin is in excellent condition! Another factor contributing to the price of this Silver coin is the type of Barber you own. Each year the coin was produced had up to three different mint locations, thus mintmarks.

The 1892-O, for example, will typically sell for around $100 while the 1892-S will sell for nearly $215 in the same condition. Some 1895 and 1896 Barber Quarters go for as much as $1,000!

SOUGHT AFTER BARBER QUARTERS

Like a lot of other coins, the most sought after Barber Quarters are either error coins (See the Error Coin Guide in this book) or coins from scarcer mintage years. Condition still plays a HUGE part of putting a value to your Barber Quarter. The better the condition, the larger the sales price.

One thing to keep in mind is the short length of time these coins were in circulation, just short of 25 years. This "smaller" window gives way to a lot of value in this series of coins! Ultimately, if you get a hold of a Barber Quarter in really good condition, you might have some big money on your hands! An early 1900s Barber Quarter might sell for $15 to upwards of $100, depending on its condition.

The key dates to look for:
- 1896-S
- 1901-S
- 1913-S

Standing Liberty Quarter

(1916 - 1930)

The public absolutely loved the **Standing Liberty Quarter** upon its release in 1916. It made many people think of the similar Seated Liberty of the 1800s. The Standing Liberty Quarter also had beautiful artwork like the earlier version!

These coins were only minted for 15 years (1916-1930), but are considered one of the most beautiful coin designs ever produced. Even with this short mintage period, these coins can be found throughout coin shops and dealers regularly.

STANDING LIBERTY QUARTER VALUES

The premium commanded by any Standing Liberty Quarter depends on how well preserved the coin is. Collectors looking for these coins usually want top tier condition coins, but that doesn't mean the beat up one you found or inherited isn't worth anything! Even poorer condition coins can be worth a few hundred dollars!

When you have a coin graded by a professional service, you will get a clearer idea of the value and an approximate grade assigned to the coin. This is done through a regimented and exacting process to determine the coins overall condition and authenticity.

HIGH VALUE STANDING LIBERTY QUARTERS

In relation to the "coin world", Standing Liberty Quarters are pretty available despite their age. Circulated copies are pretty easy to come by and add to your collection. High condition coins, not so much. So grab those up when you can!

Many collectors and enthusiasts search for San Francisco mintmark, or "S", coins due to those being more valuable with less mintage.

Bust Half Dollar
(1794 – 1839)

The Half Dollar has been produced since the very first days of the United States Mint and has always seen good circulation. The first iteration of the Half Dollar, known as the Bust Half Dollar, was first minted in 1794. Sometimes referred to as a "Capped Bust", due to the cap worn by Lady Liberty on the obverse of the coin. These were produced for almost 40 years and saw much circulation life. Due to the old age of these coins, it is difficult to find one in Good or higher condition. Their older age also drives the price of these coins as fewer and fewer are seen on the market for sale.

THE VALUE OF A BUST HALF DOLLAR

The most important factor in pricing these coins is the mintage year means a great deal when it comes to determining a price point. Of course, like any collectible, the condition does matter, but these coins are very sought after and leniency is taken in regards to condition to some degree.

Naturally, Busts produced during the 1700s and early 1800s are valued above those produced during the later parts of the series like the 1820s and 30s. Even the most recent Bust Half Dollars in Poor condition are not cheap, as they are still very old and have prominence in other manners to collectors. Bust Half Dollars can range from around $6 to $30,000! I know... I know... you're probably thinking that is a HUGE range of values for a coin! You would be right.

SOUGHT AFTER BUST HALF DOLLARS

The first Bust Half Dollar, the Flowing Hair Half Dollar, is by far the most desirable coin in this series. This particular variety of Half Dollar was minted for just two years! (1794-1795) The extremely low number of these coins, due to this sort mintage period, makes them worth thousands of dollars. You would be very, very lucky to own one of these beautiful coins!

As with any coin over 200 years old, the condition is important, but not the most important driving factor in establishing a value on your coin. Flowing Hair Bust Half Dollars are so rare that they generally sell for close to $10,000 in good condition. Now, later years are cheaper in most cases, but that depends on your definition of cheap. Capped Bust Half Dollars are usually less expensive then their Flowing Hair counterpart. These usually sell from a few hundred dollars and up.

Year after year, these coins have gained value. They are very expensive in any condition really. If you want to have one of these as part of your collection, I would suggest buying sooner then later, because there is no telling how expensive Bust Half Dollars will be in coming years!

Seated Liberty Half Dollar
(1794 – 1839)

The **Seated Liberty Half Dollar**, or Seated Half Dollar, is a wonderful coin to collect and was the third variety of half dollar. It was minted in the United States in 1839. This coin would replace the Bust Half Dollar.

The general public really liked this coin's design featuring Lady Liberty. Collectors love these coins for the immense rarity, especially in good condition. High condition coins can be worth thousands!

VALUE OF A SEATED LIBERTY HALF DOLLAR

The premium on a given Seated Liberty Half Dollar depends on a few factors. Most importantly, the condition of the coin affects its value. As a collector, you will undoubtedly want a high condition coin.

Unfortunately, not many excellent condition Seat Half Dollars even exist. The year of issue also matters with Seated Half Dollars, as with any coin. Those produced during or around the Civil War command higher prices than coins struck during more peaceful periods of time. These coins can range from $20 to well over $1,500. High condition, key date coins in excellent condition should be sent in for grade, which will really increase the value when selling.

Barber Half Dollar
(1892 – 1915)

The **Barber Half Dollar**, the third of the Barber-designed coins minted by the United States, circulated from 1892 to 1915. The public did not really love nor hate the design, but overall accepted the high detail on the obverse of the coin. Since the coin was not produced for very long, they can command really high values on the market. Collectors love these coins!

Additionally, almost every Barber Half Dollar I have ever come across in a local coin shop or auction was totally worn out. When you find these in better condition for sale and you can afford it, grab them up!

Unlike other coins of this time period, the Barber Half Dollar is so scarce it commands pretty good value in any condition. Although high condition versions of any coin are preferred by collectors, these coins are sought after in any condition.

As an example, a poorly preserved 1896 Barber Half Dollar can be worth around $15, but a high condition version of this same coin can be seen selling for over $600! In general, plan to spend somewhere around $75 to $450 on average for one of these coins.

Basically all Barber Half Dollars minted are worth collecting. You cannot really ask for much more than a great coin, with great history, and solid value year after year. Condition is still a huge driving force behind the values of these coins, even with their short mintage advantage to this detail. I love Barber Quarters though, I think you should pick up cheaper, worn out specimens as good collectibles. They are cool to have in a collection and also a great investment coin!

Walking Liberty Half Dollar
(1916-1947)

The **Walking Liberty** design is one that very few coin collectors will fail to recognize, heralded as one of the best designs to ever grace a US coin. The evocative image of Lady Liberty seemingly gliding across a sunrise landscape is something that is near and dear to every American's heart.

In addition to the coin's design, the timing of this particular coin's minting makes it especially valuable. First minted in 1916 and minted up until 1947, this coin was around during some of the most iconic periods of American history.

Nowadays, collectors are constantly striving to get their hands on these coins, though fewer and fewer of them exist with each passing year. This is something that is only going to grow truer as time moves forward.

Walking Liberty Half Dollar Values

Determining the price you might be asked to pay for a Walking Liberty Half Dollar is no more difficult than taking into consideration a few different factors. First and foremost, collectors will closely analyze the surfaces of a Half Dollar, looking to spot even the smallest imperfections. As you might expect, those coins that have been extremely well-preserved over the course of their 50+ year existence are the ones that will sell for the highest prices.

The range of prices the Walking Liberty Half Dollar falls under can range from as little as $10 to many thousands of dollars. While condition plays some role in determining the price of a Walking Liberty, the year in which the coin was minted and the type of coin it is also help determine a price. It is important to keep in mind that there were up to 3 different types of Walking Liberties produced every year, so while one Walking Liberty type from a given year will sell for x-price, another type of the same year's coin may sell for double or even triple that price. When it comes down to it, the price you are going to be asked to pay can vary quite dramatically.

Sought After Walking Liberty Half Dollars

To put it simply, the most sought after Walking Liberty Half Dollars are those that were produced first. The coins from the 1910s and 1920s take precedence simply because they are older and naturally a bit more difficult to come across. When you are referencing these older coins, it is important to point out that the absolute most sought after versions of these coins are the well-preserved ones. This is so because it is amazing for a collector to have a 90+ year old coin that looks as though it was just recently minted.

Beyond that, you will find that, generally, the most sought after pieces are those that have had their condition preserved. These coins were heavily circulated and you will find that most have been pretty beaten up through years of changing hands. For someone to say they have a coin that is will over 50 years old yet still in perfect condition, that is something that is truly remarkable.

Franklin Half Dollars
(1948-1963)

Silver **Franklin Half Dollars** were released by the United States Mint beginning in 1948 and running until 1963. The coins feature an obverse image of American inventor, author and founding father of the United States, Benjamin Franklin. The reverse of the coins depict the Liberty Bell, including its famous vertical crack.

Franklin Half Dollars were struck from 90% silver with 0.3617 ounces of the precious metal. The 12.5 gram coins have a diameter of 30.6 mm and were struck in the Philadelphia mint, San Francisco mint and Denver mint.

Prior to the release of the Franklin Half Dollar, the U.S. Mint had been producing the Walking Liberty Half Dollars, designed by artist Adolph A. Weinman.

Historical Franklin Half Dollar Silver Coin Melt Values

U.S. Mint Director Nellie Tayloe Ross implementing a new idea for the half dollar in 1947. U.S. Mint chief engraver John R. Sinnock was instructed to come up with potential designs that would feature the founding father. Sinnock passed away before he could complete them, but his assistant, Gilroy Roberts, stepped in to complete the new design.

Shown on the obverse of Franklin Half Dollars is a right facing portrait of Benjamin Franklin. Surrounding his image are the inscriptions of "LIBERTY," "IN GOD WE TRUST" and the year of minting.

The reverse showcases an image of a cracked Liberty Bell. To the right of the bell is a small eagle. The reverse also includes the inscriptions of "UNITED STATES OF AMERICA," "E PLURIBUS UNUM" and "HALF DOLLAR."

Franklin half dollar's production would end up having a short life span due to the assassination of President John F. Kennedy. Congress sought to immortalize Kennedy on a piece of currency and the new Kennedy Half Dollar appeared in 1964.

With relatively high mintage amounts, a complete collection of the Franklin Half Dollars is attainable at reasonable prices. So, beginning collectors can jump on these to have a complete set early on in the hobby. As with all other coins, higher grades demand higher values.

Those Franklin Half Dollars in such poor shape as to warrant little or no numismatic interest are still valuable owing to their intrinsic silver coin melt value.

Flowing Hair Dollar
(1794 – 1795)

The very first US Silver Dollar ever made was produced in 1794 as the **Flowing Hair Dollar**. This coin did not have a denomination indicator such as "1 D." or "One Dollar" - So the denomination was simply discerned by the diameter size of the coin and the lettering on the edge: "HUNDRED CENTS ONE DOLLAR OR UNIT". The reverse of the coin features the Small Eagle portrait. Source of example image is courtesy of Heritage Auction Galleries.

Flowing Hair Dollar Design

Obverse: Flowing Hair design with six curls, the third curl weak on most specimens. First star close to 1 in date. Second star near first curl, but does not touch it. The head of Liberty in the 1794 dollar has a fuller cheek and more pronounced jaw line than does any of 1795. Blunt tip to neck point. No head on a 1795 dollar is exactly like this head.

Reverse: Eagle perched on a rock within a wreath; 21 leaves on each branch. The wreath has 19 berries, 10 on the left branch, 9 on the right. A leaf is joined to second T in STATES, and another almost touches the right corner of F in OF. "Lobster claw" leaf pair under second T of UNITED and first A of AMERICA. Eagle's wing touches R in AMERICA. Ribbons below wreath thinner and much closer together, and branch ends thinner and straighter, than on any 1795 reverse. Ribbon around junction of the two wreath stems. Rock under eagle's

feet extends much farther to the left than on any 1795 die. This die was retired after the 1794-dated coinage and was not used in 1795. Flowing Hair Dollars are rare in most grades. These coins are known for their beautiful design and attention to detail. If you have one of these coins, please contact one of our local coin experts to have your rare coin appraised. We offer free rare coin appraisals and would love to buy your coin. Our rare coin price guide should give you all the information you need, but if you need more information, don't hesitate to reach out to our team of rare coin experts.

Draped Bust Dollar

(1795 - 1804)

Bust Silver Dollars were among the first minted silver dollars and were only produced for a short time. (1795-1803 and again in the 1850s) Due to their limited mintage, these coins are INCREDIBLY valuable. Even poor condition coins are worth good money!

Although more stuffy collectors of these coins will swear you should only look for perfect specimens. This is incorrect! If you come across any of these coins in any condition, I suggest picking them up for your collection. Not only are they beautiful coins, but they have historically gained a steady value over the years and will continue to do so.

THE VALUE OF A BUST SILVER DOLLAR

As I stated before, a Bust Silver Dollar in any condition is valuable. The higher end condition coins are generally hundreds of dollars. Lower condition coins with signs of wear and tear can be bought in the neighborhood of a whopping $1,500 - $2,400. Which is crazy! High, almost mint state coins would go for close to $5,000+.

The value of Silver Dollars is primarily based off of the condition of the coin then anything else, but also the date in some regards. Coins minted during the late 1800s can be found pretty steadily, usually for a few hundred dollars. Bust Dollars from the late 1700s are much more valuable. For example, a Bust Silver Dollar graded Uncirculated or Extremely Fine, is going to run no less than $2,100.

SOUGHT AFTER BUST SILVER DOLLARS

So, what to look for? Realistically, every Bust Silver Dollar is worth buying. They are beautiful coins and all valuable. They are an old coin, scarce in many ways, and a favorite among silver dollar coins. These factors all aid in making this coin's value continue to grow from its already high price tag.

In short, the older the Bust Silver Dollar, the more valuable. Coins minted in the late 18th century will hold the highest value. Uncirculated and Extremely Fine varieties of Bust Silver Dollars command premiums over $9,000. This is obviously not a coin sought after by beginning collectors, but if you are lucky enough to come across one or maybe inherited a collection, get the coin graded and slabbed!

Seated Liberty Dollar
(1840 - 1873)

Seated Liberty Dollars are an awesome coin to get into if you are starting collecting. It is the second silver dollar minted, but unlike its predecessor, these coins were minted for more then 30 years. This means they can generally be found pretty easily and are not crazy in price.

From a precious metal content standpoint, they contain silver of course, but the condition of the coin still plays a heavy factor into the overall value of the coin. Seated Liberty Silver Dollars are all more than a century old and most of them will show definite signs of circulation wear. Even if this is case, these coins can still have some decent value.

WHAT YOU WILL PAY

As with any collectible, Seated Liberty Dollars in good condition are ultimately going to be the coins that you want to search for. The problem for most collectors is that these coins have an incredibly variable cost. While a lower condition. The dramatic price variance has to do with the rarity of a given coin.

Naturally, an excellently preserved Seated Liberty from 1843 has greater value on the market than a similarly preserved coin from 20 years later. If a seated Liberty Dollar is something you want to add to your collection, then a semi- worn out one will cost you somewhere around $80 to $100. Higher condition coins can garner sales prices in the thousands!

I would suggest making the Seated Liberty Dollar a later coin to add into your collection due to the higher price and also the scarcity of coming across one of these coins in good condition.

THE MOST DESIRABLE SEATED LIBERTY SILVER DOLLARS

So to the really important stuff, what coins do you look for?

Coins from the 1840s are always great and really valuable. These coins are over 150 years old and are collected for both their historical and monetary values.

Seated Liberty Silver Dollars are sought after and pricey in good condition. If you are lucky enough to come across one of these, its super important to get it graded if you can. Rarity drives value, so holding onto one of these coins is always a good ideas. As I stated before, even super worn copies of these coins can go for around $100, where as good condition Seated Liberty Silver Dollars can sell for thousands.

Morgan Silver Dollar
(1878 - 1921)

The **Morgan Dollar** is a coin that means a lot to me. Not only is it regarded as one of the most beautiful coins ever produced, but my dear friend, Dustin Morgan, who got me into coin and banknote collecting years ago, loved this coin the same. Dustin may no longer be with us, but I think of him every time I see one of these coins.

Morgan Dollars were immediately embraced by everyone the moment of their release in 1878. This coins production ran through 1904 before being replaced by the Peace Dollar. Demand for its return surfaced and the Morgan Dollar return for one year in 1921. Next to the Nova Constellatio, Morgan dollars are one of my favorite coins. I have a 1921 Morgan Silver Dollar that is made into a ring.

You will want to look for Morgan Silver Dollars in quality condition as with any other collectible coin or banknote. These will command the most value. The Morgan Silver Dollar shared some design aspects of the Bust Dollar, but had a lot better detail. On lightly circulated specimens of this coin, the design features will be highly visible and exhibit minimal wear.

All of these coins are over 100 years old, so they are getting harder and harder to come by, especially in good condition. The good news is that theirs values steadily rise, making them a great coin to grab up.

MORGAN SILVER DOLLAR VALUE

The value of the Morgan Silver Dollar you have found, purchased, etc.; will be determined from a few different factors. The age of the coin and the condition will be the biggest driving forces behind higher or lower values. Coins from the earlier series are most sought after, but harder to find of course. Morgan Silver Dollars from 1921 are easy to come by. These were mass produced, with nearly 90 million of them hitting circulation. These are generally well under $100 in good condition. Other factors can apply to your coins value, as well. If you have an error coin, like a doubled die, you will add exponential value to any Morgan Silver Dollar. If the coin is in exceptionally good condition and from the late 1800's, you could potentially be sitting on thousands of dollars!

There were three varieties of the Morgan Silver Dollar struck for each year it was produced. Certain coins, such as those from the Carson City Mint (Bearing the mintmark: CC), generally have higher values then others from the same year.

Peace Dollar
(1921 - 1935)

Peace Dollars are a favorite of collectors as well as myself. These coins were minted from 1921 through 1935. You should be thrilled to have one of these if you do not only for their historical significance, but also their value. Peace Dollars were the last silver dollar minted that was meant for circulation. Until the U.S Mint began production of the Eisenhower Dollar in 1971, Peace Dollars were in production for over 30 years.

The Peace Dollar is undoubtedly one of the most known and collected coins on the market. I absolutely love the design of this coin. Collectors seek this coin for its silver content, its limited mintage and the prominence surrounding the coin.

PEACE DOLLAR DESIGN

The design of the Peace Dollar is the work of sculptor Anthony de Francisci, who was chosen through a nationwide competition, at 34 years old, de Francisci was the youngest competitor. The original design featured a few difference from the one eventually used, including variations of a sword. One of these versions featured a broken sword and was felt to be "weak" or unpatriotic. This design was altered to the one featured on the minted coin.

PEACE DOLLARS FOR COLLECTORS

For collectors, the Peace Dollar is famous not only because of its limited mintage but also its historical significance. The coin is seen as real piece of American history, which, of course, adds to its value. Condition matters a lot less in relation to this coin due to these factors.

The Peace Dollar's value is also high as one of the last silver dollars to get minted in the United States. Similar to other limited mintage coins, the value will be higher in the earlier years especially. Many of these coins can be found in decent condition and for $40 - $60. Coins minted in 1921 are most sought after and have a few errors like light striking. These coins are a bit more expensive, although you can usually pick one up for under $100.

NOTES ON THE PEACE DOLLAR:
- The design of the Peace Dollar was changed to 'low relief' in 1922
- A die break is known in the hair on the 1923
- Some 1925 coins have a missing sun ray
- The 1928 edition is the scarcest, with only 360,649 minted

Eisenhower Dollar Coins
(1971 - 1978)

Between 1971 and 1978, the United States Mint released a $1 coin with President Dwight D. Eisenhower on the obverse. Commonly called **"Ike Dollars",** these coins did not see much popularity.

Because of their bulky size, Americans tended to associate them with 90% Silver Dollars, such as the Morgan or Peace Dollar.

Eisenhower Ike Dollar Varieties

After the aborted Peace Dollar coinage in 1965, Congress mandated that no more silver dollars be coined for a period of five years. As this restriction ran out in 1970, the owners of gambling casinos were lobbying for dollar coins to replace the ones lost to silver hoarders. An omnibus bill passed at the end of that year provided for the elimination of all silver from the half dollar and production of a new dollar coin that was likewise to be of the copper-nickel-clad composition.

These dollars were of the traditional size and bore a portrait of Dwight D. Eisenhower, the late president and Army general.

The reverse carried a reproduction of the Apollo XI emblem, both Eisenhower's passing and the first moon landing having occurred in 1969.

Designed and sculpted by U. S. Mint Chief Engraver Frank Gasparro, the Eisenhower Dollar debuted in the fall of 1971. The circulating edition of the " Ike" Dollar, though it did answer the needs of casinos, was otherwise a flop with the public.

During its eight years of production, it enjoyed the same obscure status as the half dollar and was a coin rarely seen outside of areas where gambling was legal. The 1973 Eisenhower Dollar was produced solely for collectors, and there were no dollars dated 1975.

The entire production that year was devoted to a combination of back-dated 1974 coins and those bearing the dual bicentennial dates 1776-1976. These featured a distinctive reverse design by Dennis R. Williams of the Liberty Bell superimposed over the moon.

The Eisenhower Dollar series has recently found a wide base of support. The primary focus is on collecting all of the Eisenhower Dollar varieties, dates and mints, in high grades. For several issues, such examples of varieties are quite elusive.

The Philadelphia Mint Ike Dollars are especially challenging to locate on good planchets and free of numerous or heavy marks. The silver-clad collector editions of 1971-74 and 1976 Eisenhower Dollar varieties, as well as the proof coins, are likewise quite popular.

If you come across a key date, collectible and/ or error Ike Dollar, then make sure to get it graded by a professional grading service. Getting you're Eisenhower dollar graded will maximize the value when you go to sell it at auction or to a private party. Although there is small fee associated with getting a coin graded, it is worth it in most cases.

Susan B. Anthony Dollar
(1979 – 1981, 1999)

The United States Mint introduced the **Susan B. Anthony Dollar** in 1979. They had high hopes that this new smaller dollar coin would circulate well in the United States.

This coin honors a pioneer in the woman's rights movement. Chief Engraver of the United States Mint, Frank Gasparro, designed both the obverse and the reverse. His initials are located on the obverse near the lower right side of the portrait. This coin marks the first time that a portrait of a real woman (as opposed to an allegorical figure of Lady Liberty) appeared on a United States circulating coin.

Over time, demand dropped, and production ceased in 1981. Due to a request from the United States Postal Service, the mint produced another run of these one dollar coins in 1999. In the following year, the mint introduced the new "Golden Dollar" with Sacajawea on the obverse.

Mintmarks

The mint produced Susan B. Anthony dollars at three different mints: Philadelphia (**P**), Denver (**D**) and San Francisco (**S**). As illustrated in the photo in the link below, the mint mark is located on the obverse of the coin, in the lower left-hand area, just above the shoulder of Susan B Anthony.

Key Dates, Rarities, and Varieties

The following Susan B. Anthony Dollars, in any condition, are worth considerably more than common SBA dollars.

- 1979-P Wide Rim Variety
- 1979-S Proof Type 2 (clear "S" mintmark)
- 1981-S Proof Type 2 (flat "S" mintmark)

Condition or Grade

If your coin is worn and details are light due to circulation If the coin is extremely worn, it will be worth no greater than its face value. If your coin looks similar to the one illustrated in the link below and has no evidence of wear due to being in circulation, it is considered an uncirculated coin. Remember, an uncirculated coin can still have some nicks and scrapes on it due to its handling during the production process. However, these should be minimal and not due to the coin being used in circulation.

American Eagle
(1986 – Current)

The **American Eagle** bullion coin program began in 1986 and with it came the first $1 American Silver Eagles, or "ASE's." American Silver Eagles revive the obverse design of Walking Liberty, as designed by famed sculptor Adolph A. Weinman and utilized on United States silver half dollars struck from 1916 through 1947. The reverse depicts a stylized heraldic eagle design by John Mercanti.

While uncirculated (or "bullion") $1 American Silver Eagles contain one troy ounce of silver and are chiefly touted as coins designed for precious metals investors, more numismatists seem to be collecting these base-level ASEs in recent years. Many hobbyists are assembling date sets in albums or collecting certified MS specimens in registry sets.

As more collectors are paying attention to the dates of their bullion-quality American Silver Eagles, a few issues have gained recognition as scarce semi-key pieces. Among these are the first-year-of-issue ASE from 1986, the 1994 uncirculated silver eagle, and the 1996 silver eagle, all of which regularly trade for substantial premiums above their spot value.

Silver Eagle Dollar Varieties

All burnished silver eagles trade for multiples of spot value, as does the 2013-W enhanced finish ASE. The rarest uncirculated quality silver eagles are error varieties, including the 2008-W Reverse of 2007 and 2011-S burnished silver eagles. While it's become expected by many individuals in the marketplace that all American Silver Eagles are readily available in high grade, this simply isn't the case with earlier ASEs, which remain challenging to find in top Mint State grades.

All of these coins are worth holding onto. They historically gain value in any condition, but graded ones are the most expensive.

Sacagawea Dollars
(2000 - 2008)

Sacagawea or Sacajawea gold dollar coins were minted in their first iteration from 2000 until 2008. They were minted again, with different reverse designs, starting in 2009. These are popular coins but well over a billion have been minted since 2000.

There are a few of varieties that are collectible like the 2000-P Cheerios coin. Your regular strike Sacagawea coins however, are typically worth just their face value. Older rolls of Sacagawea coins can sell for a small premium to the right collector. They are made of copper, manganese, brass, zinc, and nickel.

Even though they are not crazy collectible value wise, the Sacagawea dollars are beautiful coins and many people collect them or try to complete sets of this coin.

Designs of the Sacagawea Dollar

Sacagawea has her infant in a papoose over her shoulder. Her son was named Jean Baptiste Charbonneau. The back of the coin features a more familiar design. It has a flying eagle, 17 stars, and the traditional text of E Pluribus Unum – United States of America – One Dollar. The front of the coin says LIBERTY and In God We Trust.

There will be a P, D, or S mint mark under the year. And the back of each coin also has the initials TDR for Thomas D. Rogers Sr, the mint sculptor and engraver.

Original design of the 2000 Sacagawea Dollar Coin circulated until 2008. The Eagle on the reverse was designed by Thomas D. Rogers. The obverse has not changed and was designed by Gelnna Goodcare.

Sacagawea Dollar Coin design from 2000 – 2008

2009 Design: The first change in design of the reverse side of the coin after its circulation started in 2000. It commemorates the contribution of Native American women to agriculture. The design features a Native American woman planting seeds in a field of corn, beans and squash.

Sacagawea Dollar Coin design 2009

2010 Design: The reverse design features the Hiawatha Belt with five arrows representing the five original Nations. The inscription on coin "HAUDENOSAUNEE, GREAT LAW OF PEACE, UNITED STATES OF AMERICA".

Sacagawea Dollar Coin design 2010

2011 Design: The reverse design depicts the hands of the Supreme Sachem Ousamequin Massasoit and Governor John Carver, symbolically offering the ceremonial peace pipe after the initiation of the first formal written peace alliance between the Wampanoag tribe and European settlers in 1621.

Sacagawea Dollar Coin design 2011

2012 Design: The reverse features a Native American man and horse in profile with horses running in the background, representing the historical spread of the horse.

Sacagawea Dollar Coin design 2012

2013 Design: The 2013 design commemorates the Delaware Treaty of 1778. Its reverse design features a turkey, howling wolf and turtle, symbols of the clans of the Delaware Tribe and a ring of 13 stars to represent the Colonies.

Sacagawea Dollar Coin design 2013

Presidential Dollars
(2007 - 2011)

The United States Mint honors our nation's presidents by issuing **$1 Presidential Coins** featuring their images in the order that they served. The program began in 2007 with Presidents Washington, Adams, Jefferson, and Madison.

Note: In December 2011, Secretary of the Treasury Timothy F. Geithner directed that the United States Mint suspend minting and issuing circulating Presidential $1 Coins. Regular circulating demand for the coins will be met through the Federal Reserve Bank's existing inventory of circulating coins minted prior to 2012.

The Presidential $1 Coin Act seeks to revitalize the design of United States coins and return circulating coinage to its position as an object of aesthetic beauty in its own right. Accordingly, the Presidential $1 Coins feature larger, more dramatic artwork, as well as edge-incused inscriptions of the year of minting or issuance, "E PLURIBUS UNUM," and the mint mark.

From 2007 to 2016, the Mint issued four Presidential $1 Coins per year, each with a common reverse design featuring a striking rendition of the Statue of Liberty. The composition of the Presidential $1 Coins is identical to that of the Sacagawea Golden Dollar and the Native American $1 Coins.

Native American Dollars
(2009 - Current)

Beginning in 2009, the United States Mint began issuing $1 coins featuring designs celebrating the important contributions made by Indian tribes and individual **Native Americans** to the history and development of the United States.

The obverse design remains the central figure of the "Sacagawea" design first produced in 2000, and contains the inscriptions LIBERTY and IN GOD WE TRUST.

The reverse design will change each year to celebrate an important contribution of Indian tribes, or individual Native Americans, and contain the inscriptions $1 and UNITED STATES OF AMERICA.

The law requires that at least 20 percent of all $1 coins minted and issued in any year be Native American $1 Coins. Like the Sacagawea and Presidential $1 Coins, the Native American $1 Coins will maintain their distinctive golden color. In addition, they will feature edge-lettering of the year, mint mark and E PLURIBUS UNUM.

These are extremely great coins to start collecting. Although they are not necessarily worth any collectible value currently, they will be. If we look at its counterpart coin, the Sacagawea Dollar, we can see that long term investment can flourish into really high collectible premiums to thee types of coins.

Native American Dollar Designs

2009

REVERSE OF THE 2009 NATIVE AMERICAN DOLLAR

THEME: Agriculture - The "Three Sisters Planting Method". This is an ancient method of gardening used by Native Americans where corn, squash, and beans are grown together simultaneously on the same mound of soil.

DESIGNED & ENGRAVED BY: U.S. Mint Sculptor-Engraver Norm Nemeth

MINTAGE: Philadelphia: 39,200,000; Denver: 35,700,000; San Francisco: 2,179,867

2010

REVERSE OF THE 2010 NATIVE AMERICAN DOLLAR

THEME: "Government - The Great Tree of Peace" - The Hiawatha Belt is a visual record of the creation of the Haudenosaunee, also known as the Iroquois Confederacy, with five symbols representing the five original Nations. The central figure on the belt, the Great White Pine, represents the Onondaga Nation with the four square symbols representing the Mohawk, Oneida, Cayuga and Seneca Nations.

DESIGNED BY: Artistic Infusion Master Designer Thomas Cleveland

ENGRAVED BY: U.S. Mint Sculptor-Engraver Charles Vickers

MINTAGE: Philadelphia: 32,060,000; Denver: 48,720,000; SF: 1,689,216

2011

**REVERSE OF THE 2011
NATIVE AMERICAN DOLLAR**

THEME: "Supreme Sachem Ousamequin, Massasoit of the Great Wampanoag Nation Creates Alliance with Settlers at Plymouth Bay (1621)" - The 2011 reverse design depicts hands of the Supreme Sachem Ousamequin Massasoit and Governor John Carver, symbolically offering the ceremonial peace pipe

DESIGNED BY: Artistic Infusion Master Designer Richard Masters

ENGRAVED BY: U.S. Mint Sculptor-Engraver Joseph Menna

MINTAGE: Philadelphia: 29,400,000; Denver: 48,160,000; San Francisco: 1,673,010

2012

**REVERSE OF THE 2012
NATIVE AMERICAN DOLLAR**

THEME: "Trade Routes in the 17th Century" - In keeping with the coin's theme, the 2012 reverse design features a Native American and horse in profile, with horses running in the background.

DESIGNED BY: United States Mint Artistic Infusion Program Master Designer Thomas Cleveland

ENGRAVED BY: U.S. Mint Sculptor-Engraver Phebe Hemphill

MINTAGE: Philadelphia: 2,800,000; Denver: 3,080,000; San Francisco: 1,189,445

2013

**REVERSE OF THE 2013
NATIVE AMERICAN DOLLAR**

THEME: "The Delaware Treaty" - After declaring independence, the United States signed its first formal treaty with an Indian tribe, the Delaware Tribe, at Fort Pitt, now Pittsburgh, on September 17, 1778.

DESIGNED BY: United States Mint Artistic Infusion Program Master Designer Susan Gamble

ENGRAVED BY: U.S. Mint Sculptor-Engraver Phebe Hemphill

MINTAGE: Philadelphia: 1,820,000; Denver: 1,820,000; San Francisco: 1,192,690

2014

**REVERSE OF THE 2014
NATIVE AMERICAN DOLLAR**

THEME: "Native Hospitality Ensured the Success of the Lewis and Clark Expedition" - The reverse design depicts a Native American man offering a pipe while his wife offers provisions of fish, corn, roots and gourds. In the background is a stylized image of the face of Clark's compass highlighting "NW."

DESIGNED BY: Chris Costello

ENGRAVED BY: Joseph Menna

MINTAGE: Philadelphia: 3,080,000; Denver: 5,600,000; San Francisco: 665,100

2015

**REVERSE OF THE 2015
NATIVE AMERICAN DOLLAR**

THEME: "Mohawk high iron workers, builders of New York City and other skylines (from 1886)" - The reverse design depicts a Mohawk iron worker reaching for an I-beam that is swinging into position, rivets on the left and right side of the border, and a high elevation view of the city skyline in the background.
DESIGNED BY: Ronald D. Sanders
ENGRAVED BY: U.S. Mint Sculptor-Engraver Phebe Hemphill
MINTAGE: Philadelphia: 2,800,00; Denver: 2,240,000; San Francisco: 1,050,166

2016

**REVERSE OF THE 2016
NATIVE AMERICAN DOLLAR**

THEME: "Code Talkers from both World War I and World War II (1917-1945)" - The design features two helmets with the inscriptions *WWI* and *WWII*, and two feathers that form a "V," symbolizing victory, unity, and the important role that these code talkers played.

DESIGNED BY: U.S. Mint Artist Thomas D. Rogers, Sr.
ENGRAVED BY: Renata Gordon
MINTAGE: Philadelphia: 2,800,000; Denver: 2,100,000; San Francisco: 923,414

2017

**REVERSE OF THE 2017
NATIVE AMERICAN DOLLAR**

THEME: The coin honors Sequoyah of the Cherokee Nation, creator of the Cherokee language. The reverse design features a profiled likeness of Sequoyah writing "Sequoyah from Cherokee Nation" in syllabary along the border of the design.

DESIGNED BY: Chris Costello
ENGRAVED BY: Charles L. Vickers
MINTAGE: Philadelphia: 1,820,000; Denver: 1,540,000; San Francisco: 488,460

2018

**REVERSE OF THE 2018
NATIVE AMERICAN DOLLAR**

THEME: This year's coin recognizes the accomplishments of Olympian and multi-talented athlete Jim Thorpe. The reverse design depicts Thorpe, with the foreground elements highlighting his football and Olympic achievements. Inscriptions are "JIM THORPE", and "WA-THO-HUK", his native name.
DESIGNED BY: Michael Gaudioso
ENGRAVED BY: Michael Gaudioso
MINTAGE: Philadelphia

2019

THEME: The theme of the 2019 Native American $1 Coin design is American Indians in the Space Program.

2020: Elizabeth Peratrovich

2021: Military Service

2022: Ely Parker

2023: Maria Tallchief

Liberty Head Gold Coin
(1849 - 1854)

The **Classic Liberty $2.50 Gold** coin is a really interesting one. These coins are sometimes referred to as Classic Head Quarter Eagle. Minted from 1840 to 1907, they bear the depiction of Lady Liberty on the obverse and an eagle on the reverse.

On Liberty Head $2.50 Gold coins, the mintmark appears just below the eagle's feathers on the reverse. These coins were minted at various mint facilities, and the minting location could affect the coin's value. "D" is for the Dahlonega Mint, while a "C" is for Charlotte. "S" is for San Francisco and the rare "O" indicates a coin struck in New Orleans.

Although, generally, very expensive coins all together, $2.50 Classic Liberty coins are really seen the collections of either the lucky or those with more monetary allotment. Why? These coins are 90% gold and 10% copper alloy, so their metal content alone commands great value.

LIBERTY HEAD $2.50 GOLD COIN VALUES

Uncirculated $2.50 Liberty Gold Coins are well over $4,000. That price point makes them a super expensive coin, even when talking about lower condition specimens of this coin. If you are looking to get into these coins, expect to spend at least $250 on a decent condition 1877, which is a bit more common. If you have a $2.50 Gold Liberty Head of a desirable mintage year, or one that seems to be in well-preserved condition, you may want to consider having it graded professionally by

a coin grading service such as PCGS or NGC.

So what condition or grade is your $2.50 Gold Liberty Coin? You can get a rough grade on your coin inspecting it yourself. I get it, you are not necessarily an expert grader, but with a few tips, you can get a decent idea of the starting point for condition of your coin.

For example, on the $2.50 Liberty Head Gold coin, you might focus on the eagle's olive branch and arrows. If the olive branch and arrows are considerably worn down and smoothed out, the coin is likely only in good condition. Anything further then this will put your coin in a low grade status. If your coin exhibits clear detail and the raised portions of the coin show minimal wear, you should get your coin graded. This will solidify the condition of the coin by a professional grader and ultimately maximize sales price when you go to sell it.

Not to be dramatic, but the Classic Liberty Gold Coin could very well become too expensive for the "normal" collector. I mean, you are already talking an extremely expensive coin and this coin becomes more expensive every year. With gold typically trending upward over time, it is not a bad idea to buy these coins if you can afford them as they always a make a solid investment.

Indian $2.50 Gold Coin

(1908 - 1929)

Indian $2.50 Gold Coins have gained value and over again, year after year. These are great coins to collect if you can afford the high price tag. Due to both their historic prominence and their intrinsic gold content value, these coins continue to get more and more valuable as years go by. Since their release in 1908, many of these coins have been lost in time, while any that turn up generally have a ton of wear on them. There will never be more of these coins, so if having one is something you desire, I suggest buying into them sooner then later.

With $2.50 Indian Heads, it is important to do some comparison shopping before committing to a purchase because retailer's premiums can differ by a hundred dollars or more. I know in a coin shop you will see FAR different prices than at a convention dealer or auction house. However, the latter generally does have extra fees associated with sales so this does factor into the higher price points.

INDIAN $2.50 COIN VALUE

$2.50 Indian Head Gold coins are expensive. Poor condition coins, due to the intrinsic value of their Gold content. You should prepare to pay at least $200 or more for one of these coins, though some special pieces can run as much as $4,200.

THE MOST SOUGHT-AFTER INDIAN $2.50 COINS

Several Gold Indian Quarter Eagles are considered particularly desirable by collectors, mainly those minted in certain years. The 1911 and 1914 Indian $2.50 Gold Coin are both very rare and sought after. The most valuable of the series is the 1911, but prepare to pay a high price tag. Generally well over $2,000 in good condition.

It is impossible to tell exactly what the value of a $2.50 Gold Indian may be the future, but historically their values have steadily increased. Collecting these can never be a bad idea. They are pricey to get into but will never see a period of losing money in the coin market simply due to their gold content value. Gold has been on a steady rise, despite fluctuation in spot value, over the last 100 or so years. This makes any gold coin worth collecting!

$3 Gold Coin
(1854 - 1889)

These were a dud upon release! The **$3 Gold Coin** was first minted in 1854. People really didn't use them as planned and they phased out after limited production. They are still a great gold coin to collect though!

The first mintage in 1854 was very large, but numbers would fall steadily until the complete stop to this coin in the 1870's. I think the $3 Gold Coin came out in a time of big changes within the currency world. The government sought to enact a lot of laws during this period when the public was still getting used to gold coinage. Not only that, but the laws had changed on postage and the need for other coinage took precedence over the usage and subsequent mintage of the $3 Gold Coin. So, it was a bit doomed before birth so to speak.

$3 GOLD PIECE DESIGN

The $3 Gold Coin design is called the Indian Princess Head. Other details on the obverse include the word "Liberty" inscribed along the coronet of the headdress.

The reverse is designed with a wreath inspired by agriculture, including wheat, corn, cotton and tobacco. The wreath surrounds the date and

"3 Dollars" to indicate the face value. A point on the design in relation to condition: You can use the knotted ribbon or top of the headdress as starting points for conditioning the coin. The clearer the details, the better the condition the coin. If your coin exhibits minimal wear, it could have a baseline condition of around FINE.

$3 GOLD COIN VALUE

Like other pieces from this period, the $3 Gold coin value is swayed yup or down by the year it was minted and the condition. Higher condition coins are very hard to come by, but some Fine and Extremely Fine coins are seen regularly in stores and online sales.

Late 1870s coins are easier to come by in circulated condition whereas an earlier or release year $3 Gold Coin would be better found in a certified auction sale. I have even seen quite a few mint state coins for sale over the last few years also.

Liberty $5 Gold Coin
(1839 - 1908)

The **Liberty $5 Gold Coin**, also known as a Half Eagle, was used quite a bit more than counterpart gold coins due to $5 being common buying power at the time. These coins are extremely collectible and valuable. They generally run over $1,000 in good condition. $5 Liberty Gold coins have historic prominence as well due to being a part of the gold coin series. Their metal content is highly sought after and a driving force in their values.

The $5 Liberty Gold coin was minted for nearly 70 years and there are generally plenty of these coins on the market for interested buyers. Due to their age and popularity of these coins, they are typically found on the market in poor condition. As stated, they generally run over $1,000, but low grade coins with visible signs of wear can be seen for a few hundred dollars. It depends on what year the coin is and spot price of gold at the time of purchase, as these coins are 90% gold.

THE MOST DESIRABLE LIBERTY $5 GOLD COINS

Like many coins, there are certain versions of the $5 Gold Coin that are more valuable than others. This difference in price can be seen in different mintmarks on these coins. The mint facility that produced the coin can effect the sales price of these $5 coins immensely. For

example, the 1877-S $5 Liberty is valued between $300 and $1,500, whereas the 1877-CC minted in Carson City is worth well over $2,000. Even if these coins are expensive, you should collect them if you can. They have historically gained value year over year.

Indian $5 Gold Coin
(1908 - 1929)

The **$5 Gold Indian coin**, sometimes called a Gold Half Eagle, was first minted in the early 1900s and was in production for just over 20 years. As most of these coins are over a century old, their general condition may leave something to be desired. You should feel lucky if you have any one of these coins in even poor condition, because even a much lower grade $5 Gold Indian Coin will command a great value!

During its period of mintage, the $5 Indian Gold represented an extremely high face value. In that day, $5 had A LOT more buying power then today, where you can barely get lunch for $5.00! Even during their general circulation not every citizen used Gold Half Eagles regularly. Even so, there are fewer of these coins on the market each passing year.

THE VALUE OF A $5 INDIAN GOLD COIN

Because $5 Indians are in high demand and because of the intrinsic value of their Gold content, these coins are not typically acquired by beginning collectors or those on smaller budgets. I would suggest getting into this coin later collecting after you have gotten experience with other coins.

Rather, it is generally veteran collectors who can devote considerable resources to their collections who purchase these pieces. Consider at least $400 to acquire a $5 Gold Indian. Poor condition examples can reach over $1,000 easily.

THE MOST COVETED $5 INDIAN GOLD COINS

Realistically, ALL $5 Indian Gold Coins are sought after. Their scarcity in decent conditions makes them hard to come by, but worth picking up in any form. Seasoned collector's will still undoubtedly want high condition coins, despite higher price tags on them. Everyone wants to acquire beautiful, perfectly preserved coins for their collection, and those who desire these coins must pay the premium to have them.

The 1909-O Indian, for example, is a prized collectible and typically sells for close to $3,000 or more in auction. The 1929 $5 Gold Indian is similar in that even low condition ones can command thousands of dollars.

Liberty $10 Gold Coin
(1908 - 1929)

The **$10 Liberty Gold Coin**, known as an Eagle, generally did not see much us in circulation compared to smaller denomination counterparts. Despite this, these coins were popular among collectors then and now. For most people looking to buy and keep one of these, they will be looking for the highest quality specimens. These are worth thousands of dollars. Every one of these gold coins is more than 100 years old and almost all will exhibit wear and tear.

THE VALUE OF A $10 LIBERTY GOLD COIN

Despite its original $10 face value, $10 Liberty coins are currently worth a good deal more. The value of these coins is directly tied to spot price of gold due their metal content alone. A semi- worn example of one these runs about $400 to $600. The most coveted $10 Liberty coins are the ones in the best condition. Regardless of the year of mintage, every collector wants to find a well preserved coin, these are obviously the most valuable.

Certain mintmark coins are going to drive higher values across this series. Carson City (CC) minted coins are very sought after due to scarcer mintage and less examples being sold on the market. For example, the 1882-C Liberty has a much higher premium than its standard 1882 counterpart. These coins, even in lesser condition, cost over $2,000 generally.

Indian Head $10 Gold Coin

(1907 - 1933)

The **Indian $10 Gold Coin**, or Indian Head Eagle, was launched in 1907 and ended mintage in 1933. Even those these coins have a higher face value, they were steadily used throughout their time period. They are a great collectible coin and bear a wonderful design!

These coins have a great value not only because of their gold content, but their historical value as well. Collectors love having Indian Head Eagles due to a variety of reasons. They always have great sales value!

THE VALUE OF A $10 INDIAN GOLD COIN

I would say budgeting $500 to $800 for the purchase of one these coins would be applicable. They are pricey even in poorer condition. The better condition coins and the ones from key date years like 1907, are worth much more. Condition and date effect everything, as with many other coins or banknotes.

When we start getting into uncirculated $10 Indian Head Eagles, the price will rise significantly. Usually sitting around double, or $1,000+, for a copy of this coin in uncirculated condition.

MOST SOUGHT AFTER COINS

Like many other coins and well, collectibles for that matter, the condition and preservation of these coins plays a lot into the value of them. Obviously, the better the condition, the more money you will get when you go to sell it. I would suggest getting any and all of these coins you may have graded. That would insure the condition is preserved and give you the ability to compare sales prices of similar condition coins more effectively.

Other $10 Indian Head Eagles to Collect:

- The first and last years the coin was minted, 1907 and 1933.
- San Francisco or "S" mintmark coins

FUTURE VALUE OF $10 INDIAN GOLD COINS

The value of $10 gold coins will steadily rise over the years not only for the collectible value of the coin, but more importantly, the gold content within the coin. I still suggest buying actual gold if that is what you are looking for, but these coins are great for their precious metal content. The coins will also gain value over time due to the age and prominence of the coin.

Saint Gaudens $20 Gold Coin
(1907-1933)

I absolutely love the design on the **Saint-Gaudens $20 Double Eagle**! These coins are easily one of the most beautiful Gold coins produced in the history of the United States Mint. It is among the most popular Gold coins on the market today and sought after by many collectors and enthusiasts.

This Gold coin was produced by the U.S. Mint from 1907 to 1933. The coin is named after its renowned designer, Augustus Saint-Gaudens. The Saint-Gaudens $20 Gold coin was produced due to President Theodore Roosevelt's dissatisfaction with the artistic level of designs seen in United States coinage.

President Roosevelt felt that Saint-Gaudens was the man who could help him beautify American coinage to the level of true art. Sadly, Saint-Gaudens passed away before the designs were finalized for production. The coin's high relief made the coin difficult to strike and Chief Engraver Charles Barber modified the design slightly, allowing it to be struck in a single blow.

In 1907 Augustus Saint-Gaudens redesigned the $20 piece, employing as the obverse motif the figure of Miss Liberty striding forward. The initial Saint-Gaudens design was high relief, giving them a sculptured appearance almost. The date was expressed in Roman numerals, MCMVII. Some 11,250 of these coins were struck, afterward, the

design would be changed in order to have production take place on newer and faster coin presses.

High Relief pieces are hard to come by today, although an estimated 2,000 or 3,000 exist. Nearly anyone who aspires to form a set of gold coins desires to own at least one Saint-Gaudens $20 coin, but you are talking SERIOUS money in cost. Nevertheless, when these coins are seen in the sales market and auction houses, there is always a buyer ready to scoop it up!

Saint-Gaudens double eagles of the later modified design offer quite a few rare and valuable specimens among them. Specifically, mintmark varieties of the 1920s. Any issue of the Saint-Gaudens coin after 1928 are also really rare and valuable. Look for these as well!

Particularly hard to find is the 1927-D, of which 180,000 were minted, but only 12 or so are know to still be around today. A majority of these were melted down for redistribution of the metal content.

In the 1940s the U.S. government took the position that no 1933 $20 pieces were officially released. A requisition for any pieces in the hands of collectors were illegally held and needed to be returned for melting. Many collectors surrendered these coins and they were subsequently sent to the melting facilities.

Any and all Saint-Gaudens coins are super rare and super valuable. Always grab these up if you can!

Constellatio Nova
(1783)

For nearly two centuries, North America had been a financial Tower of Babel. English law forbade the colonies from striking gold and silver coins, and the mercantile system operated in such a way that British coinage was scarce outside the mother country. Consequently, a hodgepodge of Spanish, French, British and Portuguese currency circulated in the New World. These coins were struck to different standards of weight and fineness, and the existing European monetary systems were forced to rely upon complicated fractional math that had been in use since the Roman Empire.

The Nova Constellatio coins are the first coins struck under the authority of The United States of America. These pattern coins were struck in early 1783, and are known in three silver denominations (1,000-Units, 500-Units, 100-Units), and one copper denomination (5-Units).

All known examples bear the legend "NOVA CONSTELLATIO" with the exception of a unique silver 500-Unit piece.

The Nova Constellatio patterns were the culmination of two years of work on the part of Robert Morris, the Founding Father credited with financing the Revolutionary War. Morris was unanimously elected the Nation's first Superintendent of Finance in 1781.

On February 21 of the following year, Congress passed the following resolution:

That Congress approve of the establishment of a mint; and, that the Superintendent of finance be, and hereby is directed to prepare and report to Congress a plan for establishing and conducting the same.

The financier's plan, developed with his assistant, Gouverneur Morris, was ambitious: he hoped to unite the fledgling Nation with a monetary unit that would allow for easy conversion from British, Spanish, Portuguese, or State currencies to U.S. funds. More importantly, Morris's proposal would be the first system of coinage in Western Europe or the Americas to use decimal accounting – an innovation that has been adopted by every nation on earth in the last two centuries.

While Thomas Jefferson was in possession of the Nova Constellatio coins, he wrote a report entitled "Notes on the Establishment of a Money Unit and of Coinage for the United States"; in it, Jefferson concluded:

The Financier, therefore, in his report, well proposes that our Coins should be in decimal proportions to one another. If we adopt the Dollar for our Unit, we should strike four coins, one of gold, two of silver, and one of copper, viz.:

1. A golden piece, equal in value to ten dollars.

2. The Unit or Dollar itself, of silver.

3. The tenth of a Dollar, of silver also.

4. The hundredth of a Dollar, of copper.

This is the first written description of the monetary system ultimately adopted by the United States, clearly illustrating the historical importance of Morris's patterns.

Collecting

After being returned to Congress, the coins were dispersed. In the mid-1840s, the 1,000-unit and 500-Unit piece from the set bearing the Legend NOVA CONSTELLATIO (A NEW CONSTELLATION) were discovered by a descendant of longtime Secretary of Congress, Charles Thomson. From this point forward, Morris's coins would be called the *Nova Constellatios*.

Twenty-five years would pass before another of Morris's coins would be found. A second silver 500-Unit piece was uncovered in 1870; however, this specimen lacked the NOVA CONSTELLATIO legend. Collectors dubbed this coin the "Type-2", because its design differed from the Congressional set's 500-Unit piece

By 1900, two types of 100-unit coins were found. Both bear the NOVA CONSTELLATIO inscription, but one has a plain edge and the other engraved. In 1979, the 5-Unit piece, also bearing the legend, was discovered in Europe. The final currently known piece, a third 100-Unit coin, first appeared in a 1991 auction from Stack's. Little is known about its provenance, and it is the only piece not currently certified by a third party grading service.

Error Coins

Introduction

Error coins can command huge premiums and are one of the funnest parts of collecting currency! Errors can occur on any type of currency across the globe. In specific, this book will cover coin and banknote errors, but in this section, we will start with coins.

Error coins come in many forms, some of which are similar in look to others. It is important to know what these errors are and to keep in mind that new errors present themselves regularly, so the hobby is always growing. If you know what to look for, you might possibly find a valuable coin right in your pocket change!

I know when I search through rolls of coins from the bank or loose pocket change, I constantly have my jeweler's loupe on me to spot an error coin! I have found many off-center strikes, doubled dies, and a variety of other coins in pocket change. That is what makes this hobby great, anyone can look through a few loose pennies and find a coin worth hundreds of dollars!

The following section will outline each type of error you may find in you loose change and while searching local coin shops. I also include some historical price data for each coin, but these price charts are just examples and not meant to represent the exact prices of each coin.

Gold Coin Errors

Gold coin errors are very rare and a few have traded in the $75,000 to $100,000 range. Even a broadstruck U.S. Gold coin can easily sell for $15,000 to $30,000 compared to a broadstruck Cent, Nickel, Dime or Quarter which all sell for well under $10. Many serious collectors of Gold Errors have to wait patiently for months and sometimes even years to acquire that one special piece for their collection.

Gold coin errors – As mints around the world produce millions of coins each year, there are some that don't come out perfectly. Whether the blank planchets were placed incorrectly or the machine faulted, sometimes coins come out with imperfections. Unintended varieties on coins are called error coins, and are often a big draw with collectors.

(Price Chart on Next Page)

HISTORICAL PRICE EXAMPLES

Pricing and realized auction sales amounts change ALL THE TIME. Prices listed here are historical examples and not meant to represent current pricing.

Gold Coin Errors Price Chart

Denomination	Partial Collar	Broadstruck	Clipped Planchet	3% - 5% Off-Center	10% - 15% Off-Center
$1 Gold Type 1	$2,500	$7,500	$2,000	$10,000	$25,000
$1 Gold Type 2	$5,000	$10,000	$10,000	$20,000	$35,000
$1 Gold Type 3	$2,000	$5,000	$1,500	$7,500	$15,000
$2½ Liberty	$2,000	$7,500	$2,500	$10,000	$20,000
$2½ Indian	$2,000	$7,500	$2,500	$7,500	$17,500
$3 Indian	$5,000	$15,000	$5,000	$15,000	$35,000
$5 Liberty	$3,000	$8,500	$3,000	$12,500	$30,000
$5 Indian	$4,000	$10,000	$3,000	$30,000	$50,000
$10 Liberty	$4,000	$20,000	$3,000	$25,000	$50,000
$10 Indian	$5,000	$20,000	$5,000	$40,000	$60,000
$20 Liberty	$7,500	$40,000	$7,500	$100,000	$250,000
$20 St. Gaudens	–	–	$5,000	–	–
$5 American Eagle	$1,000	$2,000	$750	$2,500	$3,500
$10 American Eagle	$1,250	$2,500	$1,000	$3,000	$3,500
$25 American Eagle	$1,500	$3,000	$1,500	$3,500	$5,000
$50 American Eagle	$2,000	$5,000	$2,000	$5,000	$10,000

Uniface Coins

A uni face coin results when two planchets are stacked, one on top of the other, at the time of striking the coin during production. This process produces two coins: one with only an obverse image, and another coin with only the reverse image. Meaning, there is the designs intended for both sides of ONE coin on opposite sides of two separate coins. The strikes may be one complete image on each coin or positioned off-centered, producing partial images on each side.

Additional Information:

Uni face coins occur when there have been two blank planchets in the press at the same time. The other blank will obstruct the die on either the obverse or reverse side, which will prevent it from having that design on the coin. There are many different variations involving uniface errors.

In addition to having a 100% blank obverse or reverse, a coin can be struck off-center, with a blank planchet in the collar which will obstruct one side of the off-center. There are also mated pairs which have a combination of multiple errors. An example, is a mated pair, where one includes a side which is a uni- face coin.

HISTORICAL PRICE EXAMPLES

Pricing and realized auction sales amounts change ALL THE TIME. Prices listed here are historical examples and not meant to represent current pricing.

Uni Face Coins Price Chart

Denomination	Uniface Obverse XF	Uniface Obverse Unc	Uniface Reverse XF	Uniface Reverse Unc
Large Cent	$1,500	$4,000	$1,250	$2,000
Indian Cent	$1,250	$3,000	$1,000	$2,500
Lincoln Cent 1943 Steel	$250	$500	$200	$400
Lincoln Cent Wheat Ears	$50	$100	$40	$75
3 Cent Nickel	$1,500	$3,000	$1,250	$2,500
Shield Nickel	$1,750	$4,000	$1,500	$3,000
Liberty Nickel	$2,000	$3,500	$1,500	$3,000
Buffalo Nickel	$2,250	$3,000	$2,000	$2,500
Jefferson Nickel War Time	$300	$750	$250	$500
Jefferson Nickel	$20	$40	$20	$40
Barber Dime	$2,000	$3,000	$1,500	$2,500
Mercury Dime	$1,500	$2,500	$1,250	$2,250
Roosevelt Dime Silver	$100	$150	$100	$150
Roosevelt Dime Clad	$40	$75	$35	$60
Washington Quarter Silver	$400	$750	$350	$500
Washington Quarter Clad	$100	$125	$75	$100
State Quarter	NA	$300	NA	$500
Kennedy Half Clad	$750	$1,000	$500	$750
IKE Dollar	NA	$4,000	NA	$4,000
SBA Dollar	NA	$1,000	NA	$750
Sac Dollar	NA	$1,500	NA	$1,000

Proof Coin Errors

Proof coins are struck by technicians who hand feed the blanks into special presses. It is very unusual to find major proof errors or varieties in the design of the proof. A few broadstrikes, off-centers, double strikes in collars and off-metals have been known to be found in sealed proof sets, but are very uncommon finds at best and would pull in great value. Proof errors are rarer and avidly sought after by collectors of all sorts.

HISTORICAL PRICE EXAMPLES

Pricing and realized auction sales amounts change ALL THE TIME. Prices listed here are historical examples and not meant to represent current pricing.

Proof Coin Price Chart

Denomination	Broadstrikes	Die Trials	Double/Triple Strikes	Off-Center Strikes	Partial Collar Errors
Proof Lincoln Cent	$1,000 - $1,500	$1,000	$3,000	$1,500 - $3,000	$500
Proof Jefferson Nickel	$2,000 - $3,000	$4,000	$4,000	$2,000 - $5,000	$1,000
Proof Clad Dime	$2,000 - $3,000	$4,000	$4,000	$2,500 - $5,000	$1,250
Proof Clad Quarter	$2,500 - $4,000	$5,000	$6,000	$7,500	$1,500
Proof Clad Half	$3,000 - $5,000	$4,000 - $5,000	$7,500	$10,000	$2,000
Proof Ike Dollar	$4,000 - $10,000	-	$25,000	-	$4,000
Presidential Dollar	-	-	-	-	3 Known

Fragments

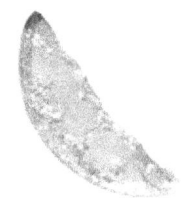

The blanking press takes the coils of metal strips and punches blanks out of it, ejecting the webbing at the other end of the press. The webbing is cut into small scrap pieces to be melted and recycled after the production process is completed. Similar to waste found at any type of metal production plant, this little "shards" of coin can be thrown, blown and tossed about during production. Occasionally, a fragment of coin will find its way into a blank planchet, and be struck into a new coin by the die hammers that lay the coin design. Fragment struck coins are very rare, especially in large denominations.

HISTORICAL PRICE EXAMPLES

Pricing and realized auction sales amounts change ALL THE TIME. Prices listed here are historical examples and not meant to represent current pricing.

Fragments Price Chart

Denomination	Uniface	Die Struck Both Sides
Indian Cent	$1,000	$2,000
Lincoln Cent Wheat Ears	$750	$2,000
Lincoln Cent Memorial	$75	$125
3 Cent Nickel	$3,000	$3,500
Jefferson Nickel	$100	$200
Roosevelt Dime Silver	$500	$1,000
Roosevelt Dime Clad	$150	$250
Washington Quarter Silver	$1,000	$1,500
Washington Quarter Clad	$200	$300
State Quarter	$750	$1,000
Kennedy Half Silver	$1,500	$2,500
Kennedy Half Clad	$750	$1,250
IKE Dollar	$3,000	$5,000
SBA Dollar	$2,000	$3,000
Sac Dollar	—	—

Partial Collars

Blanks are surrounded by collars when struck to prevent the blank from flattening and spreading. Edge and rim errors occur when collars are either out of position or are deteriorated. A wire rim occurs when excessive pressure squeezes out metal between the collar and the edge of the die producing an extremely high thin rim.

A partial collar occurs when an out-of-position collar leaves a line around the coin which is visible when looking at its edge. A partial collar is sometimes called a railroad rim when a reeded edge coin is involved as the line resembles a rail and the reeds resemble railroad ties.

(Price chart on next page.)

HISTORICAL PRICE EXAMPLES

Pricing and realized auction sales amounts change ALL THE TIME. Prices listed here are historical examples and not meant to represent current pricing.

Partial Collars Price Chart

Denomination	XF/AU	Unc
Large Cent	$100	$200
Flying Eagle Cent (1857 – 1858)	$500	$1,500
Indian Cent	$35	$100
Lincoln Cent 1930 and Earlier	$30	$100
Lincoln Cent 1943 Steel	$25	$50
Proof Lincoln Cent	N/A	$750
3 Cent Nickel	$150	$500
3 Cent Silver	$250	$750
Shield Nickel	$200	$600
Liberty Nickel	$50	$150
Buffalo Nickel	$50	$75
Jefferson Nickel War Time	$40	$60
Proof Jefferson Nickel	N/A	$1,000
Seated Half Dime Legend	$750	$1,500
Seated Dime Legend	$500	$1,250
Barber Dime	$75	$150
Mercury Dime	$30	$100
Proof Clad Dime	N/A	$1,250
Barber Quarter	$300	$750
Standing Liberty Quarter	$1,250	$2,000
Washington Quarter Silver	$40	$75
State Quarter	N/A	$15
Proof Clad Quarter	N/A	$1,500
Barber Half	$1,000	$1,500
Walking Liberty Half	$1,500	$3,500
Franklin Half	$500	$1,000
Kennedy Half Silver	$50	$100
Kennedy Half Clad	$20	$30
Proof Clad Half	N/A	$2,000
Morgan Dollar	$150	$300
Peace Dollar	$1,000	$2,500
IKE Dollar	$50	$100
SBA Dollar	$20	$30
Sac Dollar	N/A	$100
Presidential Dollar	N/A	$250
$1 Gold Type 1	$2,500	$5,000
$1 Gold Type 2	$5,000	$10,000
$1 Gold Type 3	$2,000	$3,000
$2½ Liberty	$2,000	$3,000
$2½ Indian	$2,000	$3,000
$3	$5,000	$10,000
$5 Liberty	$3,000	$5,000
$5 Indian	$4,000	$6,000
$10 Liberty	$4,000	$7,500
$10 Indian	$5,000	$7,500
$20 Liberty Type 3	$7,500	$10,000

Wrong Planchet Coins

Sometimes planchets for one coin denomination are fed into a coin- stamping press equipped with dies of another denomination, this is referred to as a "wrong planchet coin". This can occur on coins of any denomination, such as a penny on a dime or nickel on a quarter. The resulting errors are prized by collectors and coin searchers alike. Some can be quite valuable. Such errors are sometimes called "double denomination" coins, but that term is also used to refer to coins struck a second time with dies of a different denomination, or sometimes referencing a coin struck twice by the same denomination, but the appropriate name for this is a "double strike" or "multi-strike" coin.

Some examples include cents struck on dime planchets or quarters on dime planchets, but there are few, even more are examples. This type of error should not be confused with the much rarer mule which is a coin struck between dies that were never intended to be used together such as a coin with nickel obverse and a dime reverse. If you find one of these, you have done well! Wrong planchet errors may also occur when the composition of the coin itself changes. Such situations generally arise when the mint has decided to change the coin in the new coinage year. If the dies be changed for the new year occurs while the old planchets are waiting for striking and not removed yet, coins using the old design will be struck with the new year's date, forming this error coin.

HISTORICAL PRICE EXAMPLES

Pricing and realized auction sales amounts change ALL THE TIME. Prices listed here are historical examples and not meant to represent current pricing.

Denomination	Off-Metal Planchet	Circulated	AU	Unc	Choice Unc – Gem
Indian Cent	Foreign Planchet	$1,000	$1,500	$5,000	$7,500
Indian Cent	Dime Planchet	$20,000	$30,000	$50,000	$75,000
Lincoln Cent Before 1919	Dime Planchet	$4,000	$6,500	$10,000	–
Lincoln Cent Before 1919	Foreign Planchet	$750	$2,000	$4,000	–
Lincoln Cent 1919 – 1940	Dime Planchet	$2,000	$2,500	$4,000	$6,000
Lincoln Cent 1919 – 1940	Foreign Planchet	$500	$1,000	$1,500	$2,500
Lincoln Cent 1943 Steel	Dime Planchet	$1,500	$2,500	$3,500	$7,500
Lincoln Cent 1943 Transitional	Copper Cent Planchet	$75,000	100,000	$150,000	$200,000
Lincoln Cent 1944 Transitional	Steel Cent Planchet	$30,000	$50,000	$100,000	$150,000
Lincoln Cent Wheat Ears (1941-1964)	Dime Planchet	$500	$600	$1,000	$2,000
Lincoln Cent 1965 and Later	Dime Planchet	$125	$150	$200	$350
Lincoln Cent 1964 Transitional	Clad Dime Planchet	$2,500	$4,000	$7,500	$10,000
Lincoln Cent 1965 Transitional	Silver Dime Planchet	$2,750	$4,500	$6,000	$7,500
Shield Nickel	Foreign Planchet	$7,500	$12,500	–	–
Shield Nickel	Cent Planchet	$15,000	$25,000	$40,000	$60,000
Liberty Nickel	Foreign Planchet	$400	$750	$1,250	$2,000
Liberty Nickel	Cent Planchet	$2,000	$3,000	$6,000	$7,500
Buffalo Nickel	Foreign Planchet	$2,500	$7,500	$12,500	–
Buffalo Nickel	Cent Planchet	$2,000	$4,000	$6,000	$8,000
Jefferson Nickel Before 1950	Cent Planchet	$250	$500	$750	$1,000
Jefferson Nickel 1950 and Later	Cent Planchet	$125	$150	$200	$250
Jefferson Nickel 1943	Steel Cent Planchet	$1,000	$2,000	$3,000	$5,000
Jefferson Nickel 1964 and Earlier	Silver Dime Planchet	$200	$300	$350	$400
Jefferson Nickel 1965 and Later	Clad Dime Planchet	$150	$200	$225	$250
Roosevelt Dime Silver	Foreign Planchet	$2,000	$2,500	$3,000	$3,500
Roosevelt Dime Clad	Foreign Planchet	$1,500	$2,000	$2,250	$2,500
Roosevelt Dime 1964 Transitional	Clad Dime Planchet	$5,000	$6,500	$10,000	$12,500
Roosevelt Dime 1965 Transitional	Silver Dime Planchet	$5,000	$6,500	$7,500	$8,500
Washington Quarter Silver	Cent Planchet	$300	$400	$500	$750
Washington Quarter Silver	Nickel Planchet	$300	$400	$500	$600
Washington Quarter Clad	Cent Planchet	$250	$300	$400	$500
Washington Quarter Clad	Nickel Planchet	$100	$150	$200	$250
Washington Quarter	Silver Dime Planchet	$300	$400	$500	$650
Washington Quarter	Clad Dime Planchet	$250	$300	$350	$400
Washington Quarter 1964 Transitional	Clad Quarter Planchet	$5,000	$6,500	$7,500	$12,500

(continued)

Washington Quarter 1965 Transitional	Silver Quarter Planchet	$5,000	$6,500	$7,500	$8,500
State Quarter	Cent Planchet	N/A	$6,500	$7,500	$8,000
Delaware State Quarter	Nickel Planchet	N/A	$500	$650	$750
All Other State Quarters	Nickel Planchet	N/A	$1,000	$1,250	$1,500
State Quarter	Dime Planchet	N/A	$5,000	$5,500	$6,000
Walking Half	Dime Planchet	N/A	N/A	N/A	$100,000
Walking Half	Quarter Planchet	$17,500	$22,500	$40,000	$50,000
Walking Half	Foreign Planchet	$10,000	$15,000	$30,000	$40,000
Franklin Half	Cent Planchet	$3,000	$4,000	$5,000	$6,000
Franklin Half	Nickel Planchet	$3,000	$4,000	$5,000	$6,000
Franklin Half	Dime Planchet	$3,500	$4,500	$5,500	$6,500
Franklin Half	Quarter Planchet	$600	$750	$1,000	$1,250
Kennedy Half Silver 1964	Cent Planchet	$1,000	$1,250	$1,500	$2,000
Kennedy Half Silver 1964	Nickel Planchet	$1,000	$1,250	$1,500	$2,000
Kennedy Half Silver 1964	Dime Planchet	$1,000	$1,250	$2,000	$2,500
Kennedy Half Silver 1964	Quarter Planchet	$400	$500	$600	$750
Kennedy Half Clad	Cent Planchet	$750	$850	$1,000	$1,500
Kennedy Half Clad	Nickel Planchet	$750	$850	$1,000	$1,250
Kennedy Half Clad	Dime Planchet	$750	$850	$1,000	$1,400
Kennedy Half Clad	Quarter Planchet	$350	$400	$450	$500
Kennedy Half 1964 Transitional	Clad Half Planchet	$5,000	$6,000	$10,000	$12,500
Kennedy Half 1965 Transitional	Silver Half Planchet	$5,000	$6,500	$7,500	$10,000
Kennedy Half 1964 Transitional	Clad Quarter Planchet	$5,000	$7,500	$10,000	$12,500
Kennedy Half 1965 Transitional	Silver Quarter Planchet	$6,000	$7,500	$8,000	$9,000
Ike Dollar	Cent Planchet	$10,000	$12,500	$15,000	$20,000
Ike Dollar	Nickel Planchet	$10,000	$12,500	$15,000	$20,000
Ike Dollar	Dime Planchet	$7,500	$8,500	$15,000	$20,000
Ike Dollar	Quarter Planchet	$10,000	$12,500	$15,000	$20,000
Ike Dollar	Half Planchet	$1,600	$1,750	$2,000	$3,000
Ike Dollar	Foreign Planchet	$900	$1,000	$1,250	$1,500
Ike Dollar Transitional	40% Silver Planchet	$2,750	$3,000	$3,500	$5,000
SBA Dollar	Cent Planchet	N/A	$1,750	$3,000	$5,000
SBA Dollar	Nickel Planchet	N/A	$6,000	$7,000	$8,000
SBA Dollar	Dime Planchet	N/A	$6,000	$7,000	$10,000
SBA Dollar	Quarter Planchet	N/A	$600	$850	$1,000
Sac Dollar	Cent Planchet	N/A	$12,500	$15,000	$20,000
Sac Dollar	Nickel Planchet	N/A	$12,500	$15,000	$20,000
Sac Dollar	Dime Planchet	N/A	$8,000	$15,000	$20,000
Sac Dollar	Quarter Planchet	N/A	$1,500	$2,000	$2,500

Broadstrike Coins

A broadstrike error occurs when a coin is struck without the collar to form the rim and edge that is part of the shape of the coin. Coins can be broadstruck on either type one or type two planchets. When a coin is broadstruck the blank being fed into the collar will spread and distort outward as it is being struck because the collar isn't in the correct position to retain it.

(Price chart on next page.)

HISTORICAL PRICE EXAMPLES

Pricing and realized auction sales amounts change ALL THE TIME. Prices listed here are historical examples and not meant to represent current pricing.

Broadstruck Coin Price Chart

Denomination	(Small) XF/AU	(Small) Unc	(Large) XF/AU	(Large) Unc
Large Cent	$150	$300	$400	$1,500
Flying Eagle Cent (1857 – 1858)	$1,000	$2,500	$1,500	$7,500
Indian Cent	$50	$150	$200	$350
Lincoln Cent 1930 and Earlier	$50	$150	$100	$250
Lincoln Cent 1943 Steel	$40	$100	$75	$200
Proof Lincoln Cent	N/A	$1,500	N/A	$2,500
3 Cent Nickel	$250	$1,000	$400	$1,500
3 Cent Silver	$1,000	$3,500	$1,500	$5,000
Shield Nickel	$400	$1,250	$1,000	$2,500
Liberty Nickel	$150	$300	$200	$600
Buffalo Nickel	$100	$200	$200	$500
Jefferson Nickel War Time	$100	$200	$200	$500
Proof Jefferson Nickel	N/A	$2,500	N/A	$4,000
Seated Half Dime Legend	$1,500	$3,500	$2,000	$7,500
Seated Dime Legend	$1,500	$3,500	$2,000	$7,500
Barber Dime	$150	$250	$200	$400
Mercury Dime	$40	$150	$150	$250
Proof Clad Dime	N/A	$3,000	N/A	$5,000
Barber Quarter	$600	$1,250	$1,000	$2,500
Standing Liberty Quarter	$2,000	$4,000	$3,000	$7,500
Washington Quarter Silver	$75	$150	$100	$250
State Quarter	N/A	$25	N/A	$50
Proof Clad Quarter	N/A	$4,000	N/A	$5,000
Barber Half	$1,000	$2,000	$2,000	$4,000
Walking Liberty Half	$3,000	$5,000	$4,000	$7,000
Franklin Half	$1,500	$3,000	$2,000	$4,000
Kennedy Half Silver	$150	$250	$200	$300
Kennedy Half Clad	$40	$60	$50	$75
Proof Clad Half	N/A	$5,000	N/A	$7,000
Morgan Dollar	$200	$500	$400	$1,000
Peace Dollar	$5,000	$7,500	$6,000	$10,000
IKE Dollar	$100	$150	$150	$200
SBA Dollar	$50	$75	$100	$200
Sac Dollar	N/A	$300	N/A	$1,000
Presidential Dollar	N/A	$1,500	N/A	$2,500

Off Center Coins

An off center coin is produced when the coin is struck once, albeit off center. Unlike a broadstrike, the punch of an off center coin is not in the center of the coin, but rather the edge. This results in a coin which is not circular. The coin gives a freakish appearance as a result, and various amounts of blank planchet space are visible. The coins can vary in value because of how far off center they are struck, although coins with full dates are more desirable than coins without a date or missing digits.

HISTORICAL PRICE EXAMPLES

Pricing and realized auction sales amounts change ALL THE TIME. Prices listed here are historical examples and not meant to represent current pricing.

Off Center Coin Price Chart

Denomination	10% - 15% XF/AU	25% - 60% XF/AU	10% - 15% Unc	25% - 60% Unc
Large Cent	$400	$2,500	$1,000	$10,000
Flying Eagle Cent (1857 – 1858)	$2,500	$10,000	$5,000	$30,000
Indian Cent	$100	$400	$200	$600
Lincoln Cent 1930 and Earlier	$75	$300	$150	$750
Lincoln Cent 1943 Steel	$40	$250	$100	$500
Proof Lincoln Cent	N/A	N/A	$1,500	$3,000
3 Cent Nickel	$300	$1,500	$600	$3,500
3 Cent Silver	$1,000	$5,000	$2,000	$7,500
Shield Nickel	$750	$2,500	$1,000	$7,500
Liberty Nickel	$250	$1,000	$500	$2,500
Buffalo Nickel	$250	$750	$400	$1,500
Jefferson Nickel War Time	$100	$500	$200	$1,000
Proof Jefferson Nickel	N/A	N/A	$2,000	$5,000
Seated Half Dime Legend	$3,000	$7,500	$5,000	$15,000
Seated Dime Legend	$2,000	$7,000	$3,500	$10,000
Barber Dime	$300	$1,500	$500	$2,500
Mercury Dime	$100	$750	$150	$1,250
Proof Clad Dime	N/A	N/A	$2,500	$5,000
Barber Quarter	$1,500	$5,000	$2,500	$10,000
Standing Liberty Quarter	$5,000	$20,000	$20,000	$40,000
Washington Quarter Silver	$50	$100	$75	$150
State Quarter	N/A	N/A	$75	$300
Proof Clad Quarter	N/A	N/A	$3,000	$6,000
Barber Half	$4,000	$10,000	$6,000	$20,000
Walking Liberty Half	$4,000	$12,500	$7,500	$20,000
Franklin Half	$2,500	$4,000	$3,500	$7,500
Kennedy Half Silver	$100	$500	$250	$1,000
Kennedy Half Clad	$60	$250	$100	$400
Proof Clad Half	N/A	N/A	$4,000	$7,500
Morgan Dollar	$3,000	$15,000	$10,000	$75,000
Peace Dollar	$20,000	$35,000	$50,000	$100,000
IKE Dollar	$125	$1,250	$150	$2,000
SBA Dollar	N/A	N/A	$100	$500
Sac Dollar	N/A	N/A	$1,000	$3,500
Presidential Dollar	—	—	$1,500	$5,000

Multi- Struck Coins

A broadstrike error occurs when a coin is struck without the collar to form the rim and edge that is part of the shape of the coin. Coins can be broadstruck on either type one or type two planchets. When a coin is broadstruck the blank being fed into the collar will spread and distort outward as it is being struck because the collar isn't in the correct position to retain it.

HISTORICAL PRICE EXAMPLES

Pricing and realized auction sales amounts change ALL THE TIME. Prices listed here are historical examples and not meant to represent current pricing.

Denomination	(Small) XF/AU	(Small) Unc	(Large) XF/AU	(Large) Unc
Large Cent	$150	$300	$400	$1,500
Flying Eagle Cent (1857 – 1858)	$1,000	$2,500	$1,500	$7,500
Indian Cent	$50	$150	$200	$350
Lincoln Cent 1930 and Earlier	$50	$150	$100	$250
Lincoln Cent 1943 Steel	$40	$100	$75	$200
Proof Lincoln Cent	N/A	$1,500	N/A	$2,500
3 Cent Nickel	$250	$1,000	$400	$1,500
3 Cent Silver	$1,000	$3,500	$1,500	$5,000
Shield Nickel	$400	$1,250	$1,000	$2,500
Liberty Nickel	$150	$300	$200	$600
Buffalo Nickel	$100	$200	$200	$500
Jefferson Nickel War Time	$100	$200	$200	$500
Proof Jefferson Nickel	N/A	$2,500	N/A	$4,000
Seated Half Dime Legend	$1,500	$3,500	$2,000	$7,500
Seated Dime Legend	$1,500	$3,500	$2,000	$7,500
Barber Dime	$150	$250	$200	$400
Mercury Dime	$40	$150	$150	$250
Proof Clad Dime	N/A	$3,000	N/A	$5,000
Barber Quarter	$600	$1,250	$1,000	$2,500
Standing Liberty Quarter	$2,000	$4,000	$3,000	$7,500
Washington Quarter Silver	$75	$150	$100	$250
State Quarter	N/A	$25	N/A	$50
Proof Clad Quarter	N/A	$4,000	N/A	$5,000
Barber Half	$1,000	$2,000	$2,000	$4,000
Walking Liberty Half	$3,000	$5,000	$4,000	$7,000
Franklin Half	$1,500	$3,000	$2,000	$4,000
Kennedy Half Silver	$150	$250	$200	$300
Kennedy Half Clad	$40	$60	$50	$75
Proof Clad Half	N/A	$5,000	N/A	$7,000
Morgan Dollar	$200	$500	$400	$1,000
Peace Dollar	$5,000	$7,500	$6,000	$10,000
IKE Dollar	$100	$150	$150	$200
SBA Dollar	$50	$75	$100	$200
Sac Dollar	N/A	$300	N/A	$1,000
Presidential Dollar	N/A	$1,500	N/A	$2,500

Mated Coins

A mated coins set or pair is a collection of two or more coins struck at the same time and forming a "set" from the coins being "mated" or stuck together during processing. Usually, these sets are not found together due to the mint facility staff removing, separating, or destroying the error coin set prior to it leaving production. Some coins are indeed separated, and sent out through different channels into circulation.

Mated coins involve two separate coins with different errors that were fused together by being struck upon one another! These errors come in many shapes and sizes. Mated pairs can be overlapped when one of the coins is struck off-center on top of another coin.

Another type involves a brockage (see terms section or within this section for details), where a struck coin was aligned almost exactly in place and essentially re-struck entirely!

Mated pairs can also involve an off-metal error, where one coin of smaller size was struck onto a coin of larger size. (A smaller and larger planchet) These error coins are super rare.

(Continue to next page for Price Chart)

HISTORICAL PRICE EXAMPLES

Pricing and realized auction sales amounts change ALL THE TIME. Prices listed here are historical examples and not meant to represent current pricing.

MATED COINS PRICE CHART

Denomination	Overlapping	Full Brockage	Die Cap	2 Die Caps
Lincoln Cent Wheat Ears	$3,500	$4,500	$7,500	-
Lincoln Cent Memorial	$500	$750	$750	$1,250
Liberty Nickel	-	$20,000	-	-
Jefferson Nickel (pre War Time)	-	-	-	$15,000
Jefferson Nickel	$1,000	$1,250	$1,500	$2,500
Barber Dime	-	-	-	$50,000
Roosevelt Dime Silver	$3,500	$4,000	$4,000	-
Roosevelt Dime Clad	$1,000	$1,250	$2,500	$3,000
Washington Quarter Silver	$4,000	-	-	-
Washington Quarter Clad	$1,500	$2,500	$5,000	$7,500
State Quarter	$3,000	$5,000	$10,000	-
Kennedy Half Silver	$7,500	$7,500	$7,500	$12,500
Kennedy Half Clad	$5,000	$6,000	$6,000	$8,500
Kennedy Half Bicentennial	$6,000	$7,500	$7,500	$10,000
IKE Dollar	$20,000	-	-	-
SBA Dollar	$7,500	$10,000	-	-
Sac Dollar	-	-	-	-

Indent Coins

An indent coin error happens when two blanks are fed into the same collar during the minting process. One blank coin overlays over the other causing the error to occur. When the die hammer strikes the combination of the two coins in the same collar, it makes a depression similar to the blank on the top of the coin.

Modern coins are still released with hub and die errors, mainly because the defects are usually too small to be seen with the naked eye. A few exceptions exist, where the dies are used despite producing obvious flaws.

HISTORICAL PRICE EXAMPLES

Pricing and realized auction sales amounts change ALL THE TIME. Prices listed here are historical examples and not meant to represent current pricing.

Indent Coins Price Chart

Denomination	10% - 25% XF	30% - 50% XF	10% - 25% Unc	30% - 50% Unc
Large Cent	$300	$600	$750	$2,000
Indian Cent	$250	$500	$400	$750
Lincoln Cent 1943 Steel	$100	$300	$175	$500
Lincoln Cent Wheat Ears	$30	$75	$75	$125
3 Cent Nickel	$500	$1,250	$1,500	$3,000
Shield Nickel	$500	$1,500	$2,000	$3,000
Liberty Nickel	$400	$1,000	$750	$1,500
Buffalo Nickel	$300	$1,000	$600	$2,000
Jefferson Nickel War Time	$200	$400	$400	$750
Jefferson Nickel	$10	$25	$15	$30
Barber Dime	$500	$1,000	$750	$2,000
Mercury Dime	$300	$750	$500	$1,500
Roosevelt Dime Silver	$30	$60	$50	$100
Roosevelt Dime Clad	$10	$20	$15	$30
Washington Quarter Silver	$100	$200	$150	$300
Washington Quarter Clad	$25	$50	$35	$100
State Quarter	N/A	N/A	$200	$350
Kennedy Half Clad	$150	$300	$200	$400
IKE Dollar	$350	$1,000	$500	$1,500
SBA Dollar	$200	$400	$250	$500
Sac Dollar	$300	$500	$400	$750

Martha Washington and Test Pieces

Dies with images of Martha Washington and Mount Vernon were first made around 1965 to create a unique set of coins, using new and unused metal alloys. Mint officials claim that all of the 1965 experimental pieces were either destroyed or otherwise accounted for.

Until 2000, the only examples known were four sets of Martha Washington "Dimes", Quarter Dollars", and "Half Dollars" embedded in Lucite and given to Congress, the Mint Director and the Smithsonian Institution. These pieces are still on display.

Beginning in 2000, examples of the Martha Washington "Cent", "Dime", "Quarter Dollar" and "Golden Dollar" began showing up in coin markets online.

In 2000, there reports of a discovery of a Martha Washington Dime. News stated the dies were used in another, more recent metallurgic testing at that time.

There is one set of a Dime, Quarter and Half struck by Martha Washington dies that are permanently housed in the Smithsonian Institute, embedded in blocks of lucite. According to United States Pattern and Related Issues, by Andrew W. Pollock III, "the only trial pieces purported to have survived metallurgical testing in 1965 were the Dime, Quarter Dollar, and Half Dollar equivalent strikes in copper-nickel clad over copper."

(Continue to next page for Price Chart)

HISTORICAL PRICE EXAMPLES

Pricing and realized auction sales amounts change ALL THE TIME. Prices listed here are historical examples and not meant to represent current pricing.

Martha Washington Price Chart

Denomination	Unc	Choice	Gem
Martha Cent	$2,000	$3,000	$4,000
Martha Nickel	$2,000	$3,000	$4,000
Martha Dime	$7,500	$10,000	$12,500
Martha Quarter	$2,000	$3,000	$4,000
Martha Half Dollar	$3,000	$4,000	$5,000
Martha Dollar (SBA Planchet)	$10,000	$12,500	$15,000
Martha Dollar (Sac Planchet)	$2,000	$3,000	$4,000

Fold Over Coins

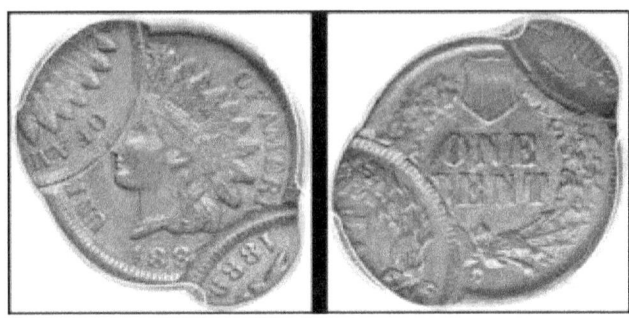

A fold-over coin is one of the most dramatic types of errors. It occurs when the blank is standing vertically between the dies. During the strike, the force is so great that it bends and folds the blank.

I have seen quite a few examples throughout the years of fold over coins and most, if not all of them, have fetched a high price at market or auction. This again, is due to the immense scarcity of the item(s).

These fold-overs can be on-center or off-center, and come in many different sizes or shapes. There are a few fold-overs with multiple errors, either with an additional strike or fold-over.

HISTORICAL PRICE EXAMPLES

Pricing and realized auction sales amounts change ALL THE TIME. Prices listed here are historical examples and not meant to represent current pricing.

Denomination	AU	AU Dated	Unc	Unc Dated
Lincoln Cent Memorial Copper	$1,000	$1,250	$1,250	$1,500
Lincoln Cent Memorial Zinc	$750	$1,000	$1,000	$1,250
Jefferson Nickel	$2,500	$3,000	$3,000	$4,000
Roosevelt Dime Silver	$4,000	$5,000	$5,000	$6,000
Roosevelt Dime Clad	$3,000	$3,500	$3,500	$4,500
Washington Quarter Silver	$4,000	$5,000	$5,000	$10,000
Washington Quarter Clad	$3,500	$4,000	$4,000	$5,000
State Quarter	$5,000	$6,000	$6,000	$8,500

Die Caps

Die caps are caused when a struck coin sticks to the upper hammer die. Once the coin is stuck to the die face, the reverse of the struck coin becomes the new die face. When the next blank is fed into the collar and the strike occurs, the reverse design of the adhered struck coin impresses itself into the new blank.

This struck coin is a brockage strike. The coin that adhered to the upper die is known as a die cap. This process repeats itself as more coins are struck by the cap. The greater the number of strikes, the higher the cap metal will be pushed around the upper die shaft. Eventually, the cap brakes away from the die in the shape of a thimble.

HISTORICAL PRICE EXAMPLES

Pricing and realized auction sales amounts change ALL THE TIME. Prices listed here are historical examples and not meant to represent current pricing.

(Continue to next page for Price Chart)

Die Caps Price Chart

Denomination	Obverse Cap XF	Obverse Cap Unc	Reverse Cap XF	Reverse Cap Unc
Large Cent	$30,000	$75,000	–	–
Indian Cent 1859	$20,000	$60,000	–	–
Indian Cent 1860-1864	$15,000	$50,000	–	–
Indian Cent 1864-1909	$15,000	$50,000	–	–
Lincoln Cent 1943 Steel	–	–	–	–
Lincoln Cent Wheat Ears	$1,000	$2,500	$500	$1,000
Lincoln Cent Memorial	$150	$200	$50	$100
2 Cent Piece	$20,000	$50,000	$15,000	$30,000
3 Cent Nickel	–	–	–	–
Shield Nickel	–	–	–	–
Liberty Nickel	$12,500	$25,000	–	–
Buffalo Nickel (1 Known)	–	$30,000	–	–
Jefferson Nickel War Time	$10,000	–	–	–
Jefferson Nickel	$200	$350	$150	$250
Barber Dime	$25,000	$30,000	$17,500	$20,000
Mercury Dime (2 Known)	$5,000	$7,500	–	–
Roosevelt Dime Silver	$750	$1,250	$500	$750
Roosevelt Dime Clad	$200	$400	$200	$250
Barber Quarter	$30,000	$75,000	–	–
Washington Quarter Silver	$1,500	$4,000	$1,500	$2,000
Washington Quarter Clad	$350	$750	$250	$350
State Quarter	N/A	$1,000	N/A	$600
Kennedy Half Silver	$3,000	$5,000	$2,000	$3,000
Kennedy Half Clad	$2,000	$3,500	$1,500	$2,000
Kennedy Half Bicentennial	$2,500	$4,000	$1,750	$2,500
IKE Dollar	–	$30,000	–	–
SBA Dollar	N/A	$20,000	N/A	$15,000
Sac Dollar	N/A	$20,000	N/A	$15,000

154

Double Denomination Coins

A double denomination coin is one that has been struck twice between different denomination dies such as once between nickel dies and again between quarter dies. The term is sometimes used to refer to a coin struck on the wrong planchet of another coin or similar error.

One of the most expensive, popular, and desired types of errors are the double denomination coins. Again, this error happens when a coin is struck on a previously struck coin of a smaller denomination, or vice versa. Examples are a cent on a struck quarter, and a dime on a cent, etc.

(Price chart on next page.)

HISTORICAL PRICE EXAMPLES

Pricing and realized auction sales amounts change ALL THE TIME. Prices listed here are historical examples and not meant to represent current pricing.

Double Denomination Coins Price Chart

Denomination	Struck On	Circulated	AU	Unc
Lincoln Cent Wheat Ears	Mercury Dime	$6,000	$12,500	$20,000
Lincoln Cent Wheat Ears	Roosevelt Dime	$4,000	$5,000	$6,000
Lincoln Cent Wheat Ears	Foreign Coin	$2,000	$2,500	–
Lincoln Cent Memorial	Roosevelt Dime Silver	$3,000	$4,500	$6,000
Lincoln Cent Memorial	Roosevelt Dime Clad	N/A	N/A	$750
Lincoln Cent Memorial	Foreign Coin	N/A	$600	$750
Jefferson Nickel	Lincoln Cent Wheat Ears	$1,500	$2,000	$2,500
Jefferson Nickel	Lincoln Cent Memorial	N/A	$750	$1,000
Jefferson Nickel	Foreign Coin	$1,000	$1,250	$1,500
Jefferson Nickel	Roosevelt Dime	$1,000	$1,250	$1,500
Roosevelt Dime Silver	Foreign Coin	$4,000	$5,000	$7,500
Roosevelt Dime Clad	Foreign Coin	$3,000	$4,000	$5,000
Washington Quarter Silver	Lincoln Cent Wheat Ears	$3,000	$4,000	$6,000
Washington Quarter Silver	Lincoln Cent Memorial	$2,500	$3,000	$3,500
Washington Quarter Silver	Foreign Coin	$2,500	$3,000	$3,500
Washington Quarter Silver	Jefferson Nickel	$3,000	$4,000	$6,000
Washington Quarter Silver	Roosevelt Dime Silver	$2,500	$3,000	$3,500
Washington Quarter Clad	Lincoln Cent Memorial	$2,500	$3,000	$3,500
Washington Quarter Clad	Foreign Coin	$2,000	$2,500	$3,000
Washington Quarter Clad	Jefferson Nickel	$2,500	$3,000	$3,500
Washington Quarter Clad	Roosevelt Dime Clad	$2,000	$2,500	$3,000
State Quarter	Jefferson Nickel	N/A	$7,500	$10,000
State Quarter (Extremely Rare)	Any Other Denomination	N/A	$10,000	$12,500
Franklin Half	Lincoln Cent Wheat Ears	$7,500	$12,500	$20,000
Kennedy Half (Extremely Rare)	Any Denomination	$7,500	$10,000	$12,500
IKE Dollar (Extremely Rare)	Any Denomination	–	–	–
Sac Dollar	Maryland State Quarter	N/A	$3,000	$4,000

Adjustment Strikes

An adjustment strike error is rare and weird by itself! When the U.S. Mint begins coining a new series of coins or sets new dies, they must calibrate the pressure used to make the design on each coin. If it's too much pressure on the coin, then it can break the die. If this pressure is too low, the coin is struck too weak. It's called die adjustments and they strike planchets until they get the appropriate striking pressure for the coin series.

Die adjustment strike error is also known as "die trials" to many collectors. This error occurs when a coin is struck from the press with very little pressure. When the press is being set up and adjusted, extremely weak strikes occur as the strike pressure reaches its optimum level.

These die trials are destroyed after being struck and are rarely found in circulation, although multiple types have made their way onto the market in other forms and can fetch in upward of $15,000.

(Price chart on next page.)

HISTORICAL PRICE EXAMPLES

Pricing and realized auction sales amounts change ALL THE TIME. Prices listed here are historical examples and not meant to represent current pricing.

Adjustment Strike Error Price Chart

Denomination	XF/AU	Unc
Indian Cent	$1,000	$2,000
Lincoln Cent Wheat Ear	$200	$300
Lincoln Cent 1943 Steel	$750	$1,500
Lincoln Cent Memorial	$50	$75
2 Cent	$5,000	–
Liberty Nickel	$3,000	$5,000
Buffalo Nickel	$4,000	$7,500
Jefferson Nickel War Time	$1,250	$2,000
Jefferson Nickel	$75	$100
Proof Jefferson Nickel	N/A	$4,000
Barber Dime	$2,500	$3,500
Mercury Dime	$1,000	$1,500
Roosevelt Dime Silver	$350	$500
Roosevelt Dime Clad	$100	$125
Seated Quarter	$5,000	$7,500
Standing Liberty Quarter	$15,000	$20,000
Washington Quarter Silver	$500	$750
Washington Quarter Clad (Pre-State)	$125	$150
State Quarter	N/A	$200
Walking Liberty Half	$2,500	$5,000
Kennedy Half Silver	$500	$750
Kennedy Half Clad	$200	$250
Proof Kennedy Half 40% Silver	N/A	$5,000
Proof Kennedy Half Clad	N/A	$4,000
Morgan Dollar	$5,000	$7,500
Peace Dollar	$10,000	$15,000
IKE Dollar	$300	$400
IKE Dollar Bicentennial	$350	$500
SBA Dollar	N/A	$500
Sac Dollar	N/A	$1,000

Brockages

Die caps are caused when a struck coin sticks to the upper hammer die. Once the coin is stuck to the die face, the reverse of the struck coin becomes the new die face. When the next blank is fed into the collar and the strike occurs, the reverse design of the adhered struck coin impresses itself into the new blank.

This struck coin is a brockage strike. The coin that adhered to the upper die is known as a die cap. This process repeats itself as more coins are struck by the cap. The greater the number of strikes, the higher the cap metal will be pushed around the upper die shaft. Eventually, the cap brakes away from the die in the shape of a thimble.

(Price chart on next page.)

HISTORICAL PRICE EXAMPLES

Pricing and realized auction sales amounts change ALL THE TIME. Prices listed here are historical examples and not meant to represent current pricing.

Denomination	50% Brockage XF	100% Brockage XF	50% Brockage Unc	100% Brockage Unc
Large Cent	$600	$1,000	$3,000	$10,000
Indian Cent	$500	$1,250	$1,500	$4,000
Lincoln Cent 1943 Steel	$350	$500	$650	$1,000
Lincoln Cent Wheat Ears	$125	$200	$200	$350
3 Cent Nickel	$1,250	$2,000	$3,500	$5,000
3 Cent Silver	$2,000	$3,000	$3,000	$6,000
Shield Nickel	$1,500	$2,500	$3,500	$5,000
Liberty Nickel	$1,250	$2,250	$2,000	$4,000
Buffalo Nickel	$2,000	$2,500	$4,000	$12,500
Jefferson Nickel War Time	$250	$750	$750	$1,500
Jefferson Nickel	$50	$75	$50	$150
Barber Dime	$1,500	$3,500	$5,000	$12,500
Mercury Dime	$750	$3,000	$1,500	$4,000
Roosevelt Dime Silver	$100	$200	$150	$250
Roosevelt Dime Clad	$50	$100	$75	$150
Washington Quarter Silver	$200	$500	$500	$1,000
Washington Quarter Clad	$75	$150	$150	$250
State Quarter	N/A	N/A	$750	$1,500
Kennedy Half Clad	N/A	N/A	$650	$1,500
IKE Dollar	$1,500	$4,000	$3,000	$7,500
SBA Dollar	N/A	N/A	$500	$2,500
Sac Dollar	N/A	N/A	$1,500	$5,000

Counter Brockages

A counterbrockage error on a coin involves a cap die and a previously struck coin. When a cap die strikes a previously struck coin, the obverse design from that struck coin will be impressed into the cap.

The result will be a design where the cap face will be an incuse brockage. When a new blank is struck by this cap die with an incuse brockage image, the obverse will have a raised and spread image from that incuse design of the cap. This brockage impression is known as a counterbrockage.

HISTORICAL PRICE EXAMPLES

Pricing and realized auction sales amounts change ALL THE TIME. Prices listed here are historical examples and not meant to represent current pricing.

Counterbrockage Price Chart

Denomination	Circulated	AU	Unc	Choice Unc - Gem
Indian Cent	$1,000	$1,500	$2,000	$2,500
Lincoln Cent 1943 Steel	$500	$750	$1,500	$2,000
Lincoln Cent Wheat Ears	$200	$200	$300	$500
Lincoln Cent Memorial	$40	$50	$75	$100
Shield Nickel	$1,500	$2,000	$4,000	$5,000
Liberty Nickel	$1,500	$2,000	$4,000	$5,000
Jefferson Nickel	$50	$100	$150	$200
Barber Dime	$3,000	$5,000	$7,500	$10,000
Roosevelt Dime Silver	$300	$500	$750	$1,000
Roosevelt Dime Clad	$100	$150	$250	$300
Washington Quarter Silver	$500	$1,000	$1,500	$2,000
Washington Quarter Clad	$100	$200	$300	$400
State Quarter	N/A	$750	$1,250	$1,500
Kennedy Half Silver	$1,250	$2,000	$3,000	$4,000
Kennedy Half Clad	$500	$750	$1,250	$1,500
SBA Dollar	N/A	$1,500	$2,000	$2,500

Counterfeit Coins & Banknotes

What Are Counterfeit Coins?

People have been faking and counterfeiting currency since ancient artisans first minted coins in 590 BC. Back then, the materials used to make various coinage were primitive, at best. This meant that is was pretty easy to duplicate coinage at the time. In modern day, counterfeiters make fake coins especially for the collecting marketplace due to the high values attached to certain coins.

Counterfeit coins are classified as any coin that is made without the consent of the issuing country. Other coins considered as counterfeits are those that are altered physical to look like other coins. This is seen a lot with banknotes as well. A practice of "washing" or "blanking" lower denomination bills and printing larger denominations on them, is a practice that has been around for ages. Over the years that currency has been in existence, dishonest people have improved methods of counterfeiting coins and banknotes. The methods get more and more unique and despite the intended use of these methods, counterfeits are actually quite fascinating. You need to be aware of them and what to look for, however, as to not be taken advantage of when buying.

A basic understanding of good practices when buying currency and an understanding of things to look for, helps protect you from fraud:

1. **Buy from reputable dealers and reputable marketplaces with some sort of buyer protection policy**
2. **Meet friends in the numismatic community! This will help create your network of knowledgeable people to contact for help**
3. **Be weary of coins sold at flea markets and pop up shops. A lot of these are reproductions or fakes**
4. **If you think a coin or banknote is fake, get a second opinion on it before buying**

Types of Counterfeit Coins

There are three types of counterfeit coins: struck, cast, and altered counterfeit coins.

Struck Counterfeits

Counterfeiters make struck counterfeit coins the same way a mint manufactures a genuine coin by a planchet between two coin dies in a coining press. The counterfeiter can create the coin dies by engraving them by hand, using the spark erosion method, a one-to-one transfer engraving lathe, the plating method, or the impact technique. These produce probably the best quality fake/ counterfeit coins, but is an extremely expensive process. It is also the most tedious means of reproducing a coin. This type of counterfeiting is usually seen with very high end coins worth thousands.

Cast Counterfeits

Like you would see in many counterfeit products, a mold can be made to reproduce a coin. A cast is form with an impression of the obverse and reverse of a certain coin. Metal, generally a composition mimicking that of the intended coin, is poured into the mold and creates a copy of the original coin. Counterfeiters like this method because this process does not destroy the original coin. Cast coins, due to typically having a metal content that is not correct, are the easiest counterfeit coins to detect. In a lot of cases however, a centrifuge will be used to create these coins, allowing for the molten metal to spread to the edge of the copy coin. This makes for a more accurate copy, but also a more difficult one to detect.

Altered, Changed and Doctored Coins

Altering a coin to look like a more expensive coin is the most simplistic way of counterfeiting. Similar to washing smaller denominations of their depictions and printing a larger denomination atop them, carving or modifying coins has been going on for a long time!

A common example of this type of modification is on the mintmark of the coin. Rare coins, like older dollar coins and wheat cents, can be worth thousands of dollars more due to what mint facility made the coin. So, skilled counterfeiters will add a mintmark, such as "CC" for Carson City or "S" for San Francisco, to a coin in order to fake its origin mint facility. This can increase a coins value many times over. Conversely, there are instances where a mintmark may be removed in order to accomplish the same counterfeiting goal. This has been seen with Peace Dollars and many Lincoln Pennies.

How to Detect Counterfeit Currency

You may not think of the scientific method from high school as a means to detect counterfeit coins, but with it may just give you some needed insight as to whether your coin is the "real deal" or a fake. These should include size, diameter, thickness, metal composition, weight, and specific gravity. Use a high precision caliper to measure the diameter and thickness of the coin. You can use a scale on your coins, which is a common practice among collectors. Different coins have differing weights so you will need an original to compare too, or you will need to reference the correct weight of the coin in question. These weights can be referenced on the US Mint's website.

Another method of detecting a fake is with the use of a magnet. The United States only made one coin that contains steel, and that is the 1943 Lincoln Wheat Penny. (Reference that coin in this guide for more information.) If the coin does not contain steel, it should not be attracted to the magnet.

Next, take a look at the coin's color and tone, compare this to an original or photos of an original for reference. There are some rare and historic coins that are counterfeited a lot more than others. "War Time" coins like steel pennies and older, more sought after coins, like the 1909-S VDB Lincoln Cent, have lots of fakes out there. These coins will generally be off in color in a lot of cases when it comes to counterfeits. Of course, focusing on graded coins when purchasing, really discounts the possibly of a counterfeit.

The US Mint has always produced currency under rigorous and structured standards. This means that if you inspect the coin or banknote under magnification, you should see vivid and detailed markings. Coins that have soft, light pressed letters are an indication of a counterfeit coin. If your coin is lacking in the correct details, light in the impression or shows details not normally on the original coin, you may have a counterfeit. I have taken coins to my local coin shop for a second opinion a few times!

Lastly, you can spot counterfeit coins and banknotes a lot easier through magnification. I suggest getting a microscope and a jeweler's loupe (sometimes call "loop"), these are undoubtedly a necessity in collecting currency. Not only will a loupe allow you to see small details on non- counterfeit coins, but will help you spot fakes. These are sold all over the place, from local hobby shops to online sites, like Amazon and eBay. I also sell a cheap magnifier on my site VarietyErrors.com. Another great magnifier is a USB microscope. These are going to be more expensive ($50+), but are the best way to go. You can zoom in a lot more with these and interact with the image on you computer, tablet or phone.

In short, there are a lot of ways to spot altered and counterfeit coins. You do not want to get ripped off of course! Other than these tips, brush up on the coins you wish to collect and really get to know them. Familiarizing yourself is part of the hobby anyway! I personally love Lincoln Wheat Cents and Morgan Dollars. Although I usually buy graded coins now, I have spent tons of time diving deep into these coins background, mintage and details in order to avoid buying a counterfeit. Been there, done that!

The US mint has changed and improved its methods of producing coinage over the years, resulting in both different and easier ways of detecting counterfeit currency. The process of learning the extensive knowledge needed to detect counterfeits can take years. So, keep researching and familiarizing yourself with different kinds of coinage.

Unlike the first presses used to make coins, modern coin minting machinery is controlled by computers. This eliminates a lot of human error and makes it more difficult for counterfeiters to produce these coins. Even with the use of computers, automated machinery and hydraulic presses, the coin market sees more and more counterfeits each year. With some knowledge and lot of research, you can avoid purchasing counterfeit coins. Good luck!

Banknote Guide

Introduction

Let's face it... being well informed is always the best way to go about anything. This is no different in banknote collecting. Before I buy anything, I research it and make sure I really understand what I am getting into. So, let's talk about some information you may find useful in your next banknote purchase!

Small-size Federal Reserve notes are the most familiar type of United States paper currency, as these bills are still issued today. However, the most modern of these notes contain high-tech security features that were but the stuff of science fiction in the mid 20th century when these small-size notes were first issued.

Small-size Federal Reserve notes are the sole type of paper currency presently issued by the United States government. However, the types of banknotes have changed significantly since the first of the Federal Reserve notes in 1928. Over the course of time since the late 1920s, notes ranging in denominational values of $1 to $10,000 were printed, though today only $1, $5, $10, $20, $50, and $100 notes are made.

The appearance of small-size Federal Reserve notes remained relatively unchanged in their overall format until the mid 1990s. At this time, the United States began implementing advanced security features on paper currency. With the Series of 1996, the $20 Federal Reserve Notes, $50 Federal Reserve Notes, and $100 Federal Reserve Notes began having larger portraits, enhanced watermarks, and color-shifting (black and green) ink. Similar changes were made to the $5 and $10 under the Series of 1999. Further security enhancements have been made to these notes in the years since.

Obsolete, Counterfeit, and Replica Banknotes

Obsolete banknotes are collected for the historical value. This, of course, translates to monetary value as well. In the early to mid 19th century, many banks, companies, merchants, and jurisdictions had their own currency. Each of these notes are obsolete and have a devout collector group. A lot these are more expensive to purchase, but sport high values in the marketplace. They are wonderful to have in your collection with their beautiful depictions and colors!

The Condition of Obsolete Currency

Like coins and other collectibles, the condition of a banknote will play a huge part in its value. Minor imperfections on the note can cause a big change in the amount it will sell for. Many people cannot agree on the same condition for certain note, so it is important to get it graded by a professional service in order to not maximize value, but also certify the condition.

Paper Money Guaranty ("PMG") or PCGS Currency ("PCGS") are both great companies, that have been around for years. These companies also inspect the paper that the bill is made from. PMG gives notes with high-quality paper an EPQ (exceptional paper quality) notation, and PCGS grades them PPQ (premium paper quality).

Counterfeit and Replica Notes

As I stated before, these notes existing in a lot of different counties, states and municipalities. That means a lot of them were made b independent printers and counterfeited readily at the time. A "counterfeit" is a note resembling a real one by the issuing entity. A "spurious" note is one that bears the name of an actual bank but carries a design that was never issued by that specific bank. Since there were so many different notes, these were actually common!

Unique Banknotes

Replacement Banknotes: These occur when a faulty sheet is removed and replaced with a perfect 'replacement' sheet, to maintain the stack's numeracy. Common prefixes for these sheets include 'M' or 'LL', which can usually be found in the top left corner of the note.

Column Sort Banknotes: If a part-faulty sheet is removed from a stack, they're put to one side and saved. Errors are marked with a phosphorescent pen, with the good columns guillotined and kept for numbering. They can be identified by a higher prefix and/or serial number. For example, A36 900001 compared to A36 400000.

Treasury Control Banknotes: Control banknotes are easy to identify as they always carry a 'Z' prefix, which is located in the bottom right corner. The rest of the sheet usually has a regular prefix.

OTHER TYPES OF NOTES:

- There are also Red Seal bills and Blue Seal "Silver Certificate" banknotes.
- 1934 notes with yellow or brown seals. These banknotes are World War II emergency money, issued in Hawaii or North Africa.

Banknote Grading

Average circulated notes grade between Very Fine (VF) and Extremely Fine (EF). These notes contain aspects such as limited folds, semi crisp to crisp surface, no tears, and no water damage or environmental damage.

Notes of lower quality (Fair to Fine) bring lower prices generally, as their condition plays a large role in the overall appraisal. "Unc or UNC" banknotes – uncirculated or also called Crisp Uncirculated (CU) are notes in new condition with absolutely no wear, no fold marks, and have SHARP corners. These bills exhibit no issue at all.

Lastly, a "Gem or Gem Mint" condition note contains all of the aforementioned aspects, but also has deeply impressed colors with solid/ vivid tones. These bills can command a high premium over their face value in auction and are highly sought after by collectors and resellers.

The physical characteristics of a note play an important part in determining its collectible appeal and value. There are some notes that have such limited availability that they are valuable in really any

condition, but there are also many notes that have no additional monetary worth beyond their face value in ordinary Circulated condition. However, those same notes may command a premium in the highest Circulated grades and in Uncirculated condition or if they contain errors, which we cover later in the book.

Only advanced collectors and paper money professionals have the necessary training and experience to accurately and consistently grade the condition of paper currency. The following grading definitions and photos are presented as a guide only.

$1 Bill Values

Average circulated notes grade between Very Fine (VF) and Extremely Fine (EF). These notes would be at the upper echelon of condition – containing no tears, folds or creases. Notes of lower quality (Fair to Fine) bring considerably lower prices in most cases as you can imagine, as condition of anything collectible plays heavily into its overall appraisal.

"Unc or UNC" banknotes – uncirculated or in some cases referred to as Crisp Uncirculated (CU) are notes in new condition with no wear, no fold marks, and have no imperfections. Lastly, a "Gem" note contains all of the aforementioned aspects, but also has deep or hard impressed colors that "gleam". These would command a higher premium over face value.

$2 Bill Values

Average circulated notes grade between Very Fine (VF) and Extremely Fine (EF). These notes would be at the upper echelon of condition – containing no tears, folds or creases. Notes of lower quality (Fair to Fine) bring considerably lower prices in most cases as you can imagine, as condition of anything collectible plays heavily into its overall appraisal. "Unc or UNC" banknotes – uncirculated or in some cases referred to as Crisp Uncirculated (CU) are notes in new condition with no wear, no fold marks, and have no imperfections. Lastly, a "Gem" note contains all of the aforementioned aspects, but also has deep or hard impressed colors that "gleam". These would command a higher premium over face value.

$5 Bill Values

Average circulated notes grade between Very Fine (VF) and Extremely Fine (EF). These notes would be at the upper echelon of condition – containing no tears, folds or creases. Notes of lower quality (Fair to Fine) bring considerably lower prices in most cases as you can imagine, as condition of anything collectible plays heavily into its overall appraisal. "Unc or UNC" banknotes – uncirculated or in some cases referred to as Crisp Uncirculated (CU) are notes in new condition with no wear, no fold marks, and have no imperfections. Lastly, a "Gem" note contains all of the mentioned aspects. These would command a higher premium over face value.

$10 Bill Values

Average circulated notes grade between Very Fine (VF) and Extremely Fine (EF). These notes would be at the upper echelon of condition – containing no tears, folds or creases. Notes of lower quality (Fair to Fine) bring considerably lower prices in most cases as you can imagine, as condition of anything collectible plays heavily into its overall appraisal. "Unc or UNC" banknotes – uncirculated or in some cases referred to as Crisp Uncirculated (CU) are notes in new condition with no wear, no fold marks, and have no imperfections. Lastly, a "Gem" note contains all of the aforementioned aspects, but also has deep or hard impressed colors that "gleam". These would command a higher premium over face value.

$20 Bill Values

Average circulated notes grade between Very Fine (VF) and Extremely Fine (EF). These notes would be at the upper echelon of condition – containing no tears, folds or creases. Notes of lower quality (Fair to Fine) bring considerably lower prices in most cases as you can imagine, as condition of anything collectible plays heavily into its overall appraisal. "Unc or UNC" banknotes – uncirculated or in some cases referred to as Crisp Uncirculated (CU) are notes in new condition with no wear, no fold marks, and have no imperfections. Lastly, a "Gem" note contains all of the aforementioned aspects, but also has deep or hard impressed colors that "gleam". These would command a higher premium over face value.

$50 Bill Values

Average circulated notes grade between Very Fine (VF) and Extremely Fine (EF). These notes would be at the upper echelon of condition – containing no tears, folds or creases. Notes of lower quality (Fair to Fine) bring considerably lower prices in most cases as you can imagine, as condition of anything collectible plays heavily into its overall appraisal. "Unc or UNC" banknotes – uncirculated or in some cases referred to as Crisp Uncirculated (CU) are notes in new condition with no wear, no fold marks, and have no imperfections. Lastly, a "Gem" note contains all of the aforementioned aspects, but also has deep or hard impressed colors that "gleam". These would command a higher premium over face value.

$100 Bills

Average circulated notes grade between Very Fine (VF) and Extremely Fine (EF). These notes would be at the upper echelon of condition – containing no tears, folds or creases. Notes of lower quality (Fair to Fine) bring considerably lower prices in most cases as you can imagine, as condition of anything collectible plays heavily into its overall appraisal. "Unc or UNC" banknotes – uncirculated or in some cases referred to as Crisp Uncirculated (CU) are notes in new condition with no wear, no fold marks, and have no imperfections. Lastly, a "Gem" note contains all of the aforementioned aspects, but also has deep or hard impressed colors that "gleam". These would command a higher premium over face value.

$500 and $1,000 Bill Values

Average circulated notes grade between Very Fine (VF) and Extremely Fine (EF). These notes would be at the upper echelon of condition – containing no tears, folds or creases. Notes of lower quality (Fair to Fine) bring considerably lower prices in most cases as you can imagine, as condition of anything collectible plays heavily into its overall appraisal. "Unc or UNC" banknotes – uncirculated or in some cases referred to as Crisp Uncirculated (CU) are notes in new condition with no wear, no fold marks, and have no imperfections. Lastly, a "Gem" note contains all of the aforementioned aspects, but also has deep or hard impressed colors that "gleam". These would command a higher premium over face value.

Banknote Grade Examples

Gem Uncirculated: A flawless note that displays the same crispness, freshness and vibrant color as when it came off the printing press. This note must be perfectly centered, have full margins and be free of any marks or blemishes. A superb note that is perfect in all respects. If this were a coin it would be graded MS-70.

Choice Uncirculated: A near perfect note, although not quite as select as the gem note. It will be brighter and fresher than ordinarily encountered in uncirculated notes of that particular issue. It must be reasonably well-centered and free of any marks or blemishes.

Uncirculated: A note that displays no evidence of having been circulated at any time. It may have a very tiny pinhole or two, counting smudge or some other evidence of improper handling, most likely performed by bank personnel. The note may be off-centered but not obtrusively so. It must maintain some degree of the crispness that is associated with a note that has never been circulated.

About Uncirculated: Sometimes referred to as "Almost Uncirculated". This is a note that, due to its bright look and crisp feel, may at first glance appear to be uncirculated. However, upon closer examination it will show signs of very light use. This could be in the form of a corner fold or a faint crease, usually a vertical center fold. Conversely, any crease that breaks the paper fibers will only serve to reduce the note's overall grade.

Extremely Fine: A bright note that maintains a good degree of original crispness. It will show some evidence of circulation. This note may exhibit two or three minor creases or folds but may not contain any tears or discoloration.

Very Fine: A decently crisp and clean banknote that has obviously been in circulation but not for an overly extended period of time. The colors may not be as vibrant or "bold" as on a higher-graded note but they

won't appear faded or washed-out. This note may have several folds, creases or light smudges but the design in the crease must not be worn off.

Fine: A note that shows much evidence of circulation and thus exhibits considerable wear. Although numerous creases and folds are apparent, some slight degree of firmness will be present. A note in this grade will not be severely stained or soiled. At the crease areas, some portion of the design may be worn off. For some rare notes of many years ago, a fine note may well be the best one readily obtainable.

Very Good: A note displaying considerable wear. It may be dark, soiled and limp in appearance. One or two small tears may be evident on the notes margins. Other defects such as writing, foreign substances or rubber-stamp impressions, to name but a few examples, may be evident as well.

Good, Fine and Poor: Notes in these grades are seldom considered by collectors unless they are truly rare notes that are customarily seen only in these low grades. In general, collectors do not want notes grading less than very fine. But you must judge for yourself as to what you will collect and how much you can afford to spend on your hobby. If well-worn notes give you pleasure, then by all means pursue them.

Pricing

The pricing of banknotes is naturally commensurate with the grade, eye appeal, desirability and scarcity of a particular piece. For a relatively modern note that many dealers seem to have ample inventories of in gem condition, it may be foolish to pay a large premium for a gem uncirculated note over the price of its choice uncirculated counterpart.

The fact is that if there are plenty of gem notes in dealer inventory, then they can't be that scarce. Oftentimes a choice note can be had for a considerable reduction in price over gem. But if absolute perfection is your goal, I would suggest a modest 10- to 20-percent premium over a choice note in this scenario.

Many banknotes are printed by the *intaglio* (or engraved) method. This involves the designer engraving steel plates with the design elements in a "mirror image". The recessed lines will hold the inks used to print on the paper. The master plate is used to produce working plates and these working plates produce the notes.

Error
Banknotes

Introduction

I began my adventure in collecting banknotes with error bills. These are among the favored things for collectors. Error banknotes result from issues in the production process of currency. The Bureau of Engraving and Printing (BEP) produces US banknotes. During the multi- phase process of making these notes, printing errors occur and result in valuable collectors items. In this section, we will discuss each type of error banknote and the details to look for in identifying it as such.

These errors can be small and hard to see or they can be very dramatic. Errors can occur in the ink, tone, overall print, serial number and many other portions of the banknote. Each type of error has its own faults identifying it from the others. Many ink errors for example look similar, but one may be in a certain portion of the note than the other, making it much more valuable.

U.S. Banknote Errors

Let's get into each error type and what you need to look for when searching pocket change for that next big find!

Double Denomination

A double denomination note has differing face and back values, for example a $5 face with a $10 back. Double denomination errors are exceedingly rare and valuable. The number in existence is very low. If you find one on eBay or for sale from a source otherwise not confirmed to be knowledgeable, it is likely that the note is not genuine.

Faulty Alignment (aka Miscut)

Faulty alignment errors are characterized by once side of a note being properly centered, while the other is shifted to some degree. Shifting may be only minor or may be dramatic. These errors are relatively common and widely collected.

Insufficient Inking

Insufficient inking errors result from poorly or inadequately filled printing plates. As a result, the note displays an image that is faint or not fully complete. Like other currency errors, insufficient inking may be only minor, or may affect large parts of the note. Most errors of this type have insufficient inking of the 1st or 2nd printing.

Inverted Back

Inverted back errors might also be called notes with upside-down backs. This type of error is caused by a sheet being fed incorrectly (rotated 180 degrees) into the printing press for printing of the face (backs are printed first). Inverted back errors are not very common and command relatively high premiums.

Blank Back or Blank Reverse
A blank back error note is one that has printing on one side, but no printing on the other. These errors are often caused by two sheets being fed into a printing press at the same time.

189

Double or Multiple Impressions

Multiple impression errors usually display an image that appears "blurry" or "fuzzy", and may occur when a sheet is mistakenly re-fed through the press after receiving printing, or a sheet staying in place after being printed and receiving a second impression of the same design.

Obstructed Printings

Obstructed printing errors occur when a piece of material (usually a stray piece of paper, tape, wrapping, etc) comes between the printing plate and the uncut sheet. The result is a portion of a note with blank area. Obstructed printings are popular with error collectors, with value increasing dramatically when the item causing the obstruction is retained with the error note.

Offset Printing or Offset Transfer

Offset printed notes occur when an inked plate makes contact with the bed, often the cause of no sheet being fed to the press to accept the intended ink. As a result, when the next sheet passes through the press, the area impressed onto the impression cylinder is then pressed onto the opposite side of the note.

Like others, this type of error can range from minor to a complete offset, with the latter being more desirable to collectors. While a rational theory, note that the errors described or pictured here are not caused by wet sheet transfer, or ink transferring from still-wet sheets to other sheets.

Reverse Overprints (3rd Print on back)

Back overprint errors are the result of an uncut sheet being fed into a press with the obverse of the note facing the overprinting press. The information printed by the overprinting press include Treasury and Federal Reserve District seals, district numbers and serial numbers. Such a note will be missing these elements from the front, and instead have each displayed on the back.

Inverted Overprint (3rd Print)

When a sheet is fed upside down relative to the existing face print, the result is the Treasury Seal, District Seal, District Number and serial numbers being printed upside down. Inverted 3rd print errors are not especially rare.

Misaligned Overprints (Shifted 3rd Print)

When overprints (3rd printing) occur when the serial numbers and seals are out of position, vertically or horizontally, and are so far from their appropriate position that they cover unintended portions of the note. For example, a District seal might be so far misaligned that it covers the portrait on the face of the note. Again, errors range from minor, to major, with major errors being more desirable to collectors.

Missing Overprint (3rd Print)

A note with a missing overprint is easily recognizable because the bill lacks serial numbers and seals.

Missing 2nd Printing

Similar to Missing Overprints, a note with a missing 2nd print is recognizable because the note is missing its face printing. Therefore no subject or denomination is displayed on the note.

Mismatched Serial Numbers

On regular notes, both serial numbers on the front of the note are the same. Mismatched serial errors are characterized by numbers (or alpha characters) not matching on the same note. There are several different causes for this type of error. Notes with more than one digit mismatched are more valuable than those with a single mismatched number. Additionally, notes with mismatched characters are more scarce than notes with mismatched numbers.

Stuck Digits

When the serial number digits freeze in place or get otherwise stuck during the printing process, the result is a stuck digit or partially turned digit.

Cutting Errors

After printing is complete, the uncut sheets of notes are sent to be cut into single notes. Like the previous printing process many errors can occur during the process of printing, ranging from minor to quite dramatic.

Gutter Fold or Blank Crease

Gutter folds are the result of the uncut sheets being sent through the press with a wrinkle or wrinkles in the paper. A gutter fold error note may have one wrinkle or multiple wrinkles. While collectible, these errors are relatively common.

Printed Fold

A printed fold occurs when an uncut sheet folds over and remains this way during the printing process. As such, these type of errors range widely depending on the size and nature of the fold.

Ink Smears

As the name implies, an ink smear error occurs when smears of ink are passed from the press onto a note. Ink smears are not hard to duplicate or fake, so be wary when purchasing.

Gold and Silver Guide

10 RULES TO GOLD & SILVER

Rule # 1: Let's Get Physical!

Paper ETF's like the SLV silver fund are ran by banks and in short, not recommended in any way. Holding paper silver will do you no good at all in a situation where you no longer have access to this or the banks no longer function to support the value of your non physical asset.

To unlock their true potential of precious metals as a portable and anonymous investment vehicle, you need to buy the physical precious metal and not the digital, paper or fund version.

Rule # 2: Pay Spot. It's that Simple.

Remember, gold and silver are traded based upon their weight of pure metal. A tarnished and scratched up old silver round is worth as much as one in brilliant uncirculated mint condition, once they hit the melting pot of a refiner. You should be looking to pay as close to spot price as possible. Collecting precious metals has a skill and "art" to it, but it is not quite investing.

There are many costly mistakes to be made by beginners in rare coin collecting, banknote collecting and precious metals purchasing. When beginning, I would stick to the 1 oz. Rounds and silver coinage like walking liberty coins and silver maple leaf coins. Certified bars of bullion like gold and silver can be found online and in many local shops.

Avoid intellectual property items (ie, featuring cartoon characters, actors, etc.), commemorative coins or specialty coinage like holiday themed items, and use only reputable dealers for the purchase.

Rule # 3: Start Simple. Start Small.

Too many investors, upon deciding to get into precious metals, buy too much physical silver or gold at once and in the wrong types. A good strategy for a beginner is to set aside an amount each month they can afford and purchase on a schedule. For example, buying one or two silver rounds each payday. This keeps your stockpile growing gradually

and avoid getting caught losing money on a swing in the spot price of silver.

Rule # 4: Watch the Price "Highs and Lows"

New highs in gold and silver prices bring new investors and market attention to the precious metals market. This generally causes a downshift in fiat currencies backed by banks. After this period, the banks will flood the market "shorts" to drive the price back down. Forbes, as well as many other outlets online, have great information on shorts and how to understand them. Mainly here, you should familiarize yourself with how the market operated in relation to gold and silver. It will help you avoid investing too much, into the wrong metal, at the wrong time.

Rule # 5: No Fakes. No Frauds.

Historically, precious metals like silver has not been a major victim of counterfeiting due to its lower cost on the market. Gold buyers however, have seen many fakes on the market over the years. As the price of both these precious metals rise, we will continue to see an increase in the amount of counterfeit products on the market. Buyers should educate themselves before purchasing to make sure the seller is reputable and the product is as advertised.

Rule # 6: Learn. Learn. Learn.

You should always be educating yourself on important things like money, government, free markets, and how they all are connected and affect our day to day lives. You should learn more so you are better able to position yourself for what could be coming. Utilize your free time by finding new avenues to learn from. This will always pay of. Use internet resources like my website (VarietyErrors.com) to read articles and access FREE resource guides on coins, banknotes and precious metals.

Consider reading some books on the history of silver and the role it plays in society and politics. This information has played a big part in my collecting experience as you will notice trends repeating themselves over the course of human history. Like I said, things are connected and intertwined... including currency and precious metals.

As a silver investor, you are a commodities investor. You should study how the commodity market works, and how it relates to currency fluctuations and general market conditions. Knowledge is golden, and the more you have, the less you will be blown around by the winds of ignorance.

Rule # 7: Protect Your Investment

While it is wise to keep some of your silver where you can get to it easily, it is also important to keep the bulk of your precious metals in a safe place. This can be a hidden safe, buried cache (Companies like BuildandSurvive.com offer these), or a storage facility of some type. You can establish an account with a brokerage warehouse or other public storage facility, but you should make sure your holdings are kept segregated and accessible to you when you wish to inspect them. Safety deposit boxes are a good place to store physical metals. Secured storage of your metals is nice, but you must always be aware that any metals you keep in banks are subject to government confiscation. Your precious metals do absolutely nothing for you if you cannot access them.

Rule # 8: Stacking Mode

Once you have built your "insurance" stack of gold and/ or silver, and have also secured your backup metal position, then you are in "stacking mode". At this point you should be steadily buying silver and gold. Keep within budget and keep some spare cash reserves for unexpected expenses. Also have cash ready for when a good deal comes along!

Rule # 9: When to Hold 'Em, When to Fold 'Em

Just like many things in our lives, money flows in cycles. Assets go from overvalued, to undervalued, to overvalued again. Those who are willing to learn and recognize the cycles can profit by buying undervalued assets and cashing them in once they become overvalued. Buy physical gold and silver now while it is still at affordable prices.

Rule # 10: When All Else FAILS.

It is not that fun to think about a dystopian future, but should a severe economic collapse occur, leaving paper currency and other assets worthless, silver and gold will be primary currency for purchase of goods and services along with the classic trade/ barter system.

Gold will be a great resource for long term wealth stores, but silver will be the most useful for day- to- day transactions. Stock up on silver primarily, it will be super useful in the event of an economic collapse or emergency.

BUYING PRECIOUS METALS

Silver and gold are exceptionally useful elements. Especially silver! It has many unique properties that make it an invaluable resource, and yet we are consuming the world's supply of silver at a shocking rate. Pure silver is the best conductor of heat and electricity of all known metals. Silver is also the best reflector of visible light known. Silver's beauty is utilized in lots of ways. The range of uses for silver is exceptionally broad and many countries around the world use silver in various manufacturing functions.

As a precious metal, it has been a source of human adornment since the beginning of time. As the principal component of fine tableware, appropriately called 'silverware', it has served an important utility for hundreds of years. As a light-sensitive element, it is used in photography and photo- imaging. Silver is even used in medical applications!

Silver's corrosion resistance, malleability, ductility, reflectivity and conductivity are opening up new uses for silver all the time. All of these reasons have kept silver in high demand by people since the beginning of time. Problem is, silver is finite and the world is running out of it.

You cannot make more silver, although we can turn other elements into silver with a process called atomic transmutation, using particle accelerators. Similar to just how it sounds, this process is very expensive and currently far exceeds the cost of silver. There are constantly new uses for silver coming to light all of the time, so it isn't confusing to see that the availability of silver will undoubtedly continue to dwindle. It is obvious you should buy up silver, and gold if you can afford it, as much as you can!

WHAT TYPE OF GOLD AND SILVER SHOULD I BUY?

Silver Coins. My main suggestion on the type of bullion you should buy, are silver coins or rounds. For example, the Silver American Eagles and Canadian Maple Leaf coins. These coins are common, highly recognizable, composed of .999 fine or better silver, and are not prone to high premiums like rare uncirculated early US silver coins. These

coins do generally carry a $3 to $5 premium per ounce, but the free market has determined the benefits of these coins are worth this small premium. These coins are accepted world-wide as silver bullion, and undoubtedly will be a great transaction currency for trade if needed.

Government-minted coins are more easily proven as genuine compared to bars. Bars are formed from melting down precious metals and as such, are more available for counterfeiting. On the market, we have seen many occurrences where bars were faked by melting down less quality materials and posing them as the real thing. Coins minted by governments like the American silver eagles and Canadian maple leaf coins are also legal tender, at $1 USD and $5 CAD respectively. These are harder to fake and serve as a great monetary piece in a variety of situations.

Pre-1964 US 90% Silver Coins

"Junk silver" is an informal term for any silver coin that has no numismatic or collectible value above the intrinsic bullion value of the silver it contains. The term "junk silver" usually refers to US quarters, dimes, dollar and half-dollar coins minted prior to 1964. These coins are made of 90% silver, mixed with 10% copper, typically. Junk silver can usually be found with little to no premium, and have the added upside potential that some years or mintage of coins are or will become rare and more valuable than their silver content alone.

Bars. Bullion bars made of .999 Fine Silver are a great way to own silver at little to no premium. Solid bullion silver bars of .999 fine purity are a great way to buy silver. I recommend you buy 10 oz Silver Bars that are clearly marked for purity and weight, and are from a well-known dealer. Never buy silver-plated bars. 1 oz. Bars and rounds are not bad either, as the smaller volume might prove beneficial in a trade transaction, if the need arises. Some examples of well-known silver bar producers are Engelhard, Johnson and Matthey, Heraeus, Sunshine Mint and Apmex. Bullion bars generally carry the smallest premium of any form of physical silver, when you go to buy them from a dealer.

Silver Rounds. As I mentioned, silver rounds are a great form of bullion to purchase as well. If you are just getting into silver or gold buying. Silver rounds are generally sold with low premiums over the spot value. These are not considered coins, because they are privately minted instead of government-made. So they are not legal tender in a dollar value. You want to purchase .999 silver 1 oz Silver Rounds that are clearly marked for weight and purity and come from well-known mints.

Keep a Variety. You may find that a mix of generic rounds, government coins, bullion bars, and junk silver to be ideal. This will give you a wide range of use when it comes to bullion related transactions. Avoid buying commemorative coins, decorative items, and other collectibles, all of which carry large premiums and are very limited in the marketplace when being sold.

HOW TO AVOID BUYING FAKE PRECIOUS METALS

Do not buy silver plated products. Auction sites like eBay are FULL of bars that are composed of mainly copper and plated with only a minimal amount of silver. You only want to buy solid 99.9% pure silver bars. They should be clearly labeled with the weight and level of purity. Sellers of some bars try to trick you with wordplay. Do not buy things label, "mils, 10 mils, 100 mils, etc., they are worthless bars of copper. The "mils" part of this product is your major red flag.

Never buy silver from Chinese and non- certified sellers on eBay. When you are shopping for silver on eBay, you should avoid buying from sellers in China. It is not Chinese people, but the location and laws that govern coin production in that area are limited at best. With over a bullion people there, it is not confusing that despite avid efforts, the Chinese government has a difficult time stopping counterfeiters within their borders. That being said, a TON of fakes come out of China. Sites like eBay do not have a level of control capable of stopping counterfeiters. It is too easy to create phony accounts and sell fake items, so counterfeiters flood to this type of site, Amazon included.

Invest in a digital scale and find a good information source. Use my website, VarietyErrors.com or other trusted source with information

about the weight and thickness of the silver coins, and verify the coins you are buying.

Do not buy "German silver" or "Nickel-silver" bars. Beware of sellers on eBay selling bars of ".999 Fine German silver" trying to mislead potential buyers into thinking they are buying pure silver bars. German silver is another name for nickel silver, a copper alloy with nickel and often zinc, and contain no silver. Do not buy these bars!

WHEN SHOULD I SELL MY SILVER?

People understandably want a hard dollar figure for the price of silver as their target to sell. Well, the problem is the United States dollar keeps being devalued and the supply inflated, and the available above-ground silver reserves are getting smaller and smaller. So, this is the problem when it comes to putting a specific dollar amount on when to sell your bullion. I would suggest relating the point of selling your silver or gold with real world assets, rather than dollar amounts. The government of China is heavily encouraging its citizens to buy physical silver. There will come a time when silver is overvalued, but it will not be time to sell your silver for dollars to hold. In this case, I would suggest considering the weight of your precious metals reserves against real world, tangible assets like real estate.

Caring for Your Collection

Onto Your Collection!

Now that you have become a coin collector, you will be putting a lot of time, effort and money into this hobby. It is important to consider any and all preparation and storage options you have for your currency.

Invest in an Acid-Free Containers and Paper

In fact, when paper that's not acid-free breaks down, it releases chemicals that can cause discoloration, spotting, and even oxidation, all of which can damage your collection and diminish its value. This applies to any form of currency you are going to collect.

Whatever storage method a collector chooses, the container should be acid-free, so safes are usually a good idea. A safe that's fire-retardant is best, in case of an emergency involving the location of your collection.

NEVER Use Bare Hands

Even if you just washed your hands, touching rare coins, rare bills or potential collectible currency of any type for that matter, with bare hands is never a good idea. The oils from your skin ruin the value of the coin by staining the surface, and concurrently, the design/ image on the faces of the coin. Bills and coins shouldn't be handled with bare hands, that's why we recommend always using gloves when handling coins.

Store Your Currency

Coins and banknotes should be kept as close to a constant temperature and humidity level as possible. If exposed to extreme temperatures, coins and other forms of currency can have effects from oxidation and be ruined in both physical appearance and value.

Copper and silver (in coins) in particular are susceptible to tarnishing or "toning" caused by temperature and humidity fluctuations around your collection. Some collectors enjoy toning, it's a destructive force that will eventually causes the coin to become very dark and less appealing in appearance to most.

Humidity can also cause mold growth, which negatively effects all forms of documents and currency. Mold is particularly a concern for paper money collectors, but it may also grow on coins. Generally, banknotes and coins should be preserved in a low-humidity environment, preferably less than 30 percent relative humidity, as to maintain their quality and value.

With a climate-controlled storage unit or storage space, you can ward off both oxidation damages and mold growth, as you can keep your storage unit at consistent and moderate temperature, with humidity levels that are just right for coin storage.

Get Insurance

You never know what is going to happen and a total loss of a currency collection is something that many have dealt with. I remember losing my entire comic book collection (over 1,200 books!) to hurricane Florence while living in Wilmington, NC. I wish I would have had the foresight to back my collection with insurance!

Many coin experts believe insurance for your collection is something that should always be considered by anyone getting into the hobby or who already has an existing collection that is sizable or valuable enough where it makes sense to purchase coverage.

Information on "Cleaning" Coins

Since this subject has been visited a few times on my website **VarietyErrors.com**, it will be discussed here. At no time, do I suggest "washing" or "cleaning" any coin you are meaning to keep in your collection, this in a way, defeats the hobby in the sense of collecting to preserve the condition the coin was found in.

Take into mind that the piece you hold in your hand could very well be a collector's item. Does the coin even need to be cleaned? As described in many other articles from Variety & Errors, the collecting of anything is very much the same in regards to cleaning specimens found while "out on the hunt".

How to Clean Coins

There are basically two ways you can go about cleaning your (not valuable) coins. You can wash them and/or you can dip them. If you want to simply wash the coins, these are the supplies you'll need:

- Dish soap (the kind for hand-washing)
- A rag or dish towel
- A Small bowl

STEP 1: Prepare the bath

If your coin is only slightly dirty, or the dirt isn't deeply set in, you can simply rinse it off in lukewarm water. If the dirt is more set on than that, run hot water in the sink or boil it in a pan on the stove. Then take about a cup of this water and fill the small bowl. You should use the hottest water possible to clean your coin, but

use caution when running it so that you don't burn your hands. Next, add about a teaspoon of dish soap and mix it with the water until it is becomes fairly uniform solution.

STEP 2: Submerge the coin

After you've got the bath ready, take your coin and place it in the soapy water. Let it soak for a couple of minutes. If you're soaking more than one coin at a time be careful that you don't scratch the coins already in the solution as you put more in. Do not stack them up in the water and make sure they don't touch each other. If you're worried about this, you can always wash each coin separately.

STEP 3: Lightly buff the coin

If after a few minutes of leaving your coin in the water bath it still has dirt on it, first, try moving it around in the water vigorously and seeing if that shakes it off. If that doesn't work, you can use your fingers to rub the coin gently, but do not try to pick the dirt off of the coin with your fingernail or another abrasive item. You could risk scratching it that way. Also, hold the coin by the edges, never by the face.

STEP 4: Rinse the coin

Once you've gotten the coin clean, you can rinse it under the faucet. But if you want to prevent hard water deposits or spots on your coin, rinse it in distilled water instead. Just pour about a cup of it into a bowl and dunk the coin in the water for a few seconds, making sure to get all the soap off of it.

STEP 5: Dry the coin

To dry your coin, place it on a paper towel or dish towel and let it air dry. If you're too impatient or need the coin right away, you can dab it with the towel to dry it. Don't forcefully rub the coin dry or you risk scratching its surface. If you hadn't figured it out by now, they scratch very easily!

Coin Storage and Holder Ideas
Containers and Albums and Sleeves, Oh My!

There are actually several currency storage solutions on the market today. All are adequate, some being better than others. The type of storage you select has a lot to do with the type of currency you are collecting and how you personally wish to store and reference them.

For example, if you are not an avid collector, you may not want to go out and buy expensive albums for those few little Wheat Back Cents you have lying around. However, an extensive coin searcher and collector would want to invest in the more expansive storage options to maintain the quality of higher grade coins.

>**Storing coins has a wide variety of options, so the following will detail each respectively and the occasions in which you may want to use them.*

2×2 Cardboard Holders

Overall, the cheapest way to store coins, other than tubes and rolls. Cardboard coin holders are actually 2×8 pieces of cardboard paper with 2 coin-sized holes cut out and covered with plastic which forms a "window" around the coin, the holder's "window" will be cut to the size appropriate for the coin it is meant to hold. Meaning, a 2×2 holder for a US Quarter will be the size of the coin itself.

2×2 Mylar Holders

Mylar holders are the next option above cardboard holders, supplying more protection for coins. There is no cardboard in these. They are all mylar plastic material. These are generally used for lower value coins that a collector plans to sell eventually.

2×2 Plastic Holders

The next level of protection above Mylar Holders (see above). Plastic panels snap together to secure the coin in place. They are composed of thicker plastic for added protection and temperature control (in a sense).

Coin and Banknote Albums

The most common way to store currency in any form. Generally, collectors would sort their sets of coins, such as a year run of Buffalo Nickels for example, within an album, in order to maintain the series' order and value. The more common (and less expensive) Whitman albums and Harris folders for coins and other currency, generally fold out into 3 or 4 sections. These sections have multiple slots for each year of coin.

The better coin albums, such as Intercept version, and a few newer brands found online, are quite a bit more expensive, but well worth the money if you are storing higher grade coins or series of coins. These are usually made of higher grade materials and display both sides of the coin beautifully. These albums also come in a standard book form, where the pages are turned rather than the cheaper albums where the pages fold out. This feature also adds to the display aspects of the album as a whole.

Coin and Banknote Tubes

The best and most common storage container for lower grade (quality) coins. These tubes are made of plastic and hold coins in a stack nicely. They come in various colors but are generally clear or white.

Air Tight / "AirTite" Holders

I like these the best for valuable coins that aren't in one of my sets. Airtite holders are kind of like the 2×2 hard plastic holders, only a little better and they're round like the coin instead of square.

Coin Binders

These are normally 3- ring binders with pages that hold 2×2 coin holders. Albums like this are a cheaper alternative usually to binders made strictly for coins. It is also a great idea to use these if you want the ability to add pages as you go.

Many stores sell binders of course, but you will most likely need to visit your local coin or hobby store in order to purchase the coin album pages. They typically come in a multi-pack.

Coin and Banknote Slabs

"Slab" is coin collector terminology. Generally a "slab" is what a professional grading service puts your coin into after they have given it a grade. This is the best and safest way to store coins (well...other than a 3 foot thick vault).

You can buy slabs online or at a coin shop. They are made of thick plastic that snaps together like the 2×2 holders. Only with a slab, they are rectangle-shaped with a space (before you snap it together) to insert a label describing what type of coin is going to be displayed in it, along with its value.

These are similar to the slabs you get from professional grading services, but not exactly the same. A slab you receive from a grading service after they have graded your coin doesn't just snap together. Instead, they are sealed and are tamper proof.

Slab holders are an even better source of storage for your collection. They make plastic rectangular boxes with slots grooved in them to stand your slabs upright in. The absolute best protection is to have your coin graded and sealed by a grading service such as NGC then you place the coin in a snap together type slab.

HOW TO TAKE CARE OF PRECIOUS METALS

It's a simple and well-known fact that people are drawn to shiny things. (*My geek side queues a *Smeagle/ Golem* reference from Lord of the Rings). These things include bullion coins or bars kept in their "mint" condition. Investors are more willing to pay for a coin or bar that is well preserved rather than one with scratches or severe tarnishing. Therefore, mint condition bullion is a more liquid asset on the market, even though most dealers and buyers will always pay attention to the bullion's manufacturer, weight, and purity first.

For this reason, knowing how to take care of coins, bars and rounds is a must if you are or want to become a bullion collector or investor. One of the biggest concerns about precious metals is their tarnishing – a process through which your bullion loses luster.

Why do metals tarnish?

Depending on each metal's chemical properties, they can react to natural or synthetic components. High humidity climates, improper cleaning or exposure to certain chemicals may accelerate the tarnishing (toning) or oxidation process of your precious bullion. This process can be faster or slower depending on the finishing of your bullion. However, most of the time it will not affect its intrinsic value, but it may become harder to trade your bullion on the market.

Each Metal's Chemical Properties

Gold:

Gold is difficult to tarnish because it's chemically inert. Gold maintains its chemical and physical properties and it doesn't oxidize under normal conditions. Gold gets dissolved by nitro-hydrochloride, which is not easily found. Although it's resistant to scuffs and scratches, it's a soft metal, hence it is possible to dent the bullion if dropped on a hard surface or from a considerable distance.

Silver:

Silver oxidizes under normal conditions. This metal is easy to tarnish, scratch and scuff, hence it requires a little bit more care than gold. It's susceptible to hydrogen sulfide.

Copper:

Copper slowly reacts with atmospheric oxygen, soil compounds and natural water, which leads to corrosion. Copper tarnishes if it's exposed to sulfur compounds forming various copper sulfides.

Platinum and Palladium:

Platinum and Palladium are the least reactive precious metals These noble metals are resistant to corrosion and high temperatures and can be damaged only if you use synthetic chemicals. However, the metals may become dull over time.

Bar, Rounds And Coin Handling

Knowing how to handle your precious bullion properly is essential for preserving its condition. Remember, it is easier to keep your bullion clean than have to restore it once you touched it. Keep your coins sealed in storage. Avoid unnecessary handling.

In case you really need to hold your bullion, make sure that you wear soft, clean, cotton gloves. Fingerprints contain oil that can transfer to coins and bullion.

Never use:

- latex or plastic gloves – these types of gloves are coated with powders or lubricants which can damage your precious bullion.
- plastic tweezers – they may scratch or damage your bars or coins.

If you choose to handle your precious metals with your bare hands, make sure to wash them before touching your bullion. By washing your hands, you ensure that they are free of any dirt or residues. The best way to clean your hands is to use hand sanitizers since they will remove any damaging oils from your hands. When handling your coins or bars, prepare a special area by draping a soft towel before you take out your metals and start working with them.

Summarizing the above tips, here are the main rules for proper bar and coin handling:

- Avoid handling your bullion if possible – keep your coins and bars in a safe storage place – this is the place where your coins and bars should be 99.9% of the time.

- If you need to handle your bullion, wear soft, lint-free cotton gloves.

- Wash your hands and use hand sanitizers before touching your bullion.
- Lay a soft towel or a thick, soft cloth– to ensure a soft landing in case you drop your bullion.
- Always handle your bullion by edges, between your forefinger and thumb.
- Never place tarnished and untarnished metals together.
- Don't talk or breathe over your bullion.

Bar, Rounds And Coin Cleaning

You should avoid any bar or coin handling unless it is necessary to do so. Rigorous cleaning is a famous misconception – by cleaning your precious metals, you will not improve their value or condition.

The attempts to protect the quality of your bullion will only accelerate the deterioration of the metal. Cleaning a coin or a bar can damage its condition and, therefore, lower its value.

If you recently acquired coins that are difficult to read or distinguish, it doesn't mean you need to clean them. This process will spoil their pleasing tarnish and deep coloration, which may have taken centuries to be formed. So, if you have highly-graded, rare or extremely valued coins or bars that need to be cleaned – do not clean them, or, in case you feel it is necessary, seek only professional help.

Remember, coins and bars that carry evidence of cleaning, contact marks, worn features or rim blemishes have significantly lower value, especially numismatic, proof and brilliant uncirculated coins which are mostly issued in low mintage editions. Old coins that show age marks are far more desirable than the ones with surfaces stripped away by improper cleaning.

If you still want to clean your bullion – make it superficial. Wash your bullion with mild soap and water, and rinse it thoroughly to avoid any soap residue. After washing it, gently wipe your bullion dry with a soft towel or cloth.

Do not polish it excessively and aggressively because you can scratch the bullion, remove the outer layer, and cause a small loss of precious metal, hence making it lighter and reducing its value. Let your bullion completely dry before storing to prevent trapping any moisture or water on its surface.

In general, when it comes to cleaning your bullion – avoid it at any price. If you still decide to do it, make it superficial, and perhaps use an ultrasonic tank, but **<u>NEVER USE</u>**:

- Special formulate polishes, abrasives or cleaners, because they contain acidic components which can corrode the surface of your precious metal.
- Tap water, since it contains chlorine in it which may discolor the bullion. Use and rinse the bullion only in distilled water.
- Fingernail polish, soda, acetone, carbon dioxide and vinegar will react with your precious metal and will certainly damage it.
- Acid-based metal cleaners, because they will remove some of the coin or bar surface.

Bar, Rounds And Coin Storage

When it comes to bar or coin storage, you should know both how and where you need to store and protect them from any potential damages or risks. Before describing the best places for gold and silver bar storage or coins storage, it is important to know what kind of boxes, tubes or capsules you must preserve your bullion in.

The best containers in which you can store your bullion must be air tight and made of natural materials, such as protective coin slabs, lined wooden boxes, wooden shadow boxes with glass display panels, or Mylar flips and containers. If you prefer storing your coins in albums, then opt for one with cardboard folders or slots, not plastic sleeves.

Never store your coins and rounds in a binder or album with plastic sleeves, as organized and attractive as it may look, it is completely unsafe. Your coins or rounds may become discolored if you place them in these plastic sleeves, since they aren't airtight, they can potentially trap moisture and cause damage to your coins.

PVC containers are very dangerous bar and coin storage options. PVC decomposes when it reacts to light or heat, releasing hydrochloric acid that will eat away the metal in your bullion and diminish its resale value — and cause irreversible and permanent damage to your coins or bars. It's also surprising that many people use tape to stick their bullion to a piece of paper or card. Avoid sticking anything to your precious metals because it will leave marks that will destroy your bullion.

For the majority of coins, the best coin storage is the Mylar "flip"- a cardboard holder lined with Mylar - it has a circle cut out in the middle, covered with this special form of a heat-resistant plastic sheet. When the coin is placed in the Mylar "window", the other part of the cardboard holder is folded over and stapled on its three sides. This way, both sides of the coin are visible through the Mylar plastic. You should be careful and flatten the staples against the card to avoid accidentally scratching other coins.

If you choose to place your coins or bars in Mylar capsules or containers, consider placing inside them some carbon or "charcoal". Carbon will help you trap some of the hydrogen sulfides which causes tarnish. You can get carbon from pet shops because it's also used for fish tanks. You can also pack your metals (e.g. silver) with silica gel - it will stop rust, spoilage, mildew and corrosion. For large silver bar storage, use dehumidifiers.

Never store tarnished and untarnished metals together. Avoid hazardously placing them together to prevent rubbing them against each other -this can lead to friction or abrasive marks. If necessary you should stack them in piles, or separate them with plain cardboard sheets or other non-reactive materials, but the best way is to simply store them separately.

Now that you know the main rules of how to store your bullion, you must decide where you will store it. Consider that $30,000 gold can fit in your pocket, but $30,000 silver weighs about 50 lbs. Also, coins always take a little bit more space than bars, and you should never store different types of metals together.

Although many recommend using safe deposit boxes in banks, there are some certain risks associated with this storage type. Safe deposit boxes aren't FDIC or bank insured and are susceptible to "Bank Holidays". Like many times you need to access something, you do not want to have issues accessing your bullion. With banks, this will be the case.

The IRS or government can also freeze and seize your box, as it has happened in the past. This means that by law you would need to have your safety deposit boxes checked and cleared before you would have access to your holdings.

A storage type that you should consider avoiding is self-storage facilities. Even though they might seem a cost-effective option, they are not ideal for storing physical bullion. There is an increased likelihood of theft among storage employees because they aren't so rigorously checked as bank or vault officers. Second, these facilities may not be secured effectively to hold such valuable items. Also, these facilities are more subject to damage during bad weather. I have also seen storage

units go under construction and allow dozens of workers to access your unit. Do you really want strangers around the bullion you have in your "secure" unit? Probably not.

This is why you may think of storing your bullion at home. Before rushing to opt for original storage compartments, like "secret storage rooms", you should first consider buying a solid safe. The right safe must be waterproof, fireproof, and large enough to hold your potential collection.

Besides choosing the best safe for you, based on its size or features, you should also decide whether you need a standalone safe, a floor safe, or a wall safe. Also, you should think of what kind of lock you need: a digital lock, a fingerprint lock, a manual combination lock, or a combination of locks.

Once you decide on the safe that will suit you the best, keep in mind the following **tips on your home bullion's storage and safety**:

- Make sure fewer people know about your belongings – limit the number of people that know about your bullion.
- Avoid posting any images of your bullion on social media websites.
- Diversify your location – consider buying two safes – one will serve as a decoy safe for tricking robbers.
- Be creative with your home storage means – get inspired by books and posts, but avoid using the same locations. Keep in mind that if you can read about where to hide something, the burglars can read, too.
- Make sure the space is cool and dry (low humidity) – moisture and heat can lead to corrosion.
- Avoid using wood surfaces due to fire hazard – your bullion may be damaged.
- Leave a letter for your relatives - in case the worst happens, write a detailed guideline about where your bullion is stored.

Currency
Graders and Groups

Coin Associations Around the World

Numismatic associations bring together groups of numismatists. They may be commercial, hobby or professional.

- American Numismatic Society
- American Numismatic
- Anchorage Coin Club
- Bellaire Coin Club
- Blue Ridge Numismatic Association
- California State Numismatic Association
- Canada Numismatic Network
- Canadian Association of Numismatic Dealers
- Canadian Errors & Varieties Numismatic Association (CEVNA)
- Canadian Paper Money Society
- Classical & Medieval Numismatic Society
- CONECA
- Edmonton Numismatic
- Florida United Numismatis
- Friends of the Segovia Mint
- Hellenic Numismatic Society
- Indian Institute of Research in Numismatic Studies
- International Bank Note Society (IBNS)
- International Numismatic Commission
- Ontario Numismatic Association
- Oriental Numismatic Society
- Ottawa Numismatic Society

Currency Terminology

Currency Terminology

"A"

About good

- one of the lowest grades in most grading standard books. Typically an about good coin is a very worn coin with some outline of the design and a readable date. Falls below below the grade of good. Sometimes abbreviated as AG.

About Uncirculated
- Same as "Almost Uncirculated". Sometimes abbreviated as "AU".

abrasion
- marks or small scratches on the surface of a coin where another coin or object has slid across or bumped the coin. Can also be caused by the coin sliding in a holder or coin drawer. Not as deep or noticeable as bag marks. Usually found on the high parts of a coin or in the open fields (background). Sometimes the terms scuffing, light rubbing, or hairlines are also used to indicate light abrasive wear.

accumulation
- A group of coins, sometimes not of any certain type or date. Also can be a "hoard".

Ag
- elemental abbreviation for SILVER

AG
- Same as "About good".

AirTite Holder
- A popular brand of plastic found shaped holders for coins. They snap together and are often used to display, protect, and store individual coins.

Album, or coin album
- Coin albums resemble a book, with holes or openings for displaying coins on each page. Some are push in types where the coin is pushed in a hole in the cardboard page. Other albums offer plastic sleeves or protective clear places for coin storage and display.

alloy
- a mixture of two or more metals melted into one compound. For example old Liberty Head gold coins minted prior to 1933 were made of an alloy. Although they were mostly gold a small amount of other metal was added to the gold to give the resulting coins a hardness that pure gold didn't offer. Harder gold coins withstood wear better during circulation. Most coins are made of some type of alloy. Even the US nickel is made of an alloy of nickel and other metals.

Almost Uncirculated
- A coin or paper money note that is very close to being uncirculated. Upon first glance it may appear un-circulated. When inspected closely it will have a slight amount of wear or friction. Same as "About Uncirculated". Sometimes abbreviated as "AU", or "A Unc".

alteration
- intentional tampering of a coin usually to make it appear more valuable. Often deals with the coin's date or mintmark. However, it can involve changing the appearance (after a coin was minted) such as when hobo nickels were made. If the intent of altering can be viewed as an attempt to deceive or fraud, prosecution can result. Also, see altered date.

altered date
- a coin with the date manipulated or altered after the coin was produced. Often done to try to deceive someone. For example, an unscrupulous person might alter the date of a 1944-D cent to look like

a 1914-D cent, by filing off part of the first 4 to make it look like the number 1.

American Eagle
Silver, gold, and platinum gold coins released by the US government starting in Oct. 1986. Front (obverse) depicts Liberty walking and reverse side bears an American Eagle and nest design. Produced in both Uncirculated and Proof conditions. The silver coins are often called Silver Eagles, gold coins often called Gold Eagles, and Platinum are called Platinum eagles.

American Eagle Bullion Coins
These are the uncirculated - mint condition versions of the United States "American Eagles" gold, silver, or platinum coins. See "American Eagles".

American Eagle Proof Coins
Silver, gold, and platinum US gold coins that are of special "Proof" quality. Sold by the United States Mint. Proofs are made with special polished coin dies that give the coins a polished mirror-like appearance.

American Numismatic Association (ANA)
- the most popular nonprofit educational coin collectors organization in America. Encourages the study of numismatics; collecting of money. The American Numismatic Association headquarters and national 'Money Museum' are located in Colorado Springs, CO. Often called the A.N.A.

American Numismatic Society (ANS)
- another nonprofit educational organization of coin collectors and dealers. Established prior to the civil war it promotes the study of coin collecting, numismatics. Often called the A.N.S.

American Silver Eagle
- sometimes called the silver eagle dollar coin or ASE. American Silver Eagle coins were first minted by the United States government in 1986. These 1 ounce solid silver coins are sold to collectors and dealers by

the US Mint, and no versions are made for circulating through the banking system.

A.N.A.
- abbreviation for the "American Numismatic Association".

ANACS
- American Numismatic Association Certification Service. This grading and certification service certifies coins as genuine, grades, and encapsulates them. One of the original grading services. Has now changed ownership and is no longer under the direction of the American Numismatic Association (ANA).

ANS
- abbreviation for the "American Numismatic Society".

anvil die
- bottom die. A coin is struck using two dies. One for the obverse (front) of the coin and another for the reverse (back). The anvil die is the one on the bottom, which is usually the reverse. The term comes from when the die was placed on an anvil with the coin blank (planchet) on top. The hammer die (top die) was placed on top of the coin and struck with a hammer. See "hammer die" and "die".

annealing
- the process of heating coin blanks (planchlets) in a furnace to soften the metal prior to striking coins out of them.

artificial toning
- changing the color or surface tone of a coin by applying chemicals, heat, or treating a coin with something. Done to make the coin appear natural or unusual, or to cover up signs that the coin has been cleaned or polished. See toning and natural toning.

ask price
- The price a dealer or trader is asking for a coin. Often used to indicate the "wholesale" asking price between dealers or on a coin trading network.

assay
- to determine the purity of the metal by scientific means. An assay of precious metal coins (gold and silver) is often done to establish that the coins do indeed contain the proper purity and amounts of precious metal.

Authentic (authenticate)
- A coin issued by an official government or a token issued by the original entity. Authentic indicates it is not a replica or counterfeit coin. Grading services such as PCGS, NGC, and ANACS will first authenticate (determine that it is genuine) before grading the coin. See genuine,official, and Certificate of Authenticity (COA).

Avoirdupois
- official description of the weight system we use in the USA for weighing most items. This unit of weight consists of 16 ounces in a pound and 2,000 pounds in a ton. Same weight system used in US grocery stores to weigh produce.

Au
- elemental (scientific) abbreviation for the metal GOLD.

AU
- See "About Uncirculated" or "Almost Uncirculated".

"B"

bag mark
-Mark(s) on a coin that occurred during the production process or while at the mint. Bag marks may occur when coins bump into each other as they are placed in bags at the mint. Larger size coins typically exhibit more bag marks than smaller ones. A coin can still be un-circulated even if it has obvious nicks or bag marks.

bag stain
- discoloration, tarnish, or toning on the surface of a coin because of coming in contact with the cloth of a coin bag. Long term storage in canvas or cloth bags may cause such bag stains.

bank notes
- paper money. In the 1800's banks often issued their own paper money. These bank notes were backed by bank resources, rather than governments. The term banknote continues to this day, as a reference to paper currency. See paper money and paper currency.

bar
- usually an "ingot" shaped as a rectangle. Can be gold, silver, or any precious metal. Gold and silver bars vary in size from 1 gram up to thousands of ounces.

Barber
- nick name for United States dimes, quarters, and half dollars designed by Charles E. Barber. Barber coins we minted from 1892 to 1916. Originally these coins were called Liberty Head because they depict a "liberty head" design on the front (obverse) and a eagle with shield on the reverse. Although Charles Barber designed other coins, only the Barber Dimes, Barber Quarters, and Barber Half dollars have acquired this nickname. (Sometimes misspelled as barbar.)

Barber, Charles E.

- Charles E Barber was chief engraver of the US Mint in the late 1800's and early 1900's. Coins that he designed often have an almost microscopic "B" on them, often at the base of the neck on the portraits. He designed various United States coins for circulation, commemoration, and some pattern coins such as the rare $4 Flowing Hair Stella coin.

beads or beading
- round bead-like decorations on the surface of a coin. When it is placed on a coin for artistic reasons, it is often a circle of beads on the face of a coin, usually near the rim or edge.

bicentennial, or bicentennial coins
- usually refers to special coins minted for the 200th anniversary of the United States of America. US Quarters, Half Dollars and the Eisenhower dollar dated 1976 had a special commemorative type reverse designs. Some Bicentennial coins were minted in 1975 with the 1976 date.

Bid
- the price a dealer (or dealers) are offering to pay for a coin. Sometimes used to indicate a standing offer at that price from a coin dealer or on a trading network. Also, see "site unseen".

Billon
- a low grade of silver. Although sometimes silver in color, usually made of part silver and part copper.

bimetallic (Bi Metallic)
- a coin made of at least two different metals that are sealed to each other. The two different metals in a bi-metallic coin are typically observable, as in the copper-nickel-clad US coins of today.

Bison
- see buffalo nickels and buffalo gold coins.

Bit
- slang used to indicate one eighth of a dollar. In early days of the USA the Spanish Milled Dollar (pillar dollar or 8 reales) circulated. Due to a shortage of smaller coins these silver dollars were often cut into pieces shaped like slices of pizza. A small piece equal to one eighth of the dollar was called a "piece of eight" or a "bit". The nursery rime "two bits, four bits, 6 bits, a dollar" comes from this time in history."A bit would be the equivalent of 12 1/2 cents. Example, two bits equals two eighths or a quarter.

blank
- a blank piece of metal on which a coin design can be stamped. Also called a planchlet (planchet). Usually already cut into the shape of a coin - round, flat and plan, without any design. See planchet or flan.

blemish
- a surface flaw or appearance of imperfection on the surface of a coin. Bag marks, discoloration, tarnish, spots, nicks are examples of blemishes.

Blue Book
- Coin collecting price guide that lists the wholesale prices that a US coin dealer might pay. Has a blue cover, hence the term blue book. Differs from the Red Book in that the Red Book (Guide Book to US Coins) lists the approximate retail values of US coins.

Blue Sheet
- Nickname for the Certified Coin Dealer newsletter. Printed on bluish paper. The bluesheet lists various US coins and bid/ask dealer prices for some of these certified/graded coins. See grey sheet.

body bag
- identifies a coin that was returned by a coin grading/certification in a poly bag or flip and not certified/graded because of some problem with the coin. Most coin grading

services charge to examine a coin, even if they decide not to grade, slab or certify the coin.

borderline

- A coin that falls on the edge between two grades. Most often used as "borderline uncirculated", indicating a high grade almost uncirculated coin. Such a coin might fall in the range of AU55 to AU59 in the coin grading point scale.

bourse

- see "show".

branch mints

- minting branches of the U.S. government minting facility. The Philadelphia Mint has been the main mint for US coins. Other mints are considered branch mints.

brilliant uncirculated

- a descriptive term used to indicate an uncirculated coin that still retains a lot of the brilliant luster. Not a heavily toned coin. BU is used to abbreviate brilliant uncirculated.

broad strike

- When coins are minted a collar surrounds the coin blank and holds it in place. This collar keeps the metal from spreading out when the coin is struck on. If a coin blank is not properly seated in the collar, and it is struck, the result will be an odd size or broadstruck coin.

bronze

- an alloy (mixture) of copper, zinc, and tin. Color usually brownish yellow.

brown spotting

- brown or rust colored spots appearing on the surface of a coin. Often a form of tarnish or an oxidation type reaction with the coin's surface

or something that has adhered to the coin's surface. Some times brownish yellow or red.

BN
- abbreviation for Brown. A natural common color for copper coins.
brushed
- a coin that has been brushed or cleaned with a wire brush, or some other material. The surface will show fine lines, or hairline scratches from the cleaning.

BU
- Brilliant Uncirculated. A coin grading term that indicates a coin has no wear, has never been exposed to circulation, and shows a surface brilliance as that of a newly minted coin. Such mint state coins will fall between MS60 and MS70 on the coin grading scale.

buffalo gold coin
- 1 ounce bullion type of United States gold coins. First issued in 2006. Contains 1 ounce of .999 fine (99.9% pure) gold and has a $50 face value. Official US government legal tender coin issued by the US mint. Similar in gold content to the Canadian Maple Leaf gold coins. The US mint began producing smaller size buffalo gold coins in 2008, with the introduction of tenth, fourth, and half ounce gold buffalo coins.

buffalo nickel
- old buffalo US five cent coins were minted from 1913 to 1938. These old nickels depicted an Indian Head design on one side and the Buffalo or American Bison on the other. The buffalo-bison design was revived in the year 2005 for a one year special minting on the US nickel again. United States gold coins and a commemorative silver dollar have also been made with a buffalo design.

buffalo round
- buffalo rounds are sometimes call buffalo or Indian head silver rounds. Minted by private mints and refineries they usually contain one ounce of silver. Often they feature a design like that of the old Buffalo nickels with a buffalo on one side and an Indian's head on

the other. Buffalo silver rounds usually sell for close to the value of silver bullion they contain.

buffing
- a polishing of a coin sometimes with an abrasive that leaves a finish that attempts to counterfeit mint luster. See whizzed.

bullion
-term used when referring to items made of precious metal. Particularly silver, gold, and platinum. Often produced in the form of ingots, bars, rounds, and coins. Bullion value of a coin would be the "value of the metal" the coin contains.

bullion coin
- coins made of precious metal and traded at current bullion prices, or at a small premium over bullion.

Bureau of Engraving and Printing
- United States government agency that produces paper money for the U.S. and some other countries.

burnished blank or burnished die
- treatment of a coin blank or die to give it a special slightly sandy or polished look. Sometimes burnishing is done with chemicals or by special polishing. Starting in 2006 the US Mint made Silver Eagle dollar coins with special burnished coin blanks. These coins have a ' W ' mint mark.

burnishing
- polishing or rubbing the surface of a coin or coin blank to make it shiny. Burnishing of a minted coin is often considered detrimental and should be mentioned in any coin description.

bury or buried
- purchasing a coin or coins for more than you can get for them.

business strike

- a coin produced for general use and circulation. Non-business strikes would be coins such as proofs, and special uncirculated coins or sets not intended to circulate.

bust

- portrait on a coin, usually displaying the head, or head and shoulders.

buyer fee or buyers fee

- a fee imposed on the buyer in a coin or stamp auction.

" C "

cast coin

- a coin that was made by pouring melted metal into a mold or cast. Not made by striking a die against a blank like most coins.

cameo (deep cameo, ultra cameo, or cam)

- usually refers to the looks of a proof coin, where the background design has a mirror like look and the raised design has a frosted look to it. This contrast gives the resulting proof coin a cameo type affect. Deep cameo and ultra cameo describe the same cameo affect and imply that the cameo look is very pronounced and easily observed. This cameo affect is normal for modern day proofs, but it is rarely found on coins made for standard circulation.

carbon spotting or carbon spots

- Dark spots, usually black or brown, found on the surface of a coin. They can be of various sizes and shapes. These carbon colored spots are caused by oxidation on the coin's surface and will sometimes hurt the coin's value.

Carson City Mint
- A United States government branch mint found at Carson City Nevada. Minted primarily silver coins from 1870 to the early 1890's. Carson City minted coins are easily identified by a "CC" mint mark. This mint was established primarily to use the vast amounts of silver being mined in that area of the USA.

cartwheel or cart wheel
- Nickname for a US Silver Dollar or large silver dollar like coin. This term is sometimes used to describe the luster effect on some brilliant uncirculated coins, where the light reflects off the surface of the coin pattern similar to the spokes of a wagon wheel.

Cent
- one hundredth of a dollar on standard currency. Called a centime, centabo,
 centimes, or penny in some countries.

centered or centering
- describes the position of the coin design in relation to the coin blank (planchet)A well centered coin is one that is struck right in the middle of the coin blank and shows a rim that is the same width all around the coin. See "off centered".

certified or certified coin
- A coin certified as genuine by a coin certification service as genuine. Often a certified coin will be graded by a coin grading service such asPCGSS, NGC, ANACS. Often a certified coin is accompanied by a photograph certificate or sealed in a special plastic slab. Also see "slabbed".

Charlotte Mint
- A United States government branch mint in Charlotte, North Carolina. Used to mint primarily gold coins prior to the Civil War.

The mint stopped coin production in 1861. These coins have a "C" mint mark.

cherry picker (cherrypicker)
- a collector or dealer who finds hidden scarce coins by looking through collections or dealer's inventory.

chop marks
- oriental marks or characters stamped into previously made coins. Often found on silver trade dollars and other precious metal coins. When coins were used for trading purposes an oriental assayer would test a piece of the coin for purity. If it met his approval he would stamp his mark into the coin indicating to others it was pure and accurate weight. Today some collectors specialize in "Chop marked" coins. However, for many coins the chop marks may hurt the value.

Chrometophobia
- a fear of money phobia. Some types of money phobias like chrometophobia have to do with using money and making decisions with it. Other types of phobias such as Fear of Germs, Verminophobia, misophobia, mysophobia, Spermatophobia, and Germ Fear might be the real cause of someone being afraid of coins or paper money.

Chrematophobia
- another spelling for the "fear of money" type of phobia

circulation
- coins used in commerce to purchase items by the populace are in circulation. A circulated coin is one that has been used one time or often more. Coins that have any kind of wear from handling, etc are also considered circulated.

Clad
- Clad coinage is a term used to describe coins that have a core of one type of metal and an outer layer of another metal or metals. Most U.S. dimes, quarters, and half dollars since 1965 have been clad. Clad differs from a plated coin in that the clad blank (or planchlet) is treated to seal the layers of metal together. Also called sandwich or hamburger coins.

clad coin
- Coins that have a core (center layer) and outer layer made of different metals. (See bi-metallic clad or silver clad.)

coin
- object usually made of flat metal. Most often it is small and round. Issued by a government as money. Usually, accepted by the community as having value. See token.

coin cabinet
- see "cabinet".

coin show
- see "show".

coin trends
- see "trends".

collar (sometimes misspelled as coller)
- when a coin is struck the collar on the printing press surrounds the rim of the coin preventing the metal from flowing outside of the collar. This maintains the width of the finished coin as an exact size.

Colonials
- coins produced by the colony states prior to the time the United States government was formed. Most were made of copper and in small denominations.

Commemorative
- a special coin or medal issued to honor an outstanding person, place, occasion or event. Often commemorative coins are a one time or short lived production. Many times commemorative coins are not produced for general circulation.

Condition
- The physical state of a coin or medal. Usually indicating the amount of wear. (See grading standards.)

contact mark

- a mark or marks on a coin that happened from coming in contact with another coin or object. Usually contact marks are small. Often this term is used to indicate marks on a coin that are not as obvious as bag marks. However, sometimes it is used to mean the same thing. See "abrasions", "bag mark", or "gouges".

copper nickel

- A metal alloy of 88% copper and 12% nickel. This alloy was used for US Flying Eagle and Indian cents from 1856 to the middle of 1864. The alloy caused these small cents to have a pale copper color. Back then people called these cents "white cents" because of their pale color. A few other countries have used some copper nickel alloys of various percentages in their coin production. "Cupro-nickel" is a similar term. See "cupro nickel".

coppers

- nick name for older copper coins, particularly the large cents, and half cents.

Copy

- refers to a reproduction of a coin or paper note. Some copies may be illegal. Current government regulations require reproductions of US coins and paper money to be much larger or smaller than the original. For copies of tokens and non-US-government coins the "hobby protection act" requires that the item contains the word "copy" or "reproduction" in a readable visible place. Advice: Don't get caught making a copy of something without finding out exactly what is legal.

Corrosion

- chemical reaction on the surface of a coin. Corrosion can result from a coin coming in contact with other things (chemicals) including chemicals in the air. This can come about because of things coming in contact with the coin years earlier. Corrosion damages a coins surface and is usually worse in copper, nickel, zinc, and silver coins. Some experts think that toning on the surface of a coin may help slow down this harmful process. Also see "toning".

Counterfeit
- a coin or piece of currency that is fake or reproduced in order to make people think it is genuine.

counter mark (countermark)
- an impression, mark, or stamp put on a coin to verify it's use by another. Sometimes done by governments when a monetary revaluation occurs.

Crackout
- coin that is cracked out of its plastic holder. Usually refers to coin removed from a grading service holder.

Crown
- a large size silver coin. Usually from Great Britain or a former British country.

Cud
- cattle ranchers have one definition for cud. Coin collectors have a different one. When a coin is struck by a broken die the place where the die is broken or missing will often show up as extra metal on the surface of a coin. This extra piece of metal or "cud" can be from a piece of the die being missing or a still intact, but moved.

Cull
- a coin that is less desirable compared to other coins in a roll, tube, or group. Sometimes used to mean a very slick, worn, or defective coin. To "Cull-it-out" - means to separate a coin from others in a roll or group, because of its defects or low grade.

cupro-nickel
- a mixture of copper, nickel, and possibly other metals. Today this term is most often used to refer to the current coins made by fusing layers of copper and nickel or combination alloy mixtures, resulting in a "sandwich" type of coin. The current US dimes and Quarters are examples. Technically the copper nickel cents, three cent nickels, and regular nickels are cupro-nickel. See "copper nickel".

Currency
- any kind of coins or paper money that is used as a medium of exchange.

" D "

D mint mark
- mintmark used to designate that the coin was struck at the US mint in "Denver Colorado". Between 1838 and the civil war the "D" mint mark was used by the US mint in Dahlonega Georgia.

DCAM
- see "Deep Cameo".

Damaged
-A damaged coin would be one that has had something happen to it to cause a defect. Examples would be: holes, bent, major nicks, corrosion, scratches, mutilation. Usually makes the coin worth much less than one without any defects.

Denomination
- different values of coins or currency. For example US coins currently have 6 different denominations: cent, nickel, dime, quarter, half dollar and dollar.

deep cameo
- describes the appearance of some proof coins. A coin with a cameo design will have a somewhat frosted appearance to the raised features of the design, with a polished or mirror like background (field). Deep cameo means this frosted cameo effect is very obvious. Often, a proof with this attribute will be of higher quality and may be rarer, particularly in older proof coins

Denticles

- small tooth like raised areas around the edge of a coin. Particularly on older coins. Often found all around the front (obverse) and back (reverse) of the coin, right next to the edge.

Designer

- artist who creates the design. Not the engraver (who actually makes the coin producing dies). Although, in years past some designers were also engravers.

Die

- an engraved metal stamp used for stamping out the design of a coin. The die is often hardened so that when it strikes the metal blank an impression will be left indicating the coins design, value, and wording. See "anvil die" and "hammer die".

die clash

- damage to a coin die that occurs when the top and bottom dies collide without a coin in the press. The dies will may hit each other with such force that they damage each other leaving a trace of the impression on one or both dies. Resulting coins produced may exhibit "clash marks". Clash marks will show some of the reverse design on the obverse side of the coin, some of the obverse design on the reverse, or both.

die defect

- damage or defect of a coin die. The coins produced by that die will exhibit the same defects.

die variety

- an alteration in the basic design of a coin. Comes from slight differences in the designs on the dies used to stamp coins.

Disme

- a French term meaning one tenth. The US term for a tenth of a dollar, a dime, traces its roots back to this term. The term was Americanized and the s was dropped.

Doubloon
- nick name given to a popular Spanish gold coin.

Doubloon
- nick name given to a popular Spanish gold coin. Often associated with pirates and buried treasure.

double die
- a coin that shows numbers or letters doubled. Caused by the coin die having been made with a doubled design on parts of it.

double dime
- nickname for the United States 20 cent piece coin made during the mid-late 1800's. ruicenea coin that shows numbers or letters doubled.

double eagle
- used to describe a twenty dollar gold piece, the likes of those made between 1850 and 1932. Called a double eagle because the gold content was twice that of an "eagle" $10 gold piece. Double Eagle gold pieces contain "almost" an ounce of gold

double edge lettering
- describes and error found on some US Presidential dollar coins. The date, motto, and mintmark are impressed into the coin edges of presidential dollar after the coins are minted by running them through an edge lettering machine. When run through the edge lettering machine twice some of the edge letters will be doubled.

" E "

eagle
- nick name for the old gold $10 coins made up until 1932. These

older gold coins contained "almost" 1/2 ounce of gold and featured an eagle design on the back. Note: the "eagle" gold coin is different than the new AMERICAN EAGLE gold bullion coin. See "American Eagle".The eagle term is also used in reference to the US Silver 1 ounce coins currently minted by the US government mint. They are often called "silver eagle coins".

Edge
- the side of the coin. Currently US dimes and quarters have a "reeded" edge, which is an edge with small lines on it. Some coins will have lettering, ornamental designs, or plain edges. The new Presidential Dollar coins have an edge lettering.

edge lettering
- letters or designs made on the side edge of a coin. Most modern day coins have plain or reeded edges. Example of edge lettering is the old Capped Bust Half dollar coins. Sometimes called edge device. See new Presidential US dollar coin series for a modern example.

E-gold
- an electronic way of purchasing, owning, and storing gold.

Eisenhower dollar
- United States dollar made from 1971 to 1978. Sometimes called "Ike" dollars because of the portrait of President/General Dwight D Eisenhower. Ike dollars did not see a lot of use in commerce, partially because of there large silver dollar size. Although made of clad (nickel and copper), there were some special versions made of 40% silver sold by the mint to collectors.

electrotype
- a reproduction of a coin or object. Sometimes used in museums. Produced using an electro-deposition process.

Engraver
- an artist who creates a coin's design as a model or sculpture. In

earlier days the engraver would actually cut out the design onto the die. The engraver may not necessarily be the designer or artist who conceptualized the coin.

Exergue
- bottom portion of a coin's design. Normally separated by a line and sometimes containing a date (year) or other information.

error coin
- a coin that has some type of production defect on it. The difference between a coin error and a coin variety is that an error is considered a "mistake" that escaped the quality control of the US mint inspectors. Modern production procedures attempt to keep error coins from being released. US Presidential dollar errors have been found with plain edge errors and double edge lettering. Double edge lettering exists as overlapped edge lettered errors and inverted edge lettered errors.

extra fine
- Coin grading term indicating a coin with wear on the higher points. Most details of the coin design are visible and readable. Sometimes called extremely fine.

" F "

face value
- the exchange value for which a coin is intended to be spent or exchanged. Example: A US quarter's face value, or spendable value, is 25 cents. Note that if a coin is silver (or a rare date) the collector value or silver content may be worth more than the face value. Face Value is Not its collector or precious metal value. It is a coin's spendable value.

fair
- A very heavily worn coin. Date may only be partially visible. One of the lowest grades of a coin, F-2.

fiat money
- currency or coin that looses it's value, retaining no substantial backing. Suggested reading - "Fiat Money Inflation in France"

filler
- a coin used to "fill in" the place in a collection until a better grade coin can be found or purchased to take its place. Often a low grade or damaged coin may be used as a filler until a nice one can be found.

field
- the background surface of a coin not used for the design or inscription. Often the field is flat and may not have any design to it.

fine
- Fine is a medium grade coin. It corresponds to F-12 and F-15 of the current accepted grading standards.

fine gold
- the purity of a gold coin or metal. (See fineness below.) A .999 fine gold coin is about as pure a gold coin as you can get. .999 fine gold means the item is 99.9% pure solid gold. .999 fine silver would be 99.9% pure silver. Most US silver coins minted up through 1964 were .90 fine, or 90% pure silver.

fineness
- the purity of a coin, medal, or precious metal item. Uses a scale of 0 to 1.000. Examples: A silver coin with fineness of .999 would be as pure as a coin can be. A silver coin with fineness of .500 would be made of 50% silver. Most 1964 and earlier US silver coins were .900 fine, or 90% pure silver.

First Spouses
- gold coins issued by the US government mint beginning in 2007. Four gold coins produced each year depicting the spouses of the Presidents

of the United States. These "first lady" gold coins are sometimes called "presidential wives" or 1st spouses gold coins.

flan
- a planchet or coin blank. (Coin that has not yet been stamped with the coin's design.)

floral edge
- design on the edge of a coin that looks like flowers or tulip bulbs laid on their side in a row. Found on some older coins like the Pillar dollars. Edge designs were more common on gold and silver coins years ago. Having a design on a coin's edge prevented unscrupulous people from shaving off some of the silver or gold. Any filing of the edge would be noticeable, because the edge lettering would be missing.

Franklin Half dollar
- Franklin Half dollars are sometimes called Liberty Bell halves because of the Liberty bell design on the reverse. The United States government made the Benjamin Franklin Half dollar from 1948 to 1963. Large numbers of them were melted during the big silver meltdowns of the late 1900's.

friction
- A frontiersman might rub two sticks together and the result is a fire. The rubbing of a coin can result in a wear on its surface. Typically, friction causes various degrees of noticeable wear and results in lowering the desire (and value) of a coin. Friction can be caused by a coin sliding in a holder, coin drawer, or even by a good intending collector who tries to "clean" the coin.

frosted proof
- a proof coin that has a mirror like surface in the background with a frosted (or dull) surface on the design. Proofs prior to 1937 and again beginning in the 1970's have frosted designs. Sometimes occurs in other years although not as often. Some frosted proof coins will bring a premium price.

full bell lines
- describes a very well detailed US Franklin Half Dollar reverse. See FBL for more about full bell line Franklin halves.

" G "

Gem
- a coin with unusually high quality.

Gem BU
-Means GEM quality *Brilliant Uncirculated* coin. Indicates that this uncirculated coin shows mint brilliance and is extremely attractive for the type of coin. Some might say it sparkles like a "GEM".

Genuine
- Authentic. Minted by the issuing country.

Gold Eagle
- Gold Eagle coins were first minted by the United States government in 1986. Today several sizes of gold eagle coins are made: 1/10 oz, fourth ounce, half oz. and one ounce coins. Sometimes these coins are called "American Eagles", GE, or AGE.

gold price
- the price of gold per troy ounce or kilogram.

goloid
- an alloy of silver, gold and copper. Goloid was a metal coin alloy proposed and patented by Dr. William Wheeler Hubbell in 1877. A goloid coin would contain about 3-4% gold, 9% copper and mostly silver.

gouges

- heavy marks on a coin where the metal was gouged out from coming in contact with an abrasive or rough surface. Worse than contact markings or minor post mint damage.

grade
- a rating or clarification that indicates how much wear a circulated coin has. Grades can also indicate the degree of perfection for uncirculated coins.

grading standards
- a set of criteria indicating how much wear a coin shows.

gram
- Metric system of measuring weights. Approximately 31.1 grams in one (1) troy ounce. Abbr. =gm.

granular
- used to describe a porous appearance or surface, often visible under slight magnification. A granular appearance can be the result of many factors, such as oxidation of the metal, exposure to moisture, or chemicals intentionally or accidentally exposed to the coin.

" H "

half eagle

- another name for a United States $5.00 gold coin. (See eagle and double eagle.)

hub
- coin production term used to refer to a reverse design that is used to make the x dies that strike the coins.

hairline scratches
- very light lines or faint scratches on the surface of a coin. Sometimes caused by light cleaning or polishing.

hairlines
- very light lines or scratches on the surface of a coin. Sometimes caused by faint cleaning or light polishing.

hamburger coin
- Clad coins were first minted in the USA in 1965. Clad coins have a center-layer that is a different colored material than top and bottom layers.

hammer die
- top die. The hammer die is the top die that is placed on top of the coin blank and struck. Years ago this was done with a hammer. See "anvil die" and "die".

hammered coins
- coins minted by hammering the dies together. A coin blank was inserted between two coin dies and struck with a hammer-like tool. This minting method (hammering coins) was in use for centuries.

head
- the obverse or front of most coins. Usually with a portrait of someone, but not always present on every coin.

heavy gold electroplate
- heavy gold electroplate is in reality a very thin layer of gold placed on the surface of a coin or object by means of electroplating. Often gives the appearance of solid gold. Although heavier than typical electroplating, heavy gold electroplate is still very thin, often amounting to much less than 1% gold on the total object. Sometimes abbreviated as HGE.

incuse

- the part of a coin's design that is pressed into the surface. Opposite of <u>relief</u>. Example: the $2 1/2 and $5 Indian US gold coins are incuse design. Rather than the design being raised up off of the surface of the coin, it is pressed into the metal. See "<u>reeded edge</u>" and "lettered edge"

ingot

- see "bars"

Ike dollar

- see Eisenhower dollar

inscription

- the words stamped (or written) on a coin.

intrinsic value

- the value of the precious metal that a coin is made of. Often called "bullion value". Not to be confused with "face value".

inverted date

-normally a coin error where the date is punched into a coin die backwards or upside down. The result is that all coins minted from that coin die will show the date mistake. Often the mint employee will try to cover up their mistake by re-punching the same die correctly. The result may be called an overdate error, where one numeral is stamped over another.

inverted edge lettering error

-"Inverted" edge lettering means that the second set of edge letters are "upside down" when compared with the first set of edge letters. Also see "overlapped edge lettering".

investment grade

-used to indicate a high grade of coin that might make a good investment.

iron dollar

-nickname for a US silver dollar. The "iron" dollar terminology was primarily used in northeastern USA. This uncomplimentary phrase was used by people who disliked carrying silver dollars due to their heavy weight.

" J "

junk silver

- silver coins of circulated quality. Often used to describe bags of coins or common United States silver coins that were pulled out of circulation when silver coinage was disappearing. Does not mean the coins are damaged. Junk silver rolls or bags usually will not contain scarce dates, low mintages, or high quality coins.

" K "

keel boat

- United States five cent nickel issued in 2004. Features a picture of the keel boat that Lewis and Clark used on their expedition. Captains Lewis and Clark can be seen in full uniform in the bow of the keel boat.

Kennedy Half

- US Half dollars first minted in 1964. Design depicts former President John F. Kennedy on the obverse. The first year of

Kennedy 50 cent coins, 1964, were made of 90% silver. Kennedy halves (made of copper nickel clad) continue to be minted today.

key date
- a scarce date that is often hard to find to complete a collection. Usually more difficult to find, of lower mintage, or more expensive.

Kilogram
- one thousand grams. Equals about 32.15 troy ounces. Also see "gram".

" L "

Laureate
- coin design of a head crowned with a laurel wreath.

Luster
-a frosty and shiny appearance found on some uncirculated (mint state) coins.

legal tender
- coins, paper money, or other currency issued by a government and used as money. The legal tender value of a coin is the value placed on it by the government. It may be different than the intrinsic value (bullion value) or collector value.

Legend
- the main lettering on a coin or paper money. For instance the phrase "United States of America".

lettered edge
- The edge of a coin that has lettering on the outside of it. Usually it is raised, but sometimes incused. (Also see edge lettering.) Most coins today have a plain edge or "reeded" edge. Having something inscribed or a design on the edge of a coin was

prevalent when coins were made of precious metals such as gold or silver.

Liberty Head
- term used to indicate a design on the face of coins similar to the Statue of Liberty in the United States. Many different US coins have a Liberty Head design, in fact.

logo punch
- metal coin punch (usually a number). Used by mint employees to punch numbers (the year of issue) into coin dies.

Lynn Coins
- internet coin shop catering to the coin collector.

" M "

Matte
- describes a coin's surface. A matte finish often appears to be slightly grainy or has a slight "sandblasted" texture or appearance.
matte proof
- matte proof coins are special proofs that have a granular or "hazy" appearance on the surface.

Medal
- Like the Olympic Medals made for athletes during the Olympic Games. This is an object made of metal that resembles a coin or coin-like design. Often medals are made or given to recognize a person, place, or occasion.

medium of exchange
- something accepted by people as having a certain value that is used to exchange or trade. Often coins and paper money are used as

mediums of exchange for goods or services, but this is more common with regular circulated currency rather than collections or rare coins.

mercury dime
- nick name for the US 10 cent pieces made between 1916 and 1945. Although originally called the Winged Liberty Head dime, the name "mercury" dime caught on with the public when it was compared to the Roman god "mercury".

Milky
- describes the appearance on the surface of a coin that is whited out or faded, maybe hazy looking on the surface.

milled edge
- coin production process that produces the edge of the coin itself.

Mint
- place where coins are produced (manufactured). The U.S. Mint produces most coins for the U.S. government in Philadelphia and Denver, but mint facilities in San Francisco and West Point (United States) are used to produce some of the Proof sets and commemorative coin series.

mint luster
- a frosty, satiny, unique shine found on uncirculated and high grade coins. Mint luster gradually disappears as a coin receives wear.

mint mark
- a small letter on a coin that identifies which of the U.S. Mints the coin was produced at. Some other coins will also use mint marks to distinguish the specific minting facilities where their coins are struck. A US coin with no mint mark means it was usually minted at the Philadelphia US minting facility.

mint proofing piece
- ingots of high purity gold used by the mint to mix with and melt together with gold that was less than 90% pure. The purpose of melting it with less than pure gold was to bring up the gold content to .900 fine, in order for the gold to be made into coins.

Mint proofing pieces were also used in making batches of silver bullion a higher purity. In the 19th century the US government mints served as places where gold and silver could be exchanged for paper money and coins.

mint set
- a complete set of coins produced by a particular mint (contains one of each denomination). Mint sets usually contain "uncirculated" non-proof coins.

mint state
- uncirculated

mintage
- the number of coins produced (the quantity made for that country, date, mintmark, and type of coin)

Morgan dollar
- United States silver dollar made during some of the years 1878 to 1921. Originally called the "Liberty Head" silver dollar. It developed the nickname "Morgan" dollar after the US mint engraver George T. Moran, who designed it.

Morgan coin
- this term was used to identify "Barber" dimes, quarters and half dollars minted in the late 1800's and early 1900's. Although designed by Charles E Barber these Liberty Head silver coins were not designed by Morgan. (Morgan designed the silver dollar.) Because they circulated at the same time as the Morgan Dollar and had some similarity in features to the Morgan dollar, people often incorrectly called them "Morgans".

Motto
- a saying, phrase, or principle sometimes found on a coin. Example: "In God We Trust", and "E Pluribus Unum"-meaning: Out of many, are one

MS69
The attribute "MS" is an abbreviation for "mint state".

Mylar
- a brand name for a clear trademark polyester material used to store coins. Similar to clear polyester film. Often cardboard 2x2 coin holders have a clear mylar window in the center of them.

" N "

national parks quarters
- name for the US 25 cent coin series began in 2010. Each year five different national parks designs are placed on United States Washington quarters.

national parks coins
- another name for the US 25 cent coin series started in 2010. Sometimes abbreviated as NPC or PC.

Nickel
- nick name for the US five cent piece. Although only 25% of the five cent piece is made of the metal nickel it gives the appearance that it is solid nickel. The nick name "nickel" came about due to its appearance of being made of the metal nickel. It is actually made of a mixture of copper (about 75%) and nickel (about 25%).

non-circulating legal tender
- non-circulating legal tender means coins or paper money that are valid and acceptable by the country that issued them, however because of age, collect-ability, or other factors they are not used or found in commerce.

numismatist
- a coin collector. Often used to indicate someone who is a serious coin hobbyist or one who studies an area of coin collecting.

Numismatic Guarantee Corporation
- a third party grading service that certifies and grades coins. One of the most popular and well respected independent coin grading companies. Often called NGC. Similar to PCGS.

Numismatic News
- One of the most popular coin publications in the USA. This newspaper-type publication is reasonably priced and is issued weekly. Contains coin collecting articles about US and world coins, with a major focus on US coins. Advertisements from major coin dealers are included in each weekly issue.

Numismatics
- hobby and study of coin collecting. It may also include paper money and things used as money, as well as similar things such as medals, ornaments and tokens.

" O "

Oddity
- when something unusual happens to a coin it is sometimes called an oddity. Can be an "error" that was made at the mint, or something that was done to a coin after the minting of the coin.

Obsolete
- a coin design or coins series that is no longer being produced.
Obverse
- the front side of a coin. Usually the obverse side of a coin has the main design, date (year of issue), and sometimes a mintmark. Sometimes called the "heads" side of a coin because many coins have a person's portrait or head design on the obverse. The back of the coin is called the reverse.

off center , or **off-center** (strike)
- describes the way a coin was struck by the printing dies. If the coin was not placed properly and the dies strike it off center then parts of the design will be missing from the coin. Sometimes an off-center coin will have part of the blank planchlet showing and part of the coin design showing.

original roll
- a group of coins that were wrapped in paper wrappers at the time of their production. In early days coins were shipped to banks in cloth bags or kegs. Sometimes later they were shipped in rolls. Silver coins stored in rolls will often have toning on and near the edges but not in the center.

Ounce
- form of measuring weight. The troy ounce that is used for weighing precious metals is different from the regular grocery store ounce.

overlapped edge lettering error
- a Presidential dollar coin that shows double edge letters on the side. Presidential $ coins have the date, mintmark, and US motto's impressed into the coin's edge. During production, when accidentally run through an edge lettering machine twice a coin will show double lettering on the side. "Overlapped" edge lettering means the error letters are facing the same direction as the first impression of the letters. See "inverted edge lettering" for and explanation of upside down edge lettering.

over strike or **overstrike**
- a coin that instead of being struck on a blank planchlet was accidentally struck on a previously struck coin. The result is the coin design pressed into the blank coin planchet twice. In rare occurrences an overstrike can be one type of coin struck over another type of coin. For example, a cent design struck on the top of a dime. This type of coin error is often somewhat scarce or rare.

" P "

PCGS
- See the "Professional Coin Grading Service".

Pattern
- a coin that was struck as an experiment or as a trial piece. Usually, of a new design or made of experimental metal alloys. U.S. Pattern coins from recent years are illegal to own because they are still considered government property.

parks quarters
- United States quarters series issued beginning in 2010 to commemorate US National Parks. Sometimes abbreviated as PQ, for parks quarters and NPQ for National Parks Quarters.

peace dollar
- United States silver dollar made during the years 1921 to 1935. This design was first minted after World War II, and has the word "peace" on the reverse. Hence the nick-name "peace" dollar caught on. Made of 90% pure silver and weighing a little less than an ounce. Peace silver dollars contain about 77% of an ounce of pure silver.

peace medal
- a U.S. five cent coin featuring a design similar to the original Indian Peace Medal commissioned for the Lewis and Clark's expedition. It depicts two symbols of peace and friendship in the center: hands shaking and crossed peace pipes.

Penny
- a small denomination coin usually made of copper. In some countries the penny is one-hundredth of a larger denomination.

Pennyweight
- a penny weight is a means of weighing precious metals. Comes from the British weight system. There are 20 pennyweights in a troy ounce.

plain edge
- a coin that does not have reading or lettering on the edge. Example, the US one cent and nickel coins. Plain edge errors can occur when the edge is not supposed to be plain edge, as with the minting of Presidential dollars coins as well. Two types of Presidential double edge lettered errors exist, overlapped errors and inverted errors. *See those terms earlier in this index.*

Planchet or **planchlet**
- a blank round piece of metal from which the coin is struck. A planchet or coin blank is a coin before the design is added to it during the minting process.

Platinum
- a precious metal rarer than gold! Metallic silver-like in color. Hard to find but very valuable!

Population or **pop**
-Used in reference to the population, or number, of coins graded or certified by a grading service for a specific date or mintmark.

PR69
-The attribute "PR" is an abbreviation for "proof". The numbers that follow (in this example 69) indicate the quality of the coin. The quality numbers run from 1 to 70, with a 70 being an absolutely prefect coin. See related topic- " MS69 ".

precious metal
- metals of value. Typically gold, silver, platinum. However, can include palladium and rhodium.

Presidential Dollars
- Series of United States Dollar coins beginning in the year 2007. Four $ coins are to be issued each year honoring the Presidents of the United States. Coins are produced for circulation (P+D mint marks), as well as proof versions sold in sets to collectors.

Presidential Wives
- another name given for the First Spouses gold coins issued by the United States government mint beginning in 2007.

price guide
- coin collecting book that lists typical selling prices of coins in various grades.

Professional Coin Grading Service (PCGS)
- one of the most popular and respected independent coin grading services in the USA. For a fee they will grade, certify a coin as genuine, and seal it in a protective capsule type display holder.

Proof
- a coin produced from polished dies and/or planchlets. Most often each proof coin is struck twice/or more which gives the coin a very sharp degree of detail and mirror like surface. Proof coins are usually made for numismatic purposes, presentations, or souvenirs. Proofs are usually not made to circulated in commerce.

proof gold
- same thing as "proof silver" below, only made of pure gold. Also see "mint proofing piece".

proof set
- a group of the different denominations of the proof coins made for one year. Sometimes packaged as a set by the mint. Example: One of each proof: cent, nickel, dime, quarter, and half. Occasionally there will be some coins that are not included in the proof sets.

proof silver
- unlike a similar term "proof silver coins" which indicates that a silver coin is in proof condition, "proof silvers" refer to samples of pure silver. These are used to test and make comparisons during the coin assaying process.

proofing piece
- see "mint proofing piece"

Poly Vinyl Chloride (PVC)
- a substance put in plastic to add softness and clarity to the material. Over time PVC has been found to Leach out and damage coins. **DO NOT USE Plastic holders that contain PVC.**

" Q "

Quarter
- a coin valued at one fourth of a dollar. The US 25 cent coin.

quarter eagle
- United States $ 2.50 gold coin. Ten dollar gold coins of yester-year were nick-named "eagle" gold coins, because of the eagle reverse design. The nickname is still used today. See "double eagles".

" R "

Rare
- a coin or collectible that is very limited in availability. Can also mean that there are few in existence, very limited availability, or that the item is very uncommon. A rare does not necessarily mean a coin is very valuable.

Raw
- means the coin has not been certified, slabbed or encapsulated by a coin grading service.

rabbit coins
- Minted in 1999. First year of a series of animal coins minted in Australia. 1999 was the Chinese lunar "Year of the Rabbit". Silver and gold rabbit coins were minted to celebrate this special year.

real or reales
- Spanish money used primarily prior to the 1800's. (Sometime pronounced "ree-owl".) Spanish real silver coins were popular in the American colonial days.

Red Book
- A price guide book on US coins and their values by R.S. Yeoman. Also called the Official Guide to United States Coins.

reeded edge
- The edge of a coin that has small reed like groove lines on it. Today's US dimes and quarters are examples of reeded edge coins. Today's pennies and nickels have a plain edge, not a reeded edge.

relief
- the part of the design that is raised from the surface of the coin field (background).

repaired
- a coin or currency note that has been fixed to look like nothing has been wrong with it. The repair being done to fix damage, a hole or defects. The seller's description should mention that the coin was repaired. Often repaired coins will bring less than a coin (of equal grade) that has never had anything wrong with it, but sell for more than a fully damaged coin. The key point being, that the buyer needs to know about anything that was done to the coin in order to make a fair judgment when making a purchase decision.

replica
- a coin copy or reproduction. Sometimes called a copy of facsimile. Resembles the original in design. For a replica of a US coin or currency to be legally sold in most countries it must meet certain governmental criteria. One point being that it must have the word "copy", "replica", or "facsimile" plainly visible.

restrike (re-strike)
- a coin minted from original dies, however at a later date than originally intended.

reverse
- the back side of the coin. Sometimes called the "tails" side of the coin, because in many years there was an eagle design with it's tail feather's showing. Opposite of obverse or heads side of the coin.

reverse proof
- proof coins normally have a mirror like background (field) and a frosty or regular raised design. A reverse proof will have a mirror like raised design and a frosty or normal appearance to the coins background.

riddler
- a machine used in the minting process that sorts out wrong size/defective blanks (planchlets).

rim
- the raised edge of a coin created by the upsetting mill. The idea being that if the edge on both sides of the coin is raised like the design it will help protect the coins design from wear.

roll
- a group of coins in the same denomination in a paper wrapper package by banks, dealers, or the US Mint. Sometimes a coin rolls are put into a plastic coin tube. The number of coins in a roll depend on the denomination. For US Cents there are typically 50 coins in a roll, nickels- 40, dimes- 50, quarters- 40, halves- 20, dollars- 25.

rounds
- coin shaped silver pieces. Not official legal tender.

rust
- rust is an oxidizing reaction causing the surface of a metal coin to corrode or decay. US pennies (cents) minted during World War 2 (in 1943) were made of zinc plated steel. Once the zinc plating wore off, the coin surface became exposed to the air and often rusted. Other coins, such as copper and even silver are subject to similar oxidation when exposed to air, moisture, or environmental chemicals.

rust spot
- Reddish or rust color spots can appear on gold coins, as well as coins made of other metals. Spotting can be from something on the surface of the coin or actually from impurities in the coin's metal.

" S "

SBA
- See Susan B. Anthony dollar coin.

Sacagewea dollars
- United States small dollar coins with a design of the Indian Sacagewea on the obverse. Reverse depicts an eagle in flight. First year of mintage was in the year 2000.

Saint-Gaudens
- Augustus Saint-Gaudens was a well know artist and coin designer of the early 1900's. Perhaps his most famous coin design is the US $20 gold piece last minted in 1933. Depicting a standing "Liberty walking toward you", this US twenty dollar coin has been honored as one of the best US coin designs from the last century.

sandwich coin
- nick name for clad coins that were first made in the US in 1965.

seller fees
- fees imposed on the seller when auctioning coins or selling them on consignment. Also see buyers fees.

series
- collection of coins of one denomination that contains all the dates and mint marks of that design. For example a Lincoln Cent Wheat back series would contain one of each date cent minted from 1909 to 1958.

show
- to display or show a group of coins. Coin shows (or bourses) occur often in many areas. There dealers may set up tables to display their inventory in an attempt to sell, buy, or trade coins with the public and / or other dealers.

silver Clad
- term referring to US Half Dollars made from 1965 to 1970. Made with an outer layer of 80% silver and 20% copper bonded to an inner core of 20.9% silver and .791% copper. Overall 40% silver.

silver eagle
- nickname given to one ounce United States "Silver" dollars made from 1986 to the present. Design is of a walking liberty on the obverse (front) and eagle on the reverse.

silver price
- the value of silver in the commodity market. Usually refers to the market price of one "troy ounce" of silver.

site unseen
- an offer to purchase a coin at a certain price without seeing the item. Although site unseen bids are common, the coin will still have to meet the grading criteria from the bidder's perspective.

slab or slabbed
- slang term for a holding device for a coin that has been encapsulated by a coin grading service. Usually, the coin will graded, authenticated, and encapsulated in a sonically sealed holder, often by a 3rd party grading service. See PNG, NCG, ANACS, PCGS.

slab
- term used to identify a hard plastic encapsulation method that some coin grading services use to package/protect a coin. Usually a slabbed coin is graded and certified by the grading service.

slider
-a term meaning the coin simulates a higher grade than it really is. Often a slider has been cleaned, treated, or whizzed to give the appearance of being uncirculated. Worth less than the coin that has not been cleaned or treated.

split grade
- a different grade for a coins front (obverse) and back (reverse).

spot

- the price quoted for large transactions of precious metal. These large metal bars are stored in a certified warehouse. The spot price does not include broker commissions, shipping, postal insurance, etc. Spot prices may change by the minute during active trading.

spotting or spot
- a mark or marks on a coin of a different color. Often looking like spots of something on the coin. Usually, it is a form of tarnish or staining. Spotting may have a negative effect on the value of a coin depending on how severe it is, etc.

spread
- The difference in price between a dealer's buy price and sell price. Example, someone might buy a coin for $30 and sell the same coin for $40. The coin's spread would be 40-30, or $10.

state quarters
- The 50 State Quarter program was started in 1999 by the US government mint. 5 quarters were produced each year commemorating the joining of states to the United States of America. George Washington's portrait was used for the obverse (front) of each coin. Quarters were issued in the order that states joined the union, through the final year in 2008. In 2009 the fifty state quarters program was replaced with quarters commemorating the US Territories and Washington DC (District of Columbia).

statehood quarters
- same as 50 "State Quarters". Sometimes abbreviated as SHQ.

striation
- fine slightly raised lines on the surface of a coin. Often best seen with magnification and usually in the background of the coin's design. Most often caused by polishing the coin die.

strike
- a process of stamping a design into a coin planchet (blank). Usually metal dies with designs engraved in them are used. If the dies are struck weakly or just average it may effect the coin's value negatively

vs. a well struck coin. Some U.S. mints were known for making weakly stuck coins during certain years.

Susan B. Anthony dollar
- The United States government made a silver dollar with Susan B. Anthony's portrait in 1979 to 1981, and then again in one more year, 1999. These "SBA" dollars were short lived and saw little use in commerce.

sweating
- illegal process of removing gold or silver from the surface of a coin in order to repurosee or sell the yielded precious metal. This method was used during the times when precious metal coins circulated in everyday commerce. Sweaters would treat a coin (often a gold coin) in an acid bath to dissolve some of the surface of the coin. Later the dissolved gold would be removed from the solution and sold.

" T "

tail
- the reverse or back side of a coin

third party grading
- third party grading services will grade and/or certify coins as genuine. Often the coin will be encapsulated in a plastic holder (or slab) by the grading service to protect it. Called "third party" grading when the service is independent of any dealer or collector's influence. They provide a grading opinion based on established criteria. Examples may include PCGS, NGC, and ANACS.

three cent piece, or three cent coin
- common term used for the US coin with the value of three cents. Two different metals were used for these coins back in the 1800's. Prior to 1865 the US made three cent pieces out of an alloy of mostly silver. Hence the name "three cent silver". The public complained because the 3 cent silvers were small and thin. By 1865 the US government changed the composition and design of the three cent coins.

thrip
- British term for the English three pence coin. See "trime".

token
- Something that looks like a coin, but is not legal tender issued by an official government. For example, parking tokens, video game machine tokens, and casino tokens. Some coin collectors shy away from collecting tokens. However, there are a few small groups of serious token collectors.

toning
- Shading of color on coins. Toning can be in many forms from dark or brown to various shade of other colors. It can cover the whole coin or more often part of the coin. Toning results when the surface of the coin comes in contact with the air and environment it is exposed to.

trends
- a price guide section in a coin magazine or publication that lists current prices of coins. Often includes a + or - sign by a coin's value, which indicates the change from the previous price list.

trime
- a nickname for the US three cent coin, made by the US mint in the 1800s. See "thrip".

troy ounce
   - a weigh to measure weight. Differs from a regular "grocery store" ounce.

turkey

- a sorry coin. One that is worse than it first appears. Also, used to mean something that won't sell despite it's appearance.

twenty cent piece
- a 20-cent coin issued by the United States government. Minted in the mid-late 1800's this large copper coin circulated and had a face value of 20 cents. Sometimes call the "double-dime" in coin catalogs. After a number of years the US government decided to stop making 20 cent pieces due to their unpopularity and lack of use.

two bits
- see "bits"

two by two
- nickname for a typical holder for one coin. Measures 2 inches by 2 inches. Often made of cardboard with a clear mylar material in the center. Cardboard 2x2s are not the best way to store coins for the long term.

two cent piece
- a US coin with the value of two cents. Common term used for the copper Shield design two-cent coin made from 1864 to 1873.

type
- coins containing the same or a similar characteristic. Often in a type collection or set the dates do not matter. Rather the collector is interested in obtaining one of each representative design. For example a collector may want one of each "type" of coin in US circulation today. Such a type set would consist of a cent, nickel, dime, quarter, half, and dollar. A collector may decide to collect one representative of each type of coin by size. For example, a cent type set may include a Lincoln Memorial cent, wheat back cent, Indian cent, etc.

type set

- collection of coins of one denomination. For example, a Quarter type set would consist of one of each design of quarter that the mint has made. (Dates and mint marks usually are not of concern.)

" U "

Unc or **unk** or **UN**
- abbreviation for uncirculated.

uncirculated or un-circulated
- a new condition coin that does not have any sign of wear. Sometimes also called mint or mint condition. Marks on a coin that may come from the manufacturing process do not keep a coin from being un-circulated.

undergrading
- assigning a coin a grade lower than what is really is. This practice is sometimes used by the unscrupulous to attempt to purchase coins for less than what they are really worth.
unique coin
- a coin where there is only one coin like it in existence.

upsetting mill or upsetting machine
- machine used in coin production to raise the rim on both sides of a blank (planchet).

" V "

vest pocket dealer

- old timer's term meaning a part time coin dealer. Someone who carries coins to sell/trade in their pockets.

variety or varieties
- A coin variety is typically something that all coins minted from a specific coin die will have. See also, *error coins*

vest pocket dealer
- someone who trades in coins but does not have a coin shop or store, and does not set up at coin shows.

" W "

waffle
- government process used to destroy defective coins. Coins are run through a metal waffling machine that defaces the coin so that it can be used for scrap metal. This often leaves the coin unrecognizable. The term waffle comes from the waffle like wavy surface left on the metal wafer.

walker
- nick name for the "Walking Liberty Half dollar".

walking liberty
- a half dollar with the Walking Liberty design. Made between 1916 and 1947. Thought by some to be one of the US most beautiful coin designs. The current "American Silver Eagles" have the same design on their obverse (front).

war nickel
- sometimes called "wartime" nickels. These Jefferson US five cent coins were made during part of World War II. At the time there was a concern that metal would be needed in the war effort.

wheat back cents
- United states one cent coins minted from 1909 and 1958. Nick named "Wheat Back Cents" or "wheat pennies" because the reverse of these pennies shows a design with wheat straw near the edges. In 1959 the Wheat back Lincoln cent was replaced with the Lincoln memorial cent.
white cents
- see "copper nickel.

Whitman
-Whitman Publishing company. Produces many collector's books, albums, and collecting supplies.

whizzed
- a whizzed coin has been buffed or polished to give it the appearance of the luster found on a mint coin. Often whizzing is done on a high grade coin to try to sell the coin at a higher grade than it really is. Sometimes done by using a fine brush attachment on a high speed drill. Whizzing a coin may hurt the value of it rather than help it because it actually causes wear to the surface of the coin. See buffing.

" X "

There are no coin collecting terms that start with the letter X in our glossary.

" Y "

year
- sometime called the date on a coin. Example, 1990 on a coin most often would mean the coin was made in the year 1990. In a few instances US coins had years in Roman Numerals.

year set

- coin collection consisting of one of each kind (size and style) of coin issued by a country for a given year. (Mint marks are usually not of concern when collecting year sets.)

" Z "

There are no coin collecting terms in our dictionary that start with the letter Z.

Coin Journal

Coin Journal

Just a nice little place to keep your thoughts together!

Coin & Banknote Checklists

AMERICAN SILVER EAGLE
1986-2025

Type 1
Heraldic Eagle

Mint Mark
Locations

Type 2
Landing Eagle

- ○ 1986
- ○ 1986-S Proof
- ○ 1987
- ○ 1987-P Proof
- ○ 1987-S Proof
- ○ 1988
- ○ 1988-S Proof
- ○ 1989
- ○ 1989-S Proof
- ○ 1990
- ○ 1990-S Proof
- ○ 1991
- ○ 1991-S Proof
- ○ 1992
- ○ 1992-S Proof
- ○ 1993
- ○ 1993-P Proof
- ○ 1994
- ○ 1994-P Proof
- ○ 1995
- ○ 1995-P Proof
- ○ 1995-W
- ○ 1996

- ○ 1996-P Proof
- ○ 1997
- ○ 1997-P Proof
- ○ 1998
- ○ 1998-P Proof
- ○ 1999
- ○ 1999-P Proof
- ○ 2000
- ○ 2000-P Proof
- ○ 2001
- ○ 2001-W Proof
- ○ 2002
- ○ 2002-W Proof
- ○ 2003
- ○ 2003-W Proof
- ○ 2004
- ○ 2004-W Proof
- ○ 2005
- ○ 2005-W Proof
- ○ 2006
- ○ 2006-W Burnished

- ○ 2006-W Proof
- ○ 2007
- ○ 2007- W Burnished
- ○ 2007-W Proof
- ○ 2008
- ○ 2008-W Burnished
- ○ 2008-W Proof
- ○ 2009
- ○ 2010
- ○ 2010-W Proof
- ○ 2011
- ○ 2011-W Burnished
- ○ 2011-W Proof
- ○ 2011-S Burnished
- ○ 2012
- ○ 2012-W Burnished
- ○ 2012-W Proof
- ○ 2012-S Proof
- ○ 2013
- ○ 2013-W Burnished
- ○ 2013-W Proof

- ○ 2014
- ○ 2014-W Burnished
- ○ 2014-W Proof
- ○ 2015
- ○ 2015-W Burnished
- ○ 2015-W Proof
- ○ 2016
- ○ 2016-W Burnished
- ○ 2016-W Proof
- ○ 2017
- ○ 2017-W Burnished
- ○ 2017-W Proof
- ○ 2018
- ○ 2018-W Burnished
- ○ 2018-W Proof
- ○ 2018-S Proof
- ○ 2019
- ○ 2019-W Burnished
- ○ 2019-W Proof
- ○ 2019-S Proof

- ○ 2020
- ○ 2020-W Burnished
- ○ 2020-W Proof
- ○ 2020-S Proof
- ○ 2021 Type 1 Reverse
- ○ 2021-W Type 1 Burnished
- ○ 2021-W Type 1 Proof
- ○ 2021 Type 2 Reverse
- ○ 2021-W Type 2 Proof
- ○ 2022
- ○ 2022-W Burnished
- ○ 2022-W Proof
- ○ 2023
- ○ 2023-W Burnished
- ○ 2023-W Proof
- ○ 2024
- ○ 2024-W Burnished
- ○ 2024-W Proof
- ○ 2025
- ○ 2025-W Burnished
- ○ 2025-W Proof

Uncirculated Bullion Silver Eagles are struck without a mint mark. From 1986-1999 these coins were struck at the Philadelphia Mint. In 2000, their production was moved to the West Point facility. Since 2011, the coins have been struck at both the San Francisco and West Point Mints.

Burnished: Since 2006, special-issue "burnished" American Silver Eagles have been released. Burnished coins are made to exacting standards using a special minting process. Each coin is struck on a special hand fed, burnished (polished) blank, giving it a unique shimmering finish.

BARBER DIMES
1892-1916

Mint Mark Location

◯ 1892	◯ 1896-O	◯ 1900-S	◯ 1905-O	◯ 1908-S	◯ 1912-S
◯ 1892-O	◯ 1896-S	◯ 1901	◯ 1905-S	◯ 1909	◯ 1913
◯ 1892-S	◯ 1897	◯ 1901-O	◯ 1906	◯ 1909-D	◯ 1913-S
◯ 1893	◯ 1897-O	◯ 1901-S	◯ 1906-D	◯ 1909-O	◯ 1914
◯ 1893-O	◯ 1897-S	◯ 1902	◯ 1906-O	◯ 1909-S	◯ 1914-D
◯ 1893-S	◯ 1898	◯ 1902-O	◯ 1906-S	◯ 1910	◯ 1914-S
◯ 1894	◯ 1898-O	◯ 1902-S	◯ 1907	◯ 1910-D	◯ 1915
◯ 1894-O	◯ 1898-S	◯ 1903	◯ 1907-D	◯ 1910-S	◯ 1915-S
◯ 1894-S	◯ 1899	◯ 1903-O	◯ 1907-O	◯ 1911	◯ 1916
◯ 1895	◯ 1899-O	◯ 1903-S	◯ 1907-S	◯ 1911-D	◯ 1916-S
◯ 1895-O	◯ 1899-S	◯ 1904	◯ 1908	◯ 1911-S	
◯ 1895-S	◯ 1900	◯ 1904-S	◯ 1908-D	◯ 1912	
◯ 1896	◯ 1900-O	◯ 1905	◯ 1908-O	◯ 1912-D	

Mint Mark Key: • Philadelphia – No Mint Mark   • Denver – D   • San Francisco – S   • New Orleans

BARBER HALVES
1892-1915

Mint Mark
Location

○ 1892	○ 1896-O	○ 1900-O	○ 1904-O	○ 1907-S	○ 1911-S
○ 1892-O	○ 1896-S	○ 1900-S	○ 1904-S	○ 1908	○ 1912
○ 1892-S	○ 1897	○ 1901	○ 1905	○ 1908-D	○ 1912-D
○ 1893	○ 1897-O	○ 1901-O	○ 1905-O	○ 1908-O	○ 1912-S
○ 1893-O	○ 1897-S	○ 1901-S	○ 1905-S	○ 1908-S	○ 1913
○ 1893-S	○ 1898	○ 1902	○ 1906	○ 1909	○ 1913-D
○ 1894	○ 1898-O	○ 1902-O	○ 1906-D	○ 1909-O	○ 1913-S
○ 1894-O	○ 1898-S	○ 1902-S	○ 1906-O	○ 1909-S	○ 1914
○ 1894-S	○ 1899	○ 1903	○ 1906-S	○ 1910	○ 1914-S
○ 1895	○ 1899-O	○ 1903-O	○ 1907	○ 1910-S	○ 1915
○ 1895-O	○ 1899-S	○ 1903-S	○ 1907-D	○ 1911	○ 1915-D
○ 1895-S	○ 1900	○ 1904	○ 1907-O	○ 1911-D	○ 1915-S
○ 1896					

Mint Mark Key: * Philadelphia – No Mint Mark   * Denver – **D**   * San Francisco – **S**   * New Orleans – **O**

BARBER QUARTERS
1892-1916

Mint Mark Location

○ 1892	○ 1897	○ 1902	○ 1907-D	○ 1911-S
○ 1892-O	○ 1897-O	○ 1902-O	○ 1907-O	○ 1912
○ 1892-S	○ 1897-S	○ 1902-S	○ 1907-S	○ 1912-S
○ 1893	○ 1898	○ 1903	○ 1908	○ 1913
○ 1893-O	○ 1898-O	○ 1903-O	○ 1908-D	○ 1913-D
○ 1893-S	○ 1898-S	○ 1903-S	○ 1908-O	○ 1913-S
○ 1894	○ 1899	○ 1904	○ 1908-S	○ 1914
○ 1894-O	○ 1899-O	○ 1904-O	○ 1909	○ 1914-D
○ 1894-S	○ 1899-S	○ 1905	○ 1909-D	○ 1914-S
○ 1895	○ 1900	○ 1905-O	○ 1909-O	○ 1915
○ 1895-O	○ 1900-O	○ 1905-S	○ 1909-S	○ 1915-D
○ 1895-S	○ 1900-S	○ 1906	○ 1910	○ 1915-S
○ 1896	○ 1901	○ 1906-D	○ 1910-D	○ 1916
○ 1896-O	○ 1901-O	○ 1906-O	○ 1911	○ 1916-D
○ 1896-S	○ 1901-S	○ 1907	○ 1911-D	

Mint Mark Key: • Philadelphia – No Mint Mark   • Denver – D   • San Francisco – S   • New Orleans – O

300

BUFFALO NICKELS
1913-1938

Mint Mark location

○ 1913 Variety 1
○ 1913 Variety 2
○ 1913-D Variety 1
○ 1913-D Variety 2
○ 1913-S Variety 1
○ 1913-S Variety 2
○ 1914
○ 1914-D
○ 1914-S
○ 1915
○ 1915-D
○ 1915-S
○ 1916

○ 1916-D
○ 1916-S
○ 1917
○ 1917-D
○ 1917-S
○ 1918
○ 1918-D
○ 1918-S
○ 1919
○ 1919-D
○ 1919-S
○ 1920
○ 1920-D

○ 1920-S
○ 1921
○ 1921-S
○ 1923
○ 1923-S
○ 1924
○ 1924-D
○ 1924-S
○ 1925
○ 1925-D
○ 1925-S
○ 1926
○ 1926-D

○ 1926-S
○ 1927
○ 1927-D
○ 1927-S
○ 1928
○ 1928-D
○ 1928-S
○ 1929
○ 1929-D
○ 1929-S
○ 1930
○ 1930-S
○ 1931-S

○ 1934
○ 1934-D
○ 1935
○ 1935-D
○ 1935-S
○ 1936
○ 1936-D
○ 1936-S
○ 1937
○ 1937-D
○ 1937-S
○ 1938-D

Variety 1 – FIVE CENTS on a raised mound (1913)
Variety 2 – FIVE CENTS in recessed area (1913-1938)

Mint Mark Key: • Philadelphia – No Mint Mark • Denver – D • San Francisco – S

301

FLYING EAGLE & INDIAN HEAD CENTS
1857-1858 & 1859-1909

Flying Eagle Cent

Indian Head Cent
Mint Mark Location

Flying Eagle Cents

Copper-Nickel
○ 1857
○ 1858 Large Letters
○ 1858 Small Letters

Indian Head Cents

Variety 1*
○ 1859

Variety 2♦
○ 1860
○ 1861
○ 1862
○ 1863
○ 1864

Variety 3®
○ 1864, No L
○ 1864, With L
○ 1865
○ 1866
○ 1867
○ 1868

○ 1869
○ 1870
○ 1871
○ 1872
○ 1873
○ 1874
○ 1875
○ 1876
○ 1877
○ 1878
○ 1879
○ 1880
○ 1881
○ 1882
○ 1883
○ 1884

○ 1885
○ 1886 Variety I*
○ 1886 Variety II♦
○ 1887
○ 1888
○ 1889
○ 1890
○ 1891
○ 1892
○ 1893
○ 1894
○ 1895
○ 1896
○ 1897
○ 1898
○ 1899

○ 1900
○ 1901
○ 1902
○ 1903
○ 1904
○ 1905
○ 1906
○ 1907
○ 1908
○ 1908-S
○ 1909
○ 1909-S

* **Variety 1** - Copper-Nickel, Laurel Wreath Reverse
♦ **Variety 2** - Copper-Nickel, Oak Wreath with Shield
® **Variety 3** - Bronze
● **1886 Variety 1** - The lowest feather of the Indian's headdress points to the IC of AMERICA
● **1886 Variety 2** - The same feather points to the CA of AMERICA

Mint Mark Key: • Philadelphia – No Mint Mark   • San Francisco – S

FRANKLIN HALF DOLLARS
1948-1963

Mint Mark Location

○ 1948	○ 1951-S	○ 1954	○ 1957 Proof
○ 1948-D	○ 1951 Proof	○ 1954-D	○ 1961
○ 1949	○ 1952	○ 1954-S	○ 1961-D
○ 1949-D	○ 1952-D	○ 1954 Proof	○ 1961 Proof
○ 1949-S	○ 1952-S	○ 1955	○ 1958
○ 1950	○ 1952 Proof	○ 1955 Proof	○ 1958-D
○ 1950-D	○ 1953	○ 1956	○ 1958 Proof
○ 1950 Proof	○ 1953-D	○ 1956 Proof	○ 1959
○ 1951	○ 1953-S	○ 1957	○ 1959-D
○ 1951-D	○ 1953 Proof	○ 1957-D	○ 1959 Proof
			○ 1960
			○ 1960-D
			○ 1960 Proof
			○ 1962
			○ 1962-D
			○ 1962 Proof
			○ 1963
			○ 1963-D
			○ 1963 Proof

Mint Mark Key: ○ Philadelphia – No Mint Mark   ○ Denver – D   ○ San Francisco – S

303

EISENHOWER DOLLAR
1971-1978

Mint Mark Location

1971-1974 & 1977-1978

Bicentennial 1976

○ 1971
○ 1971-D
○ 1971-S Silver Clad
○ 1971-S Silver Proof
○ 1972
○ 1972-D
○ 1972-S Silver Clad
○ 1972-S Silver Proof
○ 1973

○ 1973-D
○ 1973-S Proof
○ 1973-S Silver Clad
○ 1973-S Silver Proof
○ 1974
○ 1974-D
○ 1974-S Proof
○ 1974-S Silver Clad
○ 1974-S Silver Proof

Bicentennial Coinage

○ 1976 Variety I*
○ 1976 Variety II**
○ 1976-D Variety I*
○ 1976-D Variety II**
○ 1976-S Variety I*
○ 1976-S Variety II**
○ 1976-S Silver Clad
○ 1976-S Silver Proof

Eagle Reverse Resumed

○ 1977
○ 1977-D
○ 1977-S Proof
○ 1978
○ 1978-D
○ 1978-S Proof

INNOVATION DOLLARS
2018-2032

Mint Mark Location

2018 Washington's Signature

2020 Massachusetts Telephone

2022 Rhode Island Reliance Yacht

	Proof	P	D	S
2018				
Washington *Washington's Signature*	○	○	○	○
2019				
Delaware *Classifying the Stars*	○	○	○	○
Pennsylvania *Polio Vaccine*	○	○	○	○
New Jersey *Light Bulb*	○	○	○	○
Georgia *Trustees' Garden*	○	○	○	○
2020				
Connecticut *Gerber Variable Scale*	○	○	○	○
Massachusetts *Telephone*	○	○	○	○
Maryland *Hubble Space Telescope*	○	○	○	○
South Carolina *Septima Clark*	○	○	○	○
2021				
New Hampshire *Home Video Game System*	○	○	○	○
Virginia *Chesapeake Bay Bridge-Tunnel*	○	○	○	○
New York *Erie Canal*	○	○	○	○
North Carolina *First Public University*	○	○	○	○
2022				
Rhode Island *Reliance Yacht "Naval Innovation"*	○	○	○	○
Vermont *Snowboarding*	○	○	○	○
Kentucky *Bluegrass Music*	○	○	○	○
Tennessee *Tennessee Valley Authority and Rural Electrification*	○	○	○	○
2023				
Ohio *Underground Railroad*	○	○	○	○
Louisiana *The Higgins Boat*	○	○	○	○
Indiana *Automobile Industry*	○	○	○	○
Mississippi *The First Human Lung Transplant*	○	○	○	○
2024				
Illinois	○	○	○	○
Alabama	○	○	○	○
Maine	○	○	○	○
Missouri	○	○	○	○
2025				
Arkansas	○	○	○	○
Michigan	○	○	○	○
Florida	○	○	○	○
Texas	○	○	○	○

	Proof	P	D	S
2026				
Iowa	○	○	○	○
Wisconsin	○	○	○	○
California	○	○	○	○
Minnesota	○	○	○	○
2027				
Oregon	○	○	○	○
Kansas	○	○	○	○
West Virginia	○	○	○	○
Nevada	○	○	○	○
2028				
Nebraska	○	○	○	○
Colorado	○	○	○	○
North Dakota	○	○	○	○
South Dakota	○	○	○	○
2029				
Montana	○	○	○	○
Washington	○	○	○	○
Idaho	○	○	○	○
Wyoming	○	○	○	○
2030				
Utah	○	○	○	○
Oklahoma	○	○	○	○
New Mexico	○	○	○	○
Arizona	○	○	○	○
2031				
Alaska	○	○	○	○
Hawaii	○	○	○	○
District of Columbia	○	○	○	○
Puerto Rico	○	○	○	○
2032				
Guam	○	○	○	○
American Samoa	○	○	○	○
U.S. Virgin Islands	○	○	○	○
Northern Mariana Islands	○	○	○	○

Mint Mark Key: = Philadelphia – **P**   = Denver – **D**   = San Francisco – **S**

JEFFERSON NICKELS 1938-2025

1938-1942 & 1946-1964
1942-1945
1968-2004**
2005
2006-Date

Mint Mark Locations

Westward Journey 2004-2005

Pre-War
- ○ 1938
- ○ 1938-D
- ○ 1938-S
- ○ 1939
- ○ 1939-D
- ○ 1939-S
- ○ 1940
- ○ 1940-D
- ○ 1940-S
- ○ 1941
- ○ 1941-D
- ○ 1941-S
- ○ 1942
- ○ 1942-D

Wartime Silver Alloy
- ○ 1942-P
- ○ 1942-S
- ○ 1943-P
- ○ 1943-D
- ○ 1943-S
- ○ 1944-P
- ○ 1944-D
- ○ 1944-S
- ○ 1945-P
- ○ 1945-D
- ○ 1945-S

Pre-War Resumed
- ○ 1946

- ○ 1946-D
- ○ 1946-S
- ○ 1947
- ○ 1947-D
- ○ 1947-S
- ○ 1948
- ○ 1948-D
- ○ 1948-S
- ○ 1949
- ○ 1949-D
- ○ 1949-S
- ○ 1950
- ○ 1950-D
- ○ 1951
- ○ 1951-D
- ○ 1951-S
- ○ 1952
- ○ 1952-D
- ○ 1952-S
- ○ 1953
- ○ 1953-D
- ○ 1953-S
- ○ 1954
- ○ 1954-D
- ○ 1954-S
- ○ 1955
- ○ 1955-D
- ○ 1956
- ○ 1957

- ○ 1957-D
- ○ 1958
- ○ 1958-D
- ○ 1959
- ○ 1959-D
- ○ 1960
- ○ 1960-D
- ○ 1961
- ○ 1961-D
- ○ 1962
- ○ 1962-D
- ○ 1963
- ○ 1963-D
- ○ 1964
- ○ 1964-D
- ○ 1965
- ○ 1966
- ○ 1967
- ○ 1968-D
- ○ 1968-S
- ○ 1969-D
- ○ 1969-S
- ○ 1970-D
- ○ 1970-S
- ○ 1971
- ○ 1971-D
- ○ 1971-S Proof
- ○ 1972
- ○ 1972-D
- ○ 1972-S Proof

- ○ 1973
- ○ 1973-D
- ○ 1973-S Proof
- ○ 1974
- ○ 1974-D
- ○ 1974-S
- ○ 1975
- ○ 1975-D
- ○ 1975-S Proof
- ○ 1976
- ○ 1976-D
- ○ 1976-S Proof
- ○ 1977
- ○ 1977-D
- ○ 1977-S Proof
- ○ 1978
- ○ 1978-D
- ○ 1978-S Proof
- ○ 1979
- ○ 1979-D
- ○ 1979-S Proof, Filled "S"
- ○ 1979-S Proof, Clear "S"
- ○ 1980-P
- ○ 1980-D
- ○ 1980-S Proof
- ○ 1981-P
- ○ 1981-D
- ○ 1981-S Proof, Filled "S"
- ○ 1981-S Proof, Clear "S"
- ○ 1982-P

- ○ 1982-D
- ○ 1982-S Proof
- ○ 1983-P
- ○ 1983-D
- ○ 1983-S Proof
- ○ 1984-P
- ○ 1984-D
- ○ 1984-S Proof
- ○ 1985-P
- ○ 1985-D
- ○ 1985-S Proof
- ○ 1986-P
- ○ 1986-D
- ○ 1986-S Proof
- ○ 1987-P
- ○ 1987-D
- ○ 1987-S Proof
- ○ 1988-P
- ○ 1988-D
- ○ 1988-S Proof
- ○ 1989-P
- ○ 1989-D
- ○ 1989-S Proof
- ○ 1990-P
- ○ 1990-D
- ○ 1990-S Proof
- ○ 1991-P
- ○ 1991-D
- ○ 1991-S Proof
- ○ 1992-P

- ○ 1992-D
- ○ 1992-S Proof
- ○ 1993-P
- ○ 1993-D
- ○ 1993-S Proof
- ○ 1994-P
- ○ 1994-D
- ○ 1994-S Proof
- ○ 1995-P
- ○ 1995-D
- ○ 1995-S Proof
- ○ 1996-P
- ○ 1996-D
- ○ 1996-S Proof
- ○ 1997-P
- ○ 1997-D
- ○ 1997-S Proof
- ○ 1998-P
- ○ 1998-D
- ○ 1998-S Proof
- ○ 1999-P
- ○ 1999-D
- ○ 1999-S Proof
- ○ 2000-P
- ○ 2000-D
- ○ 2000-S Proof
- ○ 2001-P
- ○ 2001-D
- ○ 2001-S Proof
- ○ 2002-P

- ○ 2002-D
- ○ 2002-S Proof
- ○ 2003-P
- ○ 2003-D
- ○ 2003-S Proof

Westward Journey

Peace Medal
- ○ 2004-P
- ○ 2004-D
- ○ 2004-S Proof

Keelboat
- ○ 2004-P
- ○ 2004-D
- ○ 2004-S Proof

Bison
- ○ 2005-P
- ○ 2005-D
- ○ 2005-S Proof

Ocean-in-View
- ○ 2005-P
- ○ 2005-D
- ○ 2005-S Proof

Return to Monticello
- ○ 2006-P
- ○ 2006-D
- ○ 2006-S Proof
- ○ 2007-P
- ○ 2007-D
- ○ 2007-S Proof

- ○ 2008-P
- ○ 2008-D
- ○ 2008-S Proof
- ○ 2009-P
- ○ 2009-D
- ○ 2009-S Proof
- ○ 2010-P
- ○ 2010-D
- ○ 2010-S Proof
- ○ 2011-P
- ○ 2011-D
- ○ 2011-S Proof
- ○ 2012-P
- ○ 2012-D
- ○ 2012-S Proof
- ○ 2013-P
- ○ 2013-D
- ○ 2013-S Proof
- ○ 2014-P
- ○ 2014-D
- ○ 2014-S Proof
- ○ 2015-P
- ○ 2015-D
- ○ 2015-S Proof
- ○ 2016-P
- ○ 2016-D
- ○ 2016-S Proof
- ○ 2017-P
- ○ 2017-D
- ○ 2017-S Proof

- ○ 2018-P
- ○ 2018-D
- ○ 2018-S Proof
- ○ 2019-P
- ○ 2019-D
- ○ 2019-S Proof
- ○ 2020-P
- ○ 2020-D
- ○ 2020-S Proof
- ○ 2020-W Proof*
- ○ 2020-W Rev Proof*
- ○ 2021-P
- ○ 2021-D
- ○ 2021-S Proof
- ○ 2022-P
- ○ 2022
- ○ 2022-S Proof
- ○ 2023
- ○ 2023-D
- ○ 2023-S Proof
- ○ 2024
- ○ 2024-D
- ○ 2024-S Proof
- ○ 2025
- ○ 2025-D
- ○ 2025-S Proof

Mint Mark Key: * Philadelphia – No Mint Mark or **P** * Denver – **D** * San Francisco – **S** * West Point – **W**

KENNEDY HALF DOLLARS
1964-2025

Mint Mark Location 1964-1967
1968-Date

Reverse Shown Actual Size

90% Silver
- ○ 1964
- ○ 1964-D
- ○ 1964 Proof

Silver Clad
- ○ 1965
- ○ 1966
- ○ 1967
- ○ 1968-D
- ○ 1968-S Proof
- ○ 1969-D
- ○ 1969-S Proof
- ○ 1970-D
- ○ 1970-S Proof

Copper-Nickel Clad
- ○ 1971
- ○ 1971-D
- ○ 1971-S Proof
- ○ 1972
- ○ 1972-D
- ○ 1972-S Proof
- ○ 1973
- ○ 1973-D
- ○ 1973-S Proof
- ○ 1974
- ○ 1974-D
- ○ 1974-S Proof

Bicentennial
- ○ 1976 CN
- ○ 1976-D CN
- ○ 1976-S CN Proof
- ○ 1976-S Silver Clad
- ○ 1976-S Silver Clad Proof

Eagle Reverse Resumed
- ○ 1977
- ○ 1977-D
- ○ 1977-S Proof
- ○ 1978
- ○ 1978-D
- ○ 1978-S Proof
- ○ 1979
- ○ 1979-D
- ○ 1979-S Proof, Filled S
- ○ 1979-S Proof, Clear S
- ○ 1980-P
- ○ 1980-D
- ○ 1980-S Proof
- ○ 1981-P
- ○ 1981-D
- ○ 1981-S Proof
- ○ 1982-P
- ○ 1982-D
- ○ 1982-S Proof
- ○ 1983-P
- ○ 1983-D
- ○ 1983-S Proof
- ○ 1984-P
- ○ 1984-D
- ○ 1984-S Proof
- ○ 1985-P
- ○ 1985-D
- ○ 1985-S Proof

- ○ 1986-P
- ○ 1986-D
- ○ 1986-S Proof
- ○ 1987-P
- ○ 1987-D
- ○ 1987-S Proof
- ○ 1988-P
- ○ 1988-D
- ○ 1988-S Proof
- ○ 1989-P
- ○ 1989-D
- ○ 1989-S Proof
- ○ 1990-P
- ○ 1990-D
- ○ 1990-S Proof
- ○ 1991-P
- ○ 1991-D
- ○ 1991-S Proof
- ○ 1992-P
- ○ 1992-D
- ○ 1992-S Proof
- ○ 1992-S Silver Proof
- ○ 1993-P
- ○ 1993-D
- ○ 1993-S Proof
- ○ 1993-S Silver Proof
- ○ 1994-P
- ○ 1994-D
- ○ 1994-S Proof
- ○ 1994-S Silver Proof
- ○ 1995-P

- ○ 1995-D
- ○ 1995-S Proof
- ○ 1995-S Silver Proof
- ○ 1996-P
- ○ 1996-D
- ○ 1996-S Proof
- ○ 1996-S Silver Proof
- ○ 1997-P
- ○ 1997-D
- ○ 1997-S Proof
- ○ 1997-S Silver Proof
- ○ 1998-P
- ○ 1998-D
- ○ 1998-S Proof
- ○ 1998-S Silver Proof
- ○ 1999-P
- ○ 1999-D
- ○ 1999-S Proof
- ○ 1999-S Silver Proof
- ○ 2000-P
- ○ 2000-D
- ○ 2000-S Proof
- ○ 2000-S Silver Proof
- ○ 2001-P
- ○ 2001-D
- ○ 2001-S Proof
- ○ 2001-S Silver Proof
- ○ 2002-P
- ○ 2002-D
- ○ 2002-S Proof
- ○ 2002-S Silver Proof

- ○ 2003-P
- ○ 2003-D
- ○ 2003-S Proof
- ○ 2003-S Silver Proof
- ○ 2004-P
- ○ 2004-D
- ○ 2004-S Proof
- ○ 2004-S Silver Proof
- ○ 2005-P
- ○ 2005-D
- ○ 2005-S Proof
- ○ 2005-S Silver Proof
- ○ 2006-P
- ○ 2006-D
- ○ 2006-S Proof
- ○ 2006-S Silver Proof
- ○ 2007-P
- ○ 2007-D
- ○ 2007-S Proof
- ○ 2007-S Silver Proof
- ○ 2008-P
- ○ 2008-D
- ○ 2008-S Proof
- ○ 2008-S Silver Proof
- ○ 2009-P
- ○ 2009-D
- ○ 2009-S Proof
- ○ 2009-S Silver Proof
- ○ 2010-P
- ○ 2010-D
- ○ 2010-S Proof

- ○ 2010-S Silver Proof
- ○ 2011-P
- ○ 2011-D
- ○ 2011-S Proof
- ○ 2011-S Silver Proof
- ○ 2012-P
- ○ 2012-D
- ○ 2012-S Proof
- ○ 2012-S Silver Proof
- ○ 2013-P
- ○ 2013-D
- ○ 2013-S Proof
- ○ 2013-S Silver Proof
- ○ 2014-P
- ○ 2014-D
- ○ 2014-S Proof
- ○ 2014-S Silver Proof
- ○ 2015-P
- ○ 2015-D
- ○ 2015-S Proof
- ○ 2015-S Silver Proof
- ○ 2016-P
- ○ 2016-D
- ○ 2016-S Proof
- ○ 2016-S Silver Proof
- ○ 2017-P
- ○ 2017-D
- ○ 2017-S Proof
- ○ 2017-S Silver Proof
- ○ 2018-D

- ○ 2018-S Proof
- ○ 2018-S Silver Proof
- ○ 2019-P
- ○ 2019-D
- ○ 2019-S Proof
- ○ 2019-S Silver Proof
- ○ 2020-P
- ○ 2020-D
- ○ 2020-S Proof
- ○ 2020-S Silver Proof
- ○ 2021-P
- ○ 2021-D
- ○ 2021-S Proof
- ○ 2021-S Silver Proof
- ○ 2022-P
- ○ 2022-D
- ○ 2022-S Proof
- ○ 2022-S Silver Proof
- ○ 2023-P
- ○ 2023-D
- ○ 2023-S Proof
- ○ 2023-S Silver Proof
- ○ 2024-P
- ○ 2024-D
- ○ 2024-S Proof
- ○ 2024-S Silver Proof
- ○ 2025-P
- ○ 2025-D
- ○ 2025-S Proof
- ○ 2025-S Silver Proof

Mint Mark Key • Philadelphia – No Mint Mark or P • Denver – D • San Francisco – S

LIBERTY HEAD NICKELS
1883-1912

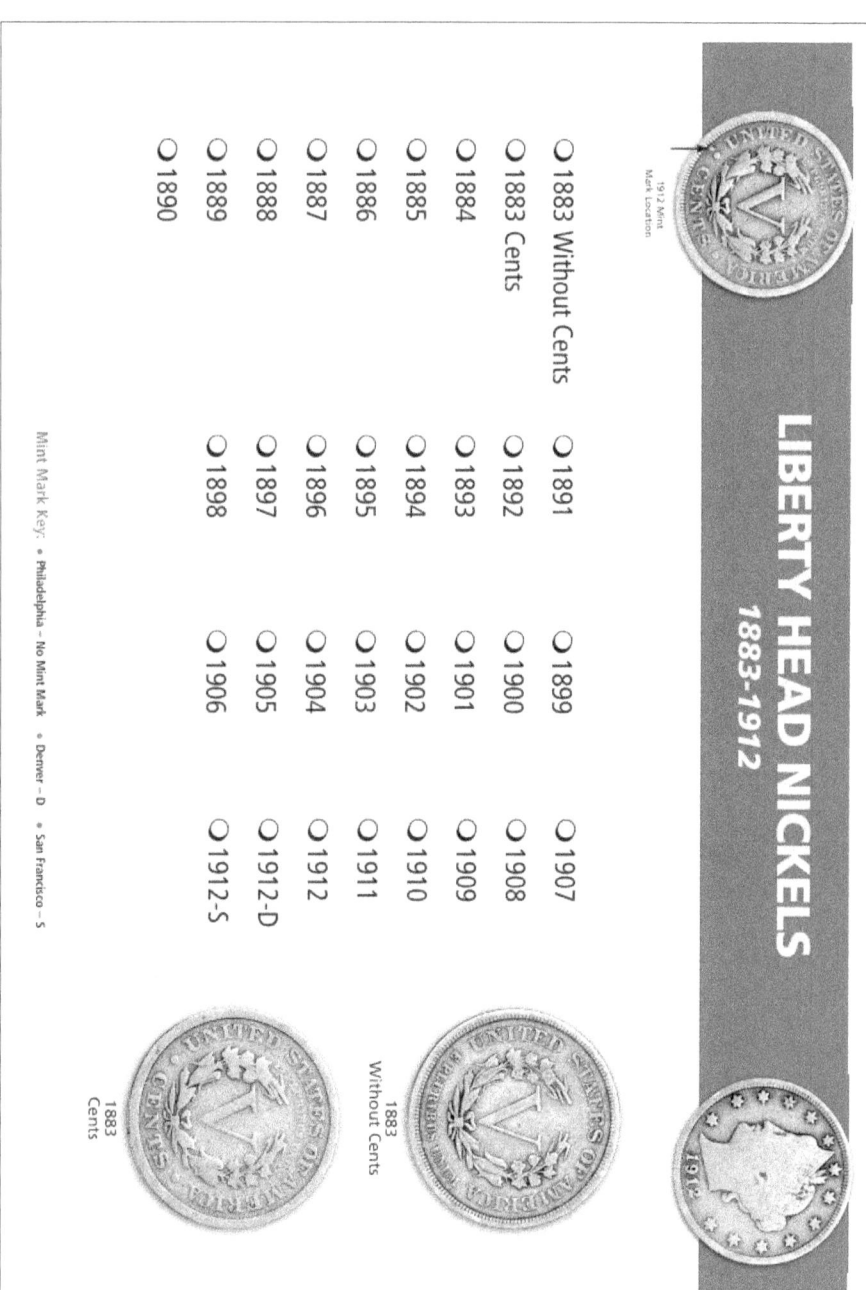

1912 Mint
Mark Location

○ 1883 Without Cents	○ 1891	○ 1899	○ 1907
○ 1883 Cents	○ 1892	○ 1900	○ 1908
○ 1884	○ 1893	○ 1901	○ 1909
○ 1885	○ 1894	○ 1902	○ 1910
○ 1886	○ 1895	○ 1903	○ 1911
○ 1887	○ 1896	○ 1904	○ 1912
○ 1888	○ 1897	○ 1905	○ 1912-D
○ 1889	○ 1898	○ 1906	○ 1912-S
○ 1890			

Mint Mark Key: • Philadelphia – No Mint Mark   • Denver – D   • San Francisco – S

1883
Cents

1883
Without Cents

LIBERTY WALKING HALVES
1916-1947

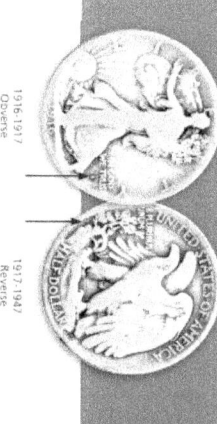

1916-1917 Obverse

1917-1947 Reverse

- ○ 1916
- ○ 1916-D
- ○ 1916-S
- ○ 1917
- ○ 1917-D Obverse
- ○ 1917-D Reverse
- ○ 1917-S Obverse
- ○ 1917-S Reverse
- ○ 1918
- ○ 1918-D
- ○ 1918-S
- ○ 1919
- ○ 1919-D

- ○ 1919-S
- ○ 1920
- ○ 1920-D
- ○ 1920-S
- ○ 1921
- ○ 1921-D
- ○ 1921-S
- ○ 1923-S
- ○ 1927-S
- ○ 1928-S
- ○ 1929-D
- ○ 1929-S
- ○ 1933-S

- ○ 1934
- ○ 1934-D
- ○ 1934-S
- ○ 1935
- ○ 1935-D
- ○ 1935-S
- ○ 1936
- ○ 1936-D
- ○ 1936-S
- ○ 1937
- ○ 1937-D
- ○ 1937-S
- ○ 1938

- ○ 1938-D
- ○ 1939
- ○ 1939-D
- ○ 1939-S
- ○ 1940
- ○ 1940-S
- ○ 1941
- ○ 1941-D
- ○ 1941-S
- ○ 1942
- ○ 1942-D
- ○ 1942-S
- ○ 1943

- ○ 1943-D
- ○ 1943-S
- ○ 1944
- ○ 1944-D
- ○ 1944-S
- ○ 1945
- ○ 1945-D
- ○ 1945-S
- ○ 1946
- ○ 1946-D
- ○ 1946-S
- ○ 1947
- ○ 1947-D

Mint Mark Key: • Philadelphia – No Mint Mark   • Denver – D   • San Francisco – S

309

Mint Mark Location

Wheat Ears

○ 1909
○ 1909-VDB
○ 1909-S
○ 1909-S VDB
○ 1910
○ 1910-S
○ 1911
○ 1911-D
○ 1911-S
○ 1912
○ 1912-D
○ 1912-S
○ 1913
○ 1913-D
○ 1913-S
○ 1914
○ 1914-D
○ 1914-S
○ 1915
○ 1915-D
○ 1915-S
○ 1916
○ 1916-D
○ 1916-S
○ 1917
○ 1917-D
○ 1917-S
○ 1918
○ 1918-D
○ 1918-S
○ 1919
○ 1919-D
○ 1919-S
○ 1920
○ 1920-D
○ 1920-S
○ 1921
○ 1921-S
○ 1922 Plain
○ 1922-D
○ 1923
○ 1923-S
○ 1924
○ 1924-D
○ 1924-S
○ 1925
○ 1925-D
○ 1925-S
○ 1926
○ 1926-D
○ 1926-S
○ 1927
○ 1927-S
○ 1928
○ 1928-D
○ 1928-S
○ 1929
○ 1929-D
○ 1929-S
○ 1930
○ 1930-D
○ 1930-S
○ 1931
○ 1931-D
○ 1931-S
○ 1932
○ 1932-D
○ 1933
○ 1933-D
○ 1934
○ 1934-D
○ 1935
○ 1935-D
○ 1935-S
○ 1936
○ 1936-D
○ 1936-S
○ 1937
○ 1937-D
○ 1937-S
○ 1938
○ 1938-D
○ 1938-S
○ 1939
○ 1939-D
○ 1939-S
○ 1940
○ 1940-D
○ 1940-S
○ 1941
○ 1941-D
○ 1941-S
○ 1942
○ 1942-D
○ 1942-S
○ 1943 Steel
○ 1943-D Steel
○ 1943-S Steel
○ 1944
○ 1944-D
○ 1944-S
○ 1945
○ 1945-D
○ 1945-S
○ 1946
○ 1946-D
○ 1946-S
○ 1947
○ 1947-D
○ 1947-S
○ 1948
○ 1948-D
○ 1948-S
○ 1949
○ 1949-D
○ 1949-S
○ 1950
○ 1950-D
○ 1950-S
○ 1951
○ 1951-D

○ 1951-S
○ 1952
○ 1952-D
○ 1952-S
○ 1953
○ 1953-D
○ 1953-S
○ 1954
○ 1954-D
○ 1954-S
○ 1955
○ 1955-D
○ 1955-S
○ 1956
○ 1956-D
○ 1957
○ 1957-D
○ 1958
○ 1958-D

Memorial

○ 1959
○ 1959-D
○ 1960 SM Date
○ 1960 LG Date
○ 1960-D SM Date
○ 1960-D LG Date
○ 1961
○ 1961-D
○ 1962
○ 1962-D
○ 1963
○ 1963-D
○ 1964
○ 1964-D
○ 1965
○ 1966
○ 1967
○ 1968
○ 1968-D
○ 1968-S Proof

○ 1969
○ 1969-D
○ 1969-S Proof
○ 1970
○ 1970-D
○ 1970-S Proof
○ 1970-S SM Date
○ 1970-S LG Date
○ 1971
○ 1971-D
○ 1971-S Proof
○ 1972
○ 1972-D
○ 1972-S Proof
○ 1973
○ 1973-D
○ 1973-S Proof
○ 1974
○ 1974-D
○ 1974-S Proof
○ 1975
○ 1975-D
○ 1975-S Proof
○ 1976
○ 1976-D
○ 1976-S Proof
○ 1977
○ 1977-D
○ 1977-S Proof
○ 1978
○ 1978-D
○ 1978-S Proof
○ 1979
○ 1979-D
○ 1979-S Proof Filled S
○ 1979-S Proof Clear S
○ 1980
○ 1980-D
○ 1980-S Proof
○ 1981
○ 1981-D

○ 1981-S Proof Filled S
○ 1981-S Proof Clear S
○ 1982 Copper LG Date
○ 1982 Copper SM Date
○ 1982-D Copper LG Date
○ 1982-S Proof
○ 1982 Zinc SM Date
○ 1982 Zinc LG Date
○ 1982-D Zinc LG Date
○ 1982-D Zinc SM Date
○ 1983
○ 1983-D
○ 1983-S Proof
○ 1984
○ 1984-D
○ 1984-S Proof
○ 1985
○ 1985-D
○ 1985-S Proof
○ 1986
○ 1986-D
○ 1986-S Proof
○ 1987
○ 1987-D
○ 1987-S Proof
○ 1988
○ 1988-D
○ 1988-S Proof
○ 1989
○ 1989-D
○ 1989-S Proof
○ 1990
○ 1990-D
○ 1990-S Proof
○ 1991
○ 1991-D
○ 1991-S Proof
○ 1992
○ 1992-D
○ 1992-S Proof
○ 1993

○ 1993-D
○ 1993-S Proof
○ 1994
○ 1994-D
○ 1994-S Proof
○ 1995
○ 1995-D
○ 1995-S Proof
○ 1996
○ 1996-D
○ 1996-S Proof
○ 1997
○ 1997-D
○ 1997-S Proof
○ 1998
○ 1998-D
○ 1998-S Proof
○ 1999
○ 1999-D
○ 1999-S Proof
○ 2000
○ 2000-D
○ 2000-S Proof
○ 2001
○ 2001-D
○ 2001-S Proof
○ 2002
○ 2002-D
○ 2002-S Proof
○ 2003
○ 2003-D
○ 2003-S Proof
○ 2004
○ 2004-D
○ 2004-S Proof
○ 2005
○ 2005-D
○ 2005-S Proof
○ 2006
○ 2006-D
○ 2006-S Proof

○ 2007
○ 2007-D
○ 2007-S Proof
○ 2008
○ 2008-D
○ 2008-S Proof

Bicentennial

Birthplace
○ 2009
○ 2009-D
○ 2009-S Proof

Formative Years
○ 2009
○ 2009-D
○ 2009-S Proof

Professional Life
○ 2009
○ 2009-D
○ 2009-S Proof

Presidency
○ 2009
○ 2009-D
○ 2009-S Proof

Shield

○ 2009
○ 2009-D
○ 2009-S Proof
○ 2010
○ 2010-D
○ 2010-S Proof
○ 2011
○ 2011-D
○ 2011-S Proof
○ 2012
○ 2012-D
○ 2012-S Proof
○ 2013
○ 2013-D
○ 2013-S Proof
○ 2014
○ 2014-D

○ 2014-S Proof
○ 2015
○ 2015-D
○ 2015-S Proof
○ 2016
○ 2016-D
○ 2016-S Proof
○ 2017-P
○ 2017-D
○ 2017-S Proof
○ 2018
○ 2018-D
○ 2018-S Proof
○ 2019
○ 2019-D
○ 2019-S Proof
○ 2019-W*
○ 2019-W Proof**
○ 2019-W Rev Proof***
○ 2020
○ 2020-D
○ 2020-S Proof
○ 2021
○ 2021-D
○ 2021-S Proof
○ 2022
○ 2022-D
○ 2022-S Proof
○ 2023
○ 2023-D
○ 2023-S Proof
○ 2024
○ 2024-D
○ 2024-S Proof
○ 2025
○ 2025-D
○ 2025-S Proof

*In Mint Set Only

Mint Mark Key: • Philadelphia – No Mint Mark or **P** • Denver – **D** • San Francisco – **S** • West Point – **W**

Wheat Ears 1909-1958

Memorial 1959-2008

Bicentennial 2009

Shield 2010-Date

MERCURY DIMES
1916-1945

Mint Mark Location
1916-1945

○ 1916	○ 1921-D	○ 1928-D	○ 1936-D	○ 1941-S
○ 1916-D	○ 1923	○ 1928-S	○ 1936-S	○ 1942 2 over 1
○ 1916-S	○ 1923-S	○ 1929	○ 1937	○ 1942
○ 1917	○ 1924	○ 1929-D	○ 1937-D	○ 1942-D 2 over 1
○ 1917-D	○ 1924-D	○ 1929-S	○ 1937-S	○ 1942-D
○ 1917-S	○ 1924-S	○ 1930.	○ 1938	○ 1942-S
○ 1918	○ 1925	○ 1930-S	○ 1938-D	○ 1943
○ 1918-D	○ 1925-D	○ 1931	○ 1938-S	○ 1943-D
○ 1918-S	○ 1925-S	○ 1931-D	○ 1939	○ 1943-S
○ 1919	○ 1926	○ 1931-S	○ 1939-D	○ 1944
○ 1919-D	○ 1926-D	○ 1934	○ 1939-S	○ 1944-D
○ 1919-S	○ 1926-S	○ 1934-D	○ 1940	○ 1944-S
○ 1920	○ 1927	○ 1935	○ 1940-D	○ 1945
○ 1920-D	○ 1927-D	○ 1935-D	○ 1940-S	○ 1945-D
○ 1920-S	○ 1927-S	○ 1935-S	○ 1941	○ 1945-S
○ 1921	○ 1928	○ 1936	○ 1941-D	○ 1945-S Micro S

Mint Mark Key • Philadelphia – No Mint Mark • Denver – D • San Francisco – S

311

MORGAN DOLLAR
1878-1921, 2021, 2023

Mint Mark Location

Common Obverse

○ 1878 all kinds*	○ 1883-CC	○ 1889-CC	○ 1894-S	○ 1901-S
○ 1878-CC	○ 1883-O	○ 1889-O	○ 1895-O	○ 1902
○ 1878-S	○ 1883-S	○ 1889-S	○ 1895-S	○ 1902-O
○ 1879	○ 1884	○ 1890	○ 1896	○ 1902-S
○ 1879-CC	○ 1884-CC	○ 1890-CC	○ 1896-O	○ 1903
○ 1879-O	○ 1884-O	○ 1890-O	○ 1896-S	○ 1903-O
○ 1879-S	○ 1884-S	○ 1890-S	○ 1897	○ 1903-S
○ 1880	○ 1885	○ 1891	○ 1897-O	○ 1904
○ 1880-CC	○ 1885-CC	○ 1891-CC	○ 1897-S	○ 1904-O
○ 1880-O	○ 1885-O	○ 1891-O	○ 1898	○ 1904-S
○ 1880-S	○ 1885-S	○ 1891-S	○ 1898-O	○ 1921
○ 1881	○ 1886	○ 1892	○ 1898-S	○ 1921-D
○ 1881-CC	○ 1886-O	○ 1892-CC	○ 1899	○ 1921-S
○ 1881-O	○ 1886-S	○ 1892-O	○ 1899-O	○ 2021
○ 1881-S	○ 1887	○ 1892-S	○ 1899-S	○ 2021-D
○ 1882	○ 1887-O	○ 1893	○ 1900	○ 2021-S
○ 1882-CC	○ 1887-S	○ 1893-CC	○ 1900-O	○ 2021-O Privy
○ 1882-O	○ 1888	○ 1893-O	○ 1900-S	○ 2021-CC Privy
○ 1882-S	○ 1888-O	○ 1893-S	○ 1901	○ 2023
○ 1883	○ 1888-S	○ 1894	○ 1901-O	○ 2023-S
	○ 1889	○ 1894-O		○ 2023-S Reverse Proof

*When first issued in 1878, the eagle on the Morgan dollar's reverse had 8 tail feathers. Instructions to change the number of tail feathers from 8 to 7 resulted in a number of exciting varieties from that year.

Mint Mark Key • Philadelphia – No Mint Mark • Denver – D • San Francisco – S • Carson City – CC • New Orleans – O

In 2021, special collector issues were released in 99.9% pure silver to honor the series' 100th anniversary. These coins will be struck in additional years at the mint's discretion. They were not issued in 2022.

Mint Mark Location

2010

Site	State or Territory	Unc		Proof	
		P	D	S	S-Slv
Hot Springs National Park	AR	P	D	S	S-Slv
Yellowstone National Park	WY	P	D	S	S-Slv
Yosemite National Park	CA	P	D	S	S-Slv
Grand Canyon National Park	AZ	P	D	S	S-Slv
Mt. Hood National Forest	OR	P	D	S	S-Slv

2011

Site	State or Territory	Unc P	Unc D	Proof S	Proof S-Slv
Gettysburg National Military Park	PA	P	D	S	S-Slv
Glacier National Park	MT	P	D	S	S-Slv
Olympic National Park	WA	P	D	S	S-Slv
Vicksburg National Military Park	MS	P	D	S	S-Slv
Chickasaw National Recreation Area	OK	P	D	S	S-Slv

2012

Site	State or Territory	Unc P	Unc D	Proof S	Proof S-Slv
El Yunque National Forest	PR	P	D	S	S-Slv
Chaco Culture National Historical Park	NM	P	D	S	S-Slv
Acadia National Park	ME	P	D	S	S-Slv
Hawai'i Volcanoes National Park	HI	P	D	S	S-Slv
Denali National Park	AK	P	D	S	S-Slv

2013

Site	State or Territory	Unc P	Unc D	Proof S	Proof S-Slv
White Mountain National Forest	NH	P	D	S	S-Slv
Perry's Victory and International Peace Memorial	OH	P	D	S	S-Slv
Great Basin National Park	NV	P	D	S	S-Slv
Fort McHenry National Monument and Historic Shrine	MD	P	D	S	S-Slv
Mount Rushmore National Memorial	SD	P	D	S	S-Slv

2014

Site	State or Territory	Unc P	Unc D	Proof S	Proof S-Slv
Great Smoky Mountains National Park	TN	P	D	S	S-Slv
Shenandoah National Park	VA	P	D	S	S-Slv
Arches National Park	UT	P	D	S	S-Slv
Great Sand Dunes National Park	CO	P	D	S	S-Slv
Everglades National Park	FL	P	D	S	S-Slv

2015

Site	State or Territory	Unc P	Unc D	Proof S	Proof S-Slv
Homestead National Monument of America	NE	P	D	S	S-Slv
Kisatchie National Forest	LA	P	D	S	S-Slv
Blue Ridge Parkway	NC	P	D	S	S-Slv
Bombay Hook National Wildlife Refuge	DE	P	D	S	S-Slv
Saratoga National Historical Park	NY	P	D	S	S-Slv

Hot Springs 2010

Tuskegee Airmen 2021

2016

Site	State or Territory	Unc		Proof	
		P	D	S	S-Slv
Shawnee National Forest	IL	P	D	S	S-Slv
Cumberland Gap National Historical Park	KY	P	D	S	S-Slv
Harpers Ferry National Historical Park	WV	P	D	S	S-Slv
Theodore Roosevelt National Park	ND	P	D	S	S-Slv
Fort Moultrie (Fort Sumter National Monument)	SC	P	D	S	S-Slv

2017

Site	State or Territory	Unc P	Unc D	Proof S	Proof S-Slv
Effigy Mounds National Monument	IA	P	D	S	S-Slv
Frederick Douglass National Historic Site	DC	P	D	S	S-Slv
Ozark National Scenic Riverways	MO	P	D	S	S-Slv
Ellis Island National Monument (Statue of Liberty)	NJ	P	D	S	S-Slv
George Rogers Clark National Historical Park	IN	P	D	S	S-Slv

2018

Site	State or Territory	Unc P	Unc D	Proof S	Proof S-Slv
Pictured Rocks National Lakeshore	MI	P	D	S	S-Slv
Apostle Islands National Lakeshore	WI	P	D	S	S-Slv
Voyageurs National Park	MN	P	D	S	S-Slv
Cumberland Island National Seashore	GA	P	D	S	S-Slv
Block Island National Wildlife Refuge	RI	P	D	S	S-Slv

2019

Site	State or Territory	Unc P	Unc D	Proof S	Proof S-Slv
Lowell National Historical Park	MA	P	D	S	S-Slv
American Memorial Park	MP	P	D	S	S-Slv
War in the Pacific National Historic Park	GU	P	D	S	S-Slv
San Antonio Missions National Historical Park	TX	P	D	S	S-Slv
Frank Church River of No Return Wilderness	ID	P	D	S	S-Slv

2020

Site	State or Territory	Unc P	Unc D	Proof S	Proof S-Slv
National Park of American Samoa	AS	P	D	S	S-Slv
Weir Farm National Historic Site	CT	P	D	S	S-Slv
Salt River Bay National Historical Park and Ecological Preserve	VI	P	D	S	S-Slv
Marsh-Billings-Rockefeller National Historical Park	VT	P	D	S	S-Slv
Tallgrass Prairie National Preserve	KS	P	D	S	S-Slv

2021

Site	State or Territory	Unc P	Unc D	Proof S	Proof S-Slv
Tuskegee Airmen National Historic Site	AL	P	D	S	S-Slv

313

PEACE DOLLARS
1921-1935, 2021 & 2023

Mint Mark Location

○ 1921   ○ 1925-S   ○ 1934-D
○ 1922   ○ 1926   ○ 1934-S
○ 1922-D   ○ 1926-D   ○ 1935
○ 1922-S   ○ 1926-S   ○ 1935-S
○ 1923   ○ 1927   ○ 2021
○ 1923-D   ○ 1927-D   ○ 2023
○ 1923-S   ○ 1927-S   ○ 2023-S Proof
○ 1924   ○ 1928   ○ 2023-S Reverse Proof
○ 1924-S   ○ 1928-S
○ 1925   ○ 1934

In 2021, special collector issues were released in 99.9% pure silver to honor the series' 100th anniversary. These coins will be struck in additional years at the mint's discretion. They were not issued in 2022.

Mint Mark Key: ● Philadelphia – No Mint Mark   ● Denver - D   ● San Francisco - S

1921 High Relief

Struck in the final days of December 1921, the first-year Peace dollar was the first and only coin in the series struck in high relief (with the design elements rising well above the coin's surface). The relief was lowered the following year due to problems in striking.

314

Mint Mark Location

2020 George H.W. Bush

2007 | Proof
George Washington | O P O D O S
John Adams | O P O D O S
Thomas Jefferson | O P O D O S
James Madison | O P O D O S

2008
James Monroe | O P O D O S
John Quincy Adams | O P O D O S
Andrew Jackson | O P O D O S
Martin Van Buren | O P O D O S

2009
William Henry Harrison | O P O D O S
John Tyler | O P O D O S
James K. Polk | O P O D O S
Zachary Taylor | O P O D O S

2010
Millard Fillmore | O P O D O S
Franklin Pierce | O P O D O S
James Buchanan | O P O D O S
Abraham Lincoln | O P O D O S

2011
Andrew Johnson | O P O D O S
Ulysses S. Grant | O P O D O S
Rutherford B. Hayes | O P O D O S
James Garfield | O P O D O S

2012
Chester Arthur | O P O D O S
Grover Cleveland (Term 1) | O P O D O S
Benjamin Harrison | O P O D O S
Grover Cleveland (Term 2) | O P O D O S

2013 | Proof
William McKinley | O P O D O S
Theodore Roosevelt | O P O D O S
William Howard Taft | O P O D O S
Woodrow Wilson | O P O D O S

2014
Warren G. Harding | O P O D O S
Calvin Coolidge | O P O D O S
Herbert Hoover | O P O D O S
Franklin D. Roosevelt | O P O D O S

2015
Harry S. Truman | O P O D O S
Dwight D. Eisenhower | O P O D O S
John F. Kennedy | O P O D O S
Lyndon B. Johnson | O P O D O S

2016
Richard M. Nixon | O P O D O S
Gerald R. Ford | O P O D O S
Ronald Reagan | O P O D O S

2020
George H.W. Bush | O P O D O S*

* In Special Edition Set Only

Mint Mark Key • **Philadelphia - P** • **Denver - D** • **San Francisco - S**

315

U.S. PROOF SETS
1955-2025

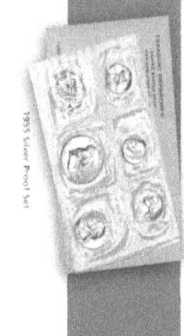

1955 Silver Proof Set

2021 Silver Proof Set

Silver Proofs

○ 1955 Proof Set
○ 1956 Proof Set
○ 1957 Proof Set
○ 1958 Proof Set
○ 1959 Proof Set
○ 1960 Proof Set
○ 1960 Proof Set Lg. Date
○ 1960 Proof Set Sm. Date
○ 1961 Proof Set
○ 1962 Proof Set
○ 1963 Proof Set
○ 1964 Proof Set

Clad & Silver Proofs

○ 1968-S Proof Set
○ 1969-S Proof Set
○ 1970-S Proof Set
○ 1971-S Proof Set
○ 1972-S Proof Set
○ 1973-S Proof Set
○ 1974-S Proof Set
○ 1975-S Proof Set
○ 1976-S Proof Set

○ 1976-S 40% Silver Proof Set
○ 1977-S Proof Set
○ 1978-S Proof Set
○ 1979-S Proof Set
○ 1980-S Proof Set
○ 1981-S Proof Set
○ 1982-S Proof Set
○ 1983-S Proof Set
○ 1984-S Proof Set
○ 1985-S Proof Set
○ 1986-S Proof Set
○ 1987-S Proof Set
○ 1988-S Proof Set
○ 1989-S Proof Set
○ 1990-S Proof Set
○ 1991-S Proof Set
○ 1992-S Proof Set
○ 1992-S 90% Silver Proof Set
○ 1993-S Proof Set
○ 1993-S 90% Silver Proof Set
○ 1994-S Proof Set
○ 1994-S 90% Silver Proof Set

○ 1995-S Proof Set
○ 1995-S 90% Silver Proof Set
○ 1996-S Proof Set
○ 1996-S 90% Silver Proof Set
○ 1997-S Proof Set
○ 1997-S 90% Silver Proof Set
○ 1998-S Proof Set
○ 1998-S 90% Silver Proof Set
○ 1999-S Proof Set
○ 1999-S 90% Silver Proof Set
○ 2000-S Proof Set
○ 2000-S 90% Silver Proof Set
○ 2001-S Proof Set
○ 2001-S 90% Silver Proof Set
○ 2002-S Proof Set
○ 2002-S 90% Silver Proof Set
○ 2003-S Proof Set
○ 2003-S 90% Silver Proof Set
○ 2004-S Proof Set
○ 2004-S 90% Silver Proof Set
○ 2005-S Proof Set
○ 2005-S 90% Silver Proof Set

○ 2006-S Proof Set
○ 2006-S 90% Silver Proof Set
○ 2007-S Proof Set
○ 2007-S 90% Silver Proof Set
○ 2008-S Proof Set
○ 2008-S 90% Silver Proof Set
○ 2009-S Proof Set
○ 2009-S 90% Silver Proof Set
○ 2010-S Proof Set
○ 2010-S 90% Silver Proof Set
○ 2011-S Proof Set
○ 2011-S 90% Silver Proof Set
○ 2012-S Proof Set
○ 2012-S 90% Silver Proof Set
○ 2013-S Proof Set
○ 2013-S 90% Silver Proof Set
○ 2014-S Proof Set
○ 2014-S 90% Silver Proof Set
○ 2015-S Proof Set
○ 2015-S 90% Silver Proof Set
○ 2016-S Proof Set
○ 2016-S 90% Silver Proof Set

○ 2017-S Proof Set
○ 2017-S 90% Silver Proof Set
○ 2018-S Proof Set
○ 2018-S 90% Silver Proof Set
○ 2019-S Proof Set
○ 2019-S 99.9% Silver Proof Set
○ 2020-S Proof Set
○ 2020-S 99.9% Silver Proof Set
○ 2021-S Proof Set
○ 2021-S 99.9% Silver Proof Set
○ 2022-S Proof Set
○ 2022-S 99.9% Silver Proof Set
○ 2023-S Proof Set
○ 2023-S 99.9% Silver Proof Set
○ 2024-S Proof Set
○ 2024-S 99.9% Silver Proof Set
○ 2025-S Proof Set
○ 2025-S 99.9% Silver Proof Set

Proof Sets were not minted from 1965-1967

Mint Mark Key: ● Philadelphia – No Mint Mark ● San Francisco – S

316

ROOSEVELT DIMES
1946-2025

Mint Mark Location (1946-1964)

Mint Mark Location (1968-Date)

90% Silver
- ○ 1946
- ○ 1946-S
- ○ 1947
- ○ 1947-D
- ○ 1947-S
- ○ 1948
- ○ 1948-S
- ○ 1948-D
- ○ 1949
- ○ 1949-D
- ○ 1949-S
- ○ 1950
- ○ 1950-D
- ○ 1950-S
- ○ 1951
- ○ 1951-D
- ○ 1951-S
- ○ 1952
- ○ 1952-S
- ○ 1953
- ○ 1953-S
- ○ 1954
- ○ 1954-D
- ○ 1954-S
- ○ 1955
- ○ 1955-D
- ○ 1955-S
- ○ 1956
- ○ 1956-D
- ○ 1957

- ○ 1957-D
- ○ 1958
- ○ 1958-D
- ○ 1959
- ○ 1959-D
- ○ 1960
- ○ 1960-D
- ○ 1961
- ○ 1961-D
- ○ 1962
- ○ 1962-D
- ○ 1963
- ○ 1963-D
- ○ 1964
- ○ 1964-D

Clad
- ○ 1965
- ○ 1966
- ○ 1967
- ○ 1968
- ○ 1968-D
- ○ 1968-S Proof
- ○ 1969
- ○ 1969-D
- ○ 1969-S Proof
- ○ 1970
- ○ 1970-D
- ○ 1970-S Proof
- ○ 1971
- ○ 1971-D
- ○ 1971-S Proof
- ○ 1972
- ○ 1972-D
- ○ 1972-S Proof

- ○ 1973
- ○ 1973-D
- ○ 1973-S Proof
- ○ 1974
- ○ 1974-D
- ○ 1974-S Proof
- ○ 1975
- ○ 1975-D
- ○ 1975-S Proof
- ○ 1976
- ○ 1976-D
- ○ 1976-S Proof
- ○ 1977
- ○ 1977-D
- ○ 1977-S Proof
- ○ 1978
- ○ 1978-D
- ○ 1978-S Proof
- ○ 1979
- ○ 1979-D
- ○ 1979-S Proof, Filled "S"
- ○ 1979-S Proof, Clear "S"
- ○ 1980-P
- ○ 1980-D
- ○ 1980-S Proof
- ○ 1981-P
- ○ 1981-D
- ○ 1981-S Proof, Filled "S"
- ○ 1981-S Proof, Clear "S"
- ○ 1982-P
- ○ 1982-D
- ○ 1982-S Proof
- ○ 1983-P

- ○ 1983-D
- ○ 1983-S Proof
- ○ 1984-P
- ○ 1984-D
- ○ 1984-S Proof
- ○ 1985-P
- ○ 1985-D
- ○ 1985-S Proof
- ○ 1986-P
- ○ 1986-D
- ○ 1986-S Proof
- ○ 1987-P
- ○ 1987-D
- ○ 1987-S Proof
- ○ 1988-P
- ○ 1988-D
- ○ 1988-S Proof
- ○ 1989-P
- ○ 1989-D
- ○ 1989-S Proof
- ○ 1990-P
- ○ 1990-D
- ○ 1990-S Proof
- ○ 1991-P
- ○ 1991-D
- ○ 1991-S Proof
- ○ 1992-P
- ○ 1992-D
- ○ 1992-S Proof
- ○ 1992-S Silver Proof
- ○ 1993-P
- ○ 1993-D
- ○ 1993-S Proof

- ○ 1993-S Silver Proof
- ○ 1994-P
- ○ 1994-D
- ○ 1994-S Proof
- ○ 1994-S Silver Proof
- ○ 1995-P
- ○ 1995-D
- ○ 1995-S Proof
- ○ 1995-S Silver Proof
- ○ 1996-P
- ○ 1996-D
- ○ 1996-W*
- ○ 1996-S Proof
- ○ 1996-S Silver Proof
- ○ 1997-P
- ○ 1997-D
- ○ 1997-S Proof
- ○ 1997-S Silver Proof
- ○ 1998-P
- ○ 1998-D
- ○ 1998-S Proof
- ○ 1998-S Silver Proof
- ○ 1999-P
- ○ 1999-D
- ○ 1999-S Proof
- ○ 1999-S Silver Proof
- ○ 2000-P
- ○ 2000-D
- ○ 2000-S Proof
- ○ 2000-S Silver Proof
- ○ 2001-P
- ○ 2001-D
- ○ 2001-S Proof

- ○ 2001-S Silver Proof
- ○ 2002-P
- ○ 2002-D
- ○ 2002-S Proof
- ○ 2002-S Silver Proof
- ○ 2003-P
- ○ 2003-D
- ○ 2003-S Proof
- ○ 2003-S Silver Proof
- ○ 2004-P
- ○ 2004-D
- ○ 2004-S Proof
- ○ 2004-S Silver Proof
- ○ 2005-P
- ○ 2005-D
- ○ 2005-S Proof
- ○ 2005-S Silver Proof
- ○ 2006-P
- ○ 2006-D
- ○ 2006-S Proof
- ○ 2006-S Silver Proof
- ○ 2007-P
- ○ 2007-D
- ○ 2007-S Proof
- ○ 2007-S Silver Proof
- ○ 2008-P
- ○ 2008-D
- ○ 2008-S Proof
- ○ 2008-S Silver Proof
- ○ 2009-P
- ○ 2009-D
- ○ 2009-S Proof
- ○ 2009-S Silver Proof

- ○ 2010-P
- ○ 2010-D
- ○ 2010-S Proof
- ○ 2010-S Silver Proof
- ○ 2011-P
- ○ 2011-D
- ○ 2011-S Proof
- ○ 2011-S Silver Proof
- ○ 2012-P
- ○ 2012-D
- ○ 2012-S Proof
- ○ 2012-S Silver Proof
- ○ 2013-P
- ○ 2013-D
- ○ 2013-S Proof
- ○ 2013-S Silver Proof
- ○ 2014-P
- ○ 2014-D
- ○ 2014-S Proof
- ○ 2014-S Silver Proof
- ○ 2015-P
- ○ 2015-D
- ○ 2015-S Proof
- ○ 2015-S Silver Proof
- ○ 2016-P
- ○ 2016-D
- ○ 2016-S Proof
- ○ 2016-S Silver Proof
- ○ 2017-P
- ○ 2017-D
- ○ 2017-S Proof
- ○ 2017-S Silver Proof
- ○ 2018-P

- ○ 2018-D
- ○ 2018-S Proof
- ○ 2018-S Silver Proof
- ○ 2019-P
- ○ 2019-D
- ○ 2019-S Proof
- ○ 2019-S Silver Proof
- ○ 2020-P
- ○ 2020-D
- ○ 2020-S Proof
- ○ 2020-S Silver Proof
- ○ 2021-P
- ○ 2021-D
- ○ 2021-S Proof
- ○ 2021-S Silver Proof
- ○ 2022-P
- ○ 2022-D
- ○ 2022-S Proof
- ○ 2022-S Silver Proof
- ○ 2023-P
- ○ 2023-D
- ○ 2023-S Proof
- ○ 2023-S Silver Proof
- ○ 2024-P
- ○ 2024-D
- ○ 2024-S Proof
- ○ 2024-S Silver Proof
- ○ 2025-P
- ○ 2025-D
- ○ 2025-S Proof
- ○ 2025-S Silver Proof

Mint Mark Key: * Philadelphia – No Mint Mark or **P** * Denver – **D** * San Francisco – **S** * West Point – **W**

SACAGAWEA AND NATIVE AMERICAN DOLLARS
2000-2025

Sacagawea Dollar
Mint Mark Location

Native American Dollar
P&D mint marks

Sacagawea	Proof	Native American	Proof		Proof
2000	O P O D O S	2009 Three Sisters	O P O D O S	2018 Jim Thorpe.	O P O D O S
2001	O P O D O S	2010 Great Law	O P O D O S	2019 American Indians in Space	O P O D O S
2002	O P O D O S	2011 Wampanoag Treaty	O P O D O S	2020 Elizabeth Peratrovich.	O P O D O S
2003	O P O D O S	2012 Trade Routes.	O P O D O S	2021 American Indians in the Military. . .	O P O D O S
2004	O P O D O S	2013 Treaty, Delawares.	O P O D O S	2022 Ely Samuel Parker.	O P O D O S
2005	O P O D O S	2014 Native Hospitality.	O P O D O S	2023 Maria Tallchief	O P O D O S
2006	O P O D O S	2015 Mohawk Ironworkers	O P O D O S	2024	O P O D O S
2007	O P O D O S	2016 Code Talkers	O P O D O S	2025	O P O D O S
2008	O P O D O S	2017 Sequoyah	O P O D O S		

Mint Mark Key: ● = Philadelphia – **P** ● = Denver – **D** ● = San Francisco – **S**

SUSAN B. ANTHONY DOLLARS
1979 - 1981 & 1999

Mint Mark Location

- 1979-P Near Date
- 1979-P Far Date
- 1979-D
- 1979-S
- 1979-S Proof (Filled S)
- 1979-S Proof (Clear S)
- 1980-P
- 1980-D
- 1980-S

- 1980-S Proof
- 1981-P
- 1981-D
- 1981-S
- 1981-S Proof (Filled S)
- 1981-S Proof (Clear S)
- 1999-P
- 1999-P Proof
- 1999-D

Filled S

Clear S

Near Date

Far Date

Mint Mark Location

Delaware 1999

Illinois 2003

Northern Mariana Islan. 2009

	Date of Statehood	Unc	Proof
1999			
Delaware	1787	O P O D	O S O S-Slv
Pennsylvania	1787	O P O D	O S O S-Slv
New Jersey	1787	O P O D	O S O S-Slv
Georgia	1788	O P O D	O S O S-Slv
Connecticut	1788	O P O D	O S O S-Slv
2000			
Massachusetts	1788	O P O D	O S O S-Slv
Maryland	1788	O P O D	O S O S-Slv
South Carolina	1788	O P O D	O S O S-Slv
New Hampshire	1788	O P O D	O S O S-Slv
Virginia	1788	O P O D	O S O S-Slv
2001			
New York	1788	O P O D	O S O S-Slv
North Carolina	1789	O P O D	O S O S-Slv
Rhode Island	1790	O P O D	O S O S-Slv
Vermont	1791	O P O D	O S O S-Slv
Kentucky	1792	O P O D	O S O S-Slv
2002			
Tennessee	1796	O P O D	O S O S-Slv
Ohio	1803	O P O D	O S O S-Slv
Louisiana	1812	O P O D	O S O S-Slv
Indiana	1816	O P O D	O S O S-Slv
Mississippi	1817	O P O D	O S O S-Slv

	Date of Statehood	Unc	Proof
2003			
Illinois	1818	O P O D	O S O S-Slv
Alabama	1818	O P O D	O S O S-Slv
Maine	1820	O P O D	O S O S-Slv
Missouri	1821	O P O D	O S O S-Slv
Arkansas	1836	O P O D	O S O S-Slv
2004			
Michigan	1837	O P O D	O S O S-Slv
Florida	1845	O P O D	O S O S-Slv
Texas	1845	O P O D	O S O S-Slv
Iowa	1846	O P O D	O S O S-Slv
Wisconsin	1848	O P O D	O S O S-Slv
2005			
California	1850	O P O D	O S O S-Slv
Minnesota	1858	O P O D	O S O S-Slv
Oregon	1859	O P O D	O S O S-Slv
Kansas	1861	O P O D	O S O S-Slv
West Virginia	1863	O P O D	O S O S-Slv
2006			
Nevada	1864	O P O D	O S O S-Slv
Nebraska	1867	O P O D	O S O S-Slv
Colorado	1876	O P O D	O S O S-Slv
North Dakota	1889	O P O D	O S O S-Slv
South Dakota	1889	O P O D	O S O S-Slv

	Date of Statehood	Unc	Proof
2007			
Montana	1889	O P O D	O S O S-Slv
Washington	1889	O P O D	O S O S-Slv
Idaho	1890	O P O D	O S O S-Slv
Wyoming	1890	O P O D	O S O S-Slv
Utah	1896	O P O D	O S O S-Slv
2008			
Oklahoma	1907	O P O D	O S O S-Slv
New Mexico	1912	O P O D	O S O S-Slv
Arizona	1912	O P O D	O S O S-Slv
Alaska	1959	O P O D	O S O S-Slv
Hawaii	1959	O P O D	O S O S-Slv
2009*			
District of Columbia	1800	O P O D	O S O S-Slv
Puerto Rico	1898	O P O D	O S O S-Slv
Guam	1898	O P O D	O S O S-Slv
American Samoa	1900	O P O D	O S O S-Slv
U.S Virgin Islands	1917	O P O D	O S O S-Slv
Northern Mariana Islands	1947	O P O D	O S O S-Slv

* Coins of 2009 were issued in order of territorial establishment, and only include the 2009 date on the reverse.

WASHINGTON QUARTERS
1932-1998 & 2021

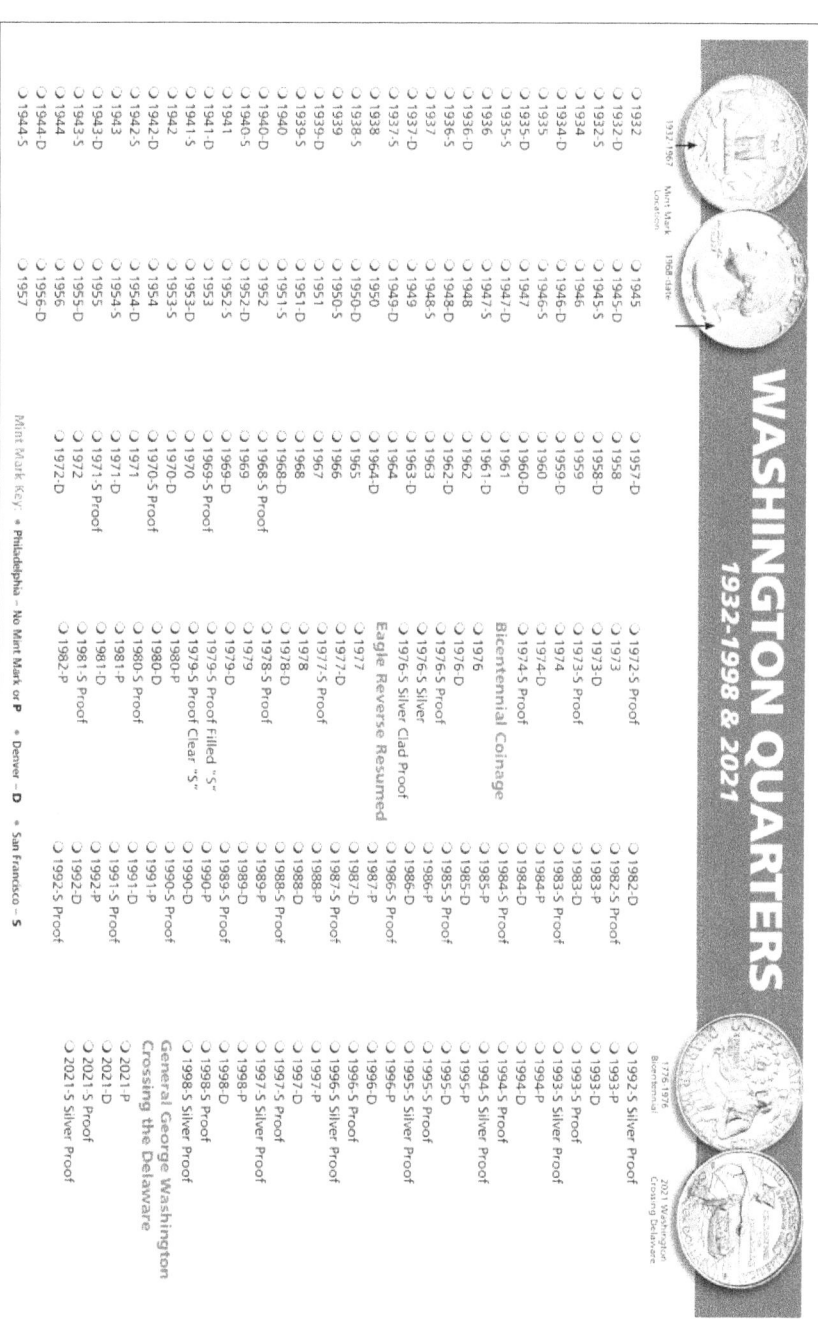

1932-1967 Mint Mark Location 1968-date

1776-1976 Bicentennial

2021 Washington Crossing Delaware

- 1932
- 1932-D
- 1932-S
- 1934
- 1934-D
- 1935
- 1935-D
- 1935-S
- 1936
- 1936-D
- 1936-S
- 1937
- 1937-D
- 1937-S
- 1938
- 1938-S
- 1939
- 1939-D
- 1939-S
- 1940
- 1940-D
- 1940-S
- 1941
- 1941-D
- 1941-S
- 1942
- 1942-D
- 1942-S
- 1943
- 1943-D
- 1943-S
- 1944
- 1944-D
- 1944-S
- 1945
- 1945-D
- 1945-S
- 1946
- 1946-D
- 1946-S
- 1947
- 1947-D
- 1947-S
- 1948
- 1948-D
- 1948-S
- 1949
- 1949-D
- 1950
- 1950-D
- 1950-S
- 1951
- 1951-D
- 1951-S
- 1952
- 1952-D
- 1952-S
- 1953
- 1953-D
- 1953-S
- 1954
- 1954-D
- 1954-S
- 1955
- 1955-D
- 1956
- 1956-D
- 1957
- 1957-D
- 1958
- 1958-D
- 1959
- 1959-D
- 1960
- 1960-D
- 1961
- 1961-D
- 1962
- 1962-D
- 1963
- 1963-D
- 1964
- 1964-D
- 1965
- 1966
- 1967
- 1968
- 1968-D
- 1968-S Proof
- 1969
- 1969-D
- 1969-S Proof
- 1970
- 1970-D
- 1970-S Proof
- 1971
- 1971-D
- 1971-S Proof
- 1972
- 1972-D
- 1972-S Proof
- 1973
- 1973-D
- 1973-S Proof
- 1974
- 1974-D
- 1974-S Proof

Bicentennial Coinage

- 1976
- 1976-D
- 1976-S Proof
- 1976-S Silver
- 1976-S Silver Clad Proof

Eagle Reverse Resumed

- 1977
- 1977-D
- 1977-S Proof
- 1978
- 1978-D
- 1978-S Proof
- 1979
- 1979-D
- 1979-S Proof Filled "S"
- 1979-S Proof Clear "S"
- 1980-P
- 1980-D
- 1980-S Proof
- 1981-P
- 1981-D
- 1981-S Proof
- 1982-P
- 1982-D
- 1982-S Proof
- 1983-P
- 1983-D
- 1983-S Proof
- 1984-P
- 1984-D
- 1984-S Proof
- 1985-P
- 1985-D
- 1985-S Proof
- 1986-P
- 1986-D
- 1986-S Proof
- 1987-P
- 1987-D
- 1987-S Proof
- 1988-P
- 1988-D
- 1988-S Proof
- 1989-P
- 1989-D
- 1989-S Proof
- 1990-P
- 1990-D
- 1990-S Proof
- 1991-P
- 1991-D
- 1991-S Proof
- 1992-P
- 1992-D
- 1992-S Proof
- 1992-S Silver Proof
- 1993-P
- 1993-D
- 1993-S Proof
- 1993-S Silver Proof
- 1994-P
- 1994-D
- 1994-S Proof
- 1994-S Silver Proof
- 1995-P
- 1995-D
- 1995-S Proof
- 1995-S Silver Proof
- 1996-P
- 1996-D
- 1996-S Proof
- 1996-S Silver Proof
- 1997-P
- 1997-D
- 1997-S Proof
- 1997-S Silver Proof
- 1998-P
- 1998-D
- 1998-S Proof
- 1998-S Silver Proof

General George Washington Crossing the Delaware

- 2021-P
- 2021-D
- 2021-S Proof
- 2021-S Silver Proof

Mint Mark Key: • **Philadelphia – No Mint Mark or P** • **Denver – D** • **San Francisco – S**

SMALL SIZE LEGAL TENDER NOTES

One Dollar Notes
Design No. 188

	Friedberg #	Series	Treasurer	Secretary of Treasury
☐	FR1500	1928	Woods	Woodin

Two Dollar Notes
Design No. 189

☐	FR1501	1928	Tate	Mellon
☐	FR1502	1928-A	Woods	Mellon
☐	FR1503	1928-B	Woods	Mills
☐	FR1504	1928-C	Julian	Morgenthau
☐	FR1505	1928-D	Julian	Morgenthau
☐	FR1506	1928-E	Julian	Vinson
☐	FR1507	1928-F	Julian	Snyder
☐	FR1508	1928-G	Clark	Snyder

Two Dollar Notes
Design No. 190

☐	FR1509	1953	Priest	Humphrey
☐	FR1510	1953-A	Priest	Anderson
☐	FR1511	1953-B	Smith	Dillon
☐	FR1512	1953-C	Granahan	Dillon

Two Dollar Notes
Design No. 191

☐	FR1513	1963	Granahan	Dillon
☐	FR1514	1963-A	Granahan	Fowler

Five Dollar Notes
Design No. 192

☐	FR1525	1928	Woods	Mellon
☐	FR1526	1928-A	Woods	Mills
☐	FR1527	1928-B	Julian	Morgenthau
☐	FR1528	1928-C	Julian	Morgenthau
☐	FR1529	1928-D	Julian	Vinson
☐	FR1530	1928-E	Julian	Snyder
☐	FR1531	1928-F	Clark	Snyder

Five Dollar Notes
Design No. 193

☐	FR1532	1953	Priest	Humphrey

SMALL SIZE LEGAL TENDER NOTES

☐	FR1533	1953-A	Priest	Anderson
☐	FR1534	1953-B	Smith	Dillon
☐	FR1535	1953-C	Granahan	Dillon

Five Dollar Notes
Design No. 194

☐	FR1536	1963	Granahan	Dillon

One Hundred Dollar Notes
Design No. 194-a

☐	FR1550	1966	Granahan	Fowler
☐	FR1551	1966-A	Elston	Kennedy

SILVER CERTIFICATES

One Dollar Notes
Design No. 195

☐	FR1600	1928	Tate	Mellon
☐	FR1601	1928-A	Woods	Mellon
☐	FR1602	1928-B	Woods	Mills
☐	FR1603	1928-C	Woods	Woodin
☐	FR1604	1928-D	Julian	Woodin
☐	FR1605	1928-E	Julian	Morgenthau

One Dollar Notes
Design No. 196

☐	FR1606	1934	Julian	Morgenthau

One Dollar Notes
Design No. 197

☐	FR1607	1935	Julian	Morgenthau
☐	FR1608	1935-A	Julian	Morgenthau
☐	FR1611	1935-B	Julian	Vinson
☐	FR1612	1935-C	Julian	Snyder
☐	FR1613N	1935-D	Clark	Snyder
☐	FR1614	1935-D	Priest	Humphrey
☐	FR1615	1935-E	Priest	Humphrey
☐	FR1616	1935-F	Priest	Anderson

One Dollar Notes
Design No. 198

☐	FR1617	1935-G	Smith	Dillon
☐	FR1618	1935-H	Granahan	Dillon
☐	FR1619	1957	Priest	Anderson
☐	FR1620	1957-A	Smith	Dillon
☐	FR1621	1957-B	Granahan	Dillon

Five Dollar Notes
Design No. 199

☐	FR1650	1934	Julian	Morgenthau
☐	FR1651	1934-A	Julian	Morgenthau
☐	FR1652	1934-B	Julian	Vinson
☐	FR1653	1934-C	Julian	Snyder
☐	FR1654	1934-D	Clark	Snyder

Ten Dollar Notes
Design No. 200

☐	FR1655	1933	Julian	Woodin
☐	FR1656	1934	Julian	Morgenthau
☐	FR1657	1953-A	Priest	Humphrey

Ten Dollar Notes
Design No. 201

☐	FR1700	1933	Julian	Woodin

SILVER CERTIFICATES

Ten Dollar Notes
Design No. 202

	Friedberg #	Series	Treasurer	Secretary of Treasury
☐	FR1700	1933	Julian	Woodin
☐	FR1701	1934	Julian	Morgenthau
☐	FR1702	1934-A	Julian	Morgenthau
☐	FR1703	1934-B	Julian	Vinson
☐	FR1704	1934-C	Julian	Snyder
☐	FR1705	1934-D	Clark	Snyder

Ten Dollar Notes
Design No. 203

☐	FR1706	1953	Priest	Humphrey
☐	FR1707	1953-A	Priest	Anderson
☐	FR1708	1953-B	Smith	Dillon

NATIONAL BANK NOTES

Five Dollar Notes
Design No. 204

☐	FR1800-1	1929	Jones	Woods
☐	FR1800-2	1929	Jones	Woods

Ten Dollar Notes
Design No. 205

☐	FR1801-1	1929	Jones	Woods
☐	FR1801-2	1929	Jones	Woods

Twenty Dollar Notes
Design No. 206

☐	FR1802-1	1929	Jones	Woods
☐	FR1802-2	1929	Jones	Woods

Fifty Dollar Notes
Design No. 207

☐	FR1803-1	1929	Jones	Woods
☐	FR1803-2	1929	Jones	Woods

One Hundred Dollar Notes
Design No. 208

☐	FR1804-1	1929	Jones	Woods
☐	FR1804-2	1929	Jones	Woods

NATIONAL BANK NOTES

States & Territories List

	State	# of Banks
☐	Alabama	107
☐	Alaska	3
☐	Arizona	11
☐	Arkansas	69
☐	California	172
☐	Colorado	93
☐	Connecticut	57
☐	Delaware	16
☐	District of Columbia	54
☐	Florida	79
☐	Georgia	54
☐	Hawaii	5
☐	Idaho	28
☐	Illinois	469
☐	Indiana	224
☐	Iowa	289
☐	Kansas	212
☐	Kentucky	141
☐	Louisiana	38
☐	Maine	56
☐	Maryland	91
☐	Massachusetts	145
☐	Michigan	145
☐	Minnesota	248
☐	Mississippi	34
☐	Missouri	119
☐	Montana	44
☐	Nebraska	132
☐	Nevada	10
☐	New Hampshire	58
☐	New Jersey	257
☐	New Mexico	23
☐	New York	522
☐	North Carolina	63
☐	North Dakota	111
☐	Ohio	336
☐	Oklahoma	214
☐	Oregon	79
☐	Pennsylvania	809
☐	Rhode Island	12
☐	South Carolina	12
☐	South Dakota	25

NATIONAL BANK NOTES

States & Territories List (continued)

	State	# of Banks
☐	Tennessee	105
☐	Texas	510
☐	Utah	17
☐	Vermont	48
☐	Virginia	151
☐	Washington	
☐	West Virginia	
☐	Wisconsin	
☐	Wyoming	

FEDERAL RESERVE BANK NOTES

Five Dollar Notes — Design No. 209
Ten Dollar Notes — Design No. 210
Twenty Dollar Notes — Design No. 211
Fifty Dollar Notes — Design No. 212
One Hundred Dollar Notes — Design No. 213

FEDERAL RESERVE NOTES

One Dollar Notes
Design No. 214

☐	FR1900	1963	Granahan	Dillon
☐	FR1901	1963	Granahan	Dillon
☐	FR1902	1963-A	Granahan	Fowler
☐	FR1903	1963-B	Granahan	Barr
☐	FR1904	1969	Elston	Kennedy
☐	FR1905	1969-A	Kabis	Kennedy
☐	FR1906	1969-B	Kabis	Connally
☐	FR1907	1969-C	Bañuelos	Connally
☐	FR1908	1969-D	Bañuelos	Shultz
☐	FR1909	1974	Neff	Simon
☐	FR1910	1977	Morton	Blumenthal
☐	FR1911	1977-A	Morton	Miller
☐	FR1912	1981	Buchanan	Regan
☐	FR1913	1981-A	Ortega	Regan
☐	FR1914	1985	Ortega	Baker
☐	FR1915	1988-A	Villalpando	Brady
☐	FR1916	1988-A	Villalpando	Brady
☐	FR1917	1988-A	Villalpando	Brady
☐	FR1918	1993	Withrow	Bentsen
☐	FR1919	1993	Withrow	Bentsen
☐	FR1920	1995	Withrow	Rubin
☐	FR1921	1995	Withrow	Rubin
☐	FR1922	1995	Withrow	Rubin
☐	FR1923	1995	Withrow	Rubin
☐	FR1924	1999	Withrow	Summers
☐	FR1925	1999	Withrow	Summers
☐	FR1926	2001	Marin	O'Neill
☐	FR1927	2001	Marin	O'Neill

FEDERAL RESERVE NOTES

Friedberg No.	Series	Treasurer	Secretary of the Treasury
FR1928	2003	Marin	Snow
FR1929		Marin	Snow
FR1930	2003	Cabral	Snow
FR1931	2003-A	Cabral	Snow

Two Dollar Notes — Design No. 214-a

FR1935	1976	Neff	Simon
FR1936	1995	Withrow	Rubin
FR1937	2003	Marin	Snow
FR1938	2003-A	Cabral	Snow

Five Dollar Notes — Design No. 215

FR1950	1928	Tate	Mellon

Five Dollar Notes — Design No. 216

FR1951	1928-A	Woods	Mellon
FR1952	1928-B	Woods	Mellon
FR1953	1928-C	Woods	Mills
FR1954	1928-D	Woods	Woodin

Five Dollar Notes — Design No. 217

FR1955	1934	Julian	Morgenthau
FR1956	1934-A	Julian	Morgenthau
FR1957	1934-B	Julian	Morgenthau
FR1958	1934-C	Julian	Vinson
FR1959	1934-D	Julian	Snyder

Five Dollar Notes — Design No. 217

FR1960	1950	Clark	Snyder
FR1961	1950-A	Priest	Humphrey
FR1962	1950-B	Priest	Anderson
FR1963	1950-C	Smith	Dillon
FR1964	1950-D	Granahan	Dillon

Five Dollar Notes — Design No. 217-a

FR1967	1963	Granahan	Dillon
FR1968	1963-A	Granahan	Fowler
FR1969	1969	Elston	Kennedy
FR1970	1969-A	Kabis	Connally
FR1971	1969-B	Bañuelos	Connally
FR1972	1969-C	Bañuelos	Shultz
FR1973	1974	Neff	Simon
FR1974	1977	Morton	Blumenthal
FR1975	1977-A	Morton	Miller

FEDERAL RESERVE NOTES

Friedberg No.	Series	Treasurer	Secretary of the Treasury

Five Dollar Notes — Design No. 217-b

FR1986	1999	Withrow	Summers
FR1987	1999	Withrow	Summers
FR1988	2001	Marin	O'Neill
FR1989	2003	Marin	Snow
FR1990	2003	Marin	Snow
FR1991	2003-A	Cabral	Snow

Ten Dollar Notes — Design No. 218

FR2000	1928	Tate	Mellon
FR2001	1928-A	Woods	Mellon

Ten Dollar Notes — Design No. 219

FR2002	1928-B	Woods	Mellon
FR2003	1928-C	Woods	Mills
FR2004	1934	Julian	Morgenthau

Ten Dollar Notes — Design No. 220

FR2005	1934	Julian	Morgenthau
FR2006	1934-A	Julian	Morgenthau
FR2007	1934-B	Julian	Vinson
FR2008	1934-C	Julian	Snyder
FR2009	1934-D	Clark	Snyder
FR2010	1950	Clark	Snyder
FR2011	1950-A	Priest	Humphrey
FR2012	1950-B	Priest	Anderson
FR2013	1950-C	Smith	Dillon
FR2014	1950-D	Granahan	Dillon
FR2015	1950-E	Granahan	Fowler

Ten Dollar Notes — Design No. 221

FR2016	1963	Granahan	Dillon
FR2017	1963-A	Granahan	Fowler
FR2018	1969	Elston	Kennedy
FR2019	1969-A	Kabis	Connally
FR2020	1969-B	Bañuelos	Connally
FR2021	1969-C	Bañuelos	Shultz
FR2022	1974	Neff	Simon
FR2023	1977	Morton	Blumenthal
FR2024	1977-A	Morton	Miller
FR2025	1981	Buchanan	Regan
FR2026	1981-A	Ortega	Regan
FR2027	1985	Ortega	Baker

Ten Dollar Notes — Design No. 221-a

FR2033	1988-A	Villalpando	Brady
FR2034	1990	Villalpando	Brady
FR2035	1993	Withrow	Bentsen
FR2036	1995	Withrow	Rubin

FEDERAL RESERVE NOTES

Friedberg No.	Series	Treasurer	Secretary of the Treasury

Ten Dollar Notes — Design No. 221-b

FR2039	2004-A	Cabral	Snow

Twenty Dollar Notes — Design No. 222

FR2050	1928	Tate	Mellon
FR2051	1928-A	Woods	Mellon

Twenty Dollar Notes — Design No. 223

FR2052	1928-B	Woods	Mellon
FR2053	1928-C	Woods	Mills
FR2054	1934	Julian	Morgenthau

Twenty Dollar Notes — Design No. 224

FR2055	1934-A	Julian	Morgenthau
FR2056	1934-B	Julian	Vinson
FR2057	1934-C	Julian	Snyder
FR2058	1934-D	Clark	Snyder

Twenty Dollar Notes — Design No. 225

FR2059	1950	Clark	Snyder
FR2060	1950-A	Priest	Humphrey
FR2061	1950-B	Priest	Anderson
FR2062	1950-C	Smith	Dillon
FR2063	1950-D	Granahan	Dillon
FR2064	1950-E	Granahan	Fowler

Twenty Dollar Notes — Design No. 225-a

FR2065	1963	Granahan	Dillon
FR2066	1963-A	Granahan	Fowler
FR2067	1969	Elston	Kennedy
FR2068	1969-A	Kabis	Connally
FR2069	1969-B	Bañuelos	Connally
FR2070	1969-C	Bañuelos	Shultz
FR2071	1974	Neff	Simon
FR2072	1977	Morton	Blumenthal
FR2073	1981	Buchanan	Regan
FR2074	1981-A	Ortega	Regan
FR2075	1985	Ortega	Baker
FR2077	1988-A	Villalpando	Brady
FR2078	1990	Villalpando	Brady
FR2079	1993	Withrow	Bentsen

Twenty Dollar Notes — Design No. 225-b

FR2083	1996	Withrow	Rubin
FR2084	1996	Withrow	Rubin
FR2085	1999	Withrow	Summers
FR2086	1999	Withrow	Summers
FR2087	2003	Marin	O'Neill

323

FEDERAL RESERVE NOTES

Friedberg #	Series	Treasurer	Secretary of Treasury
FR2088	2001	Marin	O'Neill

Twenty Dollar Notes — Design No. 225-c

Friedberg #	Series	Treasurer	Secretary of Treasury
FR2089	2004	Marin	Snow
FR2090	2004	Martin	Snow
FR2091	2004-A	Cabral	Snow
FR2092	2004-A	Cabral	Snow

Fifty Dollar Notes — Design No. 226

| FR2100 | 1928 | Woods | Mellon |
| FR2101 | 1928-A | Woods | Mellon |

Fifty Dollar Notes — Design No. 227

FR2102	1934	Julian	Morgenthau
FR2103	1934-A	Julian	Morgenthau
FR2104	1934-B	Julian	Vinson
FR2105	1934-C	Julian	Snyder
FR2106	1934-D	Clark	Snyder

Fifty Dollar Notes — Design No. 228

FR2107	1950	Clark	Snyder
FR2108	1950-A	Priest	Humphrey
FR2109	1950-B	Priest	Anderson
FR2110	1950-C	Smith	Dillon
FR2111	1950-D	Granahan	Dillon
FR2112	1950-E	Granahan	Fowler

Design No. 228-a

FR2113	1963-A	Granahan	Fowler
FR2114	1969	Elston	Kennedy
FR2115	1969-A	Kabis	Connally
FR2116	1969-B	Banuelos	Connally
FR2117	1969-C	Banuelos	Shultz
FR2118	1974	Neff	Simon

Design No. 228-b

FR2119	1977	Morton	Blumenthal
FR2120	1981	Buchanan	Regan
FR2121	1981-A	Ortega	Regan
FR2122	1985	Ortega	Baker
FR2123	1988	Ortega	Brady
FR2124	1990	Villalpando	Brady
FR2125	1993	Withrow	Bentsen

Design No. 228-c

| FR2126 | 1996 | Withrow | Rubin |
| FR2127 | 2001 | Marin | O'Neill |

Fifty Dollar Notes — Design No. 229

| FR2128 | 2004 | Marin | Snow |
| FR2129 | 2004-A | Cabral | Snow |

One Hundred Dollar Notes — Design No. 230

FR2150	1928	Woods	Mellon
FR2151	1928-A	Woods	Mellon
FR2152	1934	Julian	Morgenthau
FR2153	1934-A	Julian	Morgenthau
FR2154	1934-B	Julian	Vinson

FEDERAL RESERVE NOTES

Friedberg #	Series	Treasurer	Secretary of Treasury
FR2155	1934-C	Julian	Snyder
FR2156	1934-D	Clark	Snyder

One Hundred Dollar Notes — Design No. 231

FR2157	1950	Clark	Snyder
FR2158	1950-A	Priest	Humphrey
FR2159	1950-B	Priest	Anderson
FR2160	1950-C	Smith	Dillon
FR2161	1950-D	Granahan	Dillon
FR2162	1950-E	Granahan	Fowler

Design No. 231-a

FR2163	1963-A	Granahan	Fowler
FR2164	1969	Elston	Kennedy
FR2165	1969-A	Kabis	Connally
FR2166	1969-B	Banuelos	Shultz
FR2167	1974	Neff	Simon

Design No. 231-b

FR2168	1977	Morton	Blumenthal
FR2169	1981	Buchanan	Regan
FR2170	1981-A	Ortega	Regan
FR2171	1985	Ortega	Baker
FR2172	1988	Ortega	Brady
FR2173	1990	Villalpando	Brady
FR2179	1993	Withrow	Bentsen
FR2175	1996	Withrow	Rubin
FR2176	1999	Withrow	Summers
FR2177	2001	Marin	O'Neill
FR2178	2001	Marin	Snow
FR2179	2003-A	Cabral	Bentsen

HIGH DENOMINATION NOTES

Five Hundred Dollar Notes — Design No. 232

FR2200	1928	Woods	Mellon
FR2201	1934	Julian	Morgenthau
FR2202	1934-A	Julian	Morgenthau

One Thousand Dollar Notes — Design No. 233

FR2210	1928	Woods	Mellon
FR2211	1934	Julian	Morgenthau
FR2212	1934-A	Julian	Morgenthau

Five Thousand Dollar Notes — Design No. 234

| FR2220 | 1928 | Woods | Mellon |
| FR2221 | 1934 | Julian | Morgenthau |

Ten Thousand Dollar Notes — Design No. 235

| FR2230 | 1928 | Woods | Mellon |
| FR2231 | 1934 | Julian | Morgenthau |

WWII EMERGENCY NOTES

Friedberg #	Series	Treasurer	Secretary of Treasury

One Dollar Notes — Design No. 236

| FR2300 | 1935-A | Julian | Morgenthau |

Five Dollar Notes — Design No. 237

| FR2301 | 1934 | Julian | Morgenthau |
| FR2302 | 1934-A | Julian | Morgenthau |

Ten Dollar Notes — Design No. 238

| FR2303 | 1934-A | Julian | Morgenthau |

Twenty Dollar Notes — Design No. 239

| FR2304 | 1934 | Julian | Morgenthau |
| FR2305 | 1934-A | Julian | Morgenthau |

One Dollar Notes — Design No. 197

| FR2300b | 1935-A | Julian | Morgenthau |

Five Dollar Notes — Design No. 199

| FR2307 | 1934-A | Julian | Morgenthau |

Ten Dollar Notes — Design No. 202

| FR2308 | 1934 | Julian | Morgenthau |
| FR2309 | 1934-A | Julian | Morgenthau |

GOLD CERTIFICATES

Ten Dollar Notes — Design No. 240

| FR2400 | 1928 | Woods | Mellon |

Twenty Dollar Notes — Design No. 241

| FR2402 | 1928 | Woods | Mellon |

Fifty Dollar Notes — Design No. 242

| FR2404 | 1928 | Woods | Mellon |

One Hundred Dollar Notes — Design No. 243

| FR2405 | 1928 | Woods | Mellon |

Five Hundred Dollar Notes — Design No. 232

| FR2407 | 1928 | Woods | Mellon |

One Thousand Dollar Notes — Design No. 233

| FR2408 | 1928 | Woods | Mellon |

Closing Thoughts

First, thanks to the thousands of loving fans and subscribers on the Variety & Errors YouTube channel and website. You all are what makes this hobby so wonderful! I have met some of my best friends through this hobby and continue to meet more people through conventions and online. I hope to meet more of you soon!

Thank you to Dustin Morgan for showing me this great hobby so many years ago! You may no longer be with us, but I think of you whenever I search my coins and bills.

To Darren Hassett. You extended a welcoming invite, to a group of misfits and weirdos, when I needed it to most. I will forever be grateful for that. You are missed.

Thank you to you the reader, for taking the time to read this coin, banknote and precious metals guide. I'm just a weird collector in one of the best hobbies out there. I love writing and sharing information with fellow currency enthusiasts. It has made me very happy to have my little book out there in the world for you to enjoy!

Visit my site for FREE coin, banknote and collectibles guides:
VarietyErrors.com

About Kyle M. Franck

I live and work in North Carolina. I love nature, anything sci fi, and of course, collecting currency. I have been collecting for over 15 years and started VarietyErrors.com in 2015 to supply free educational material on coins, banknotes, and precious metals.

www.ingramcontent.com/pod-product-compliance
Lightning Source LLC
Chambersburg PA
CBHW060859120626
46553CB00001B/142